'Ooh la la! A fabulous, ~~~~~~~ ove story'
Fi Cotter Craig, author of *The Middle-class ABC*

'I loved this book; this true story of how a chance encounter took Sam from despair to delight, and from hopelessness to happiness, made me keep on reading. Apart from being a fabulous read, this book is inspiring, uplifting, funny and poignant by turns. Sam can really write; her descriptions of rural France – the colours, the scents, the food and the people – made me feel as if I was already there and made me want to decamp there immediately. It is true to say this book is a page turner; I became lost in it even though I had a hundred other things to do as it forced me to escape into the expat world of rural France and was very entertaining and uplifting. I can highly rec~~~~~~

Marisa ~~~~~~~~~~~~ ournalist

HEAD OVER HEELS IN

Copyright © Samantha Brick, 201

Samantha Brick has asserted her right to be identified as the author
in accordance with sections 77 and 78 of the Copyright, Designs and
Act 1988.

Summersdale Publishers Ltd
46 West Street
Chichester
West Sussex
PO19 1RP
UK

www.summersdale.com

Printed and bound by CPI Group (UK) Ltd, Croydon, CR0 4YY

ISBN: 978-1-84953-392-8

Substantial discounts on bulk quantities of Summersdale books are available
to corporations, professional associations and other organisations. For details
contact Nicky Douglas by telephone: +44 (0) 1243 756902, fax: +44 (0) 1243
786300 or email: nicky@summersdale.com.

Head over Heels in France

Falling in love in the Lot

SAMANTHA BRICK

summersdale

To Pascal

Note from the Author

This is a true story, based on diaries I've kept throughout my time in television and since moving to France. However certain names and details have been changed to protect the privacy of those concerned.

Acknowledgements

Mille mercis to the utterly lovely team at Summersdale for making the writing of this memoir a joy. Especially Jen, Debbie, Lucy, Suzanne and Nicky, all of whom have held my hand so gently – yet firmly – through the process.

Sally Ann, Christine, Tracey, Rosetta – thank you for the aura sprays, cupcakes and 'calorie-free' vodka; and for being there when the *merde* really did hit the fan.

Sophie and Frances: you spurred me on when you read my first attempts at writing this – I so appreciated your words of encouragement.

I blush when I think of the scrapes the family GP, Dr Hughes, has seen the Bricks through over the decades... Dr Hughes you are one of the many unsung heroes of the NHS. Thank you for getting me through the darkest period of my life.

I consider myself lucky to be part of the Rubinat family and to have The Best Stepchildren in the World: Joëlle, Hélios and Antonio. Thank you for letting me into your lives.

I daren't enter Birmingham again without a shout out to my family: Nan, Norman, Debra, Sophie, Victoria, Anthony, Lola, Dave and Sam – thank you for putting up with the flighty one. Jo and Fiona – you are The Best Li'l Sisters *ever*, the next bottle of Pinot Blush at The Fighting Cocks is on me. Madeleine, my angel – what would the doggies and I have done without you?

Dad, what can I say? Your number one girl is eternally grateful and assuming you'll be available when we move to the UK (joke).

Mum, you catch me every time I fall and yet you continually give me the confidence to carry on – I know thank you isn't enough...

Pascal, mon amour, *je t'aime à la folie*.

Contents

Prologue

September 2007

Finally, the car scrunches along the gravelled drive.

After fourteen hours on the road, the last of which was on teeny-tiny lanes approximately 2 kilometres away from our destination, the view is worth the wait.

Dense hedging gives way to reveal one dreamy, turreted, chalk-coloured chateau. The elegant country house looks straight out of a fairy tale, its round towers shooting up to protect it.

Two months ago, when I'd said 'yes' to the question that would change my life forever, booking a night's stay in a Loire Valley, dog-friendly hotel seemed like a fitting first night in France.

Having eventually parked the car, I fall out of the driver door, trying not to dislodge any of the countless essential belongings shoehorned around me when I said goodbye to my old life and the United Kingdom. A jelly baby wrapping flutters to the floor, a can of sugar-free Red Bull swiftly following.

'Look at that!' Mother cries, as she exits her side of the car, a sweater and a bottle of water rolling out behind her. 'It's beautiful, isn't it?'

My first night in France, my new home turf, and I'm spending it with Mother.

Mother, fifty-six, red-haired and with a Rubenesque figure, rubs pointedly at the back of her legs. For the last few hours she's been muttering about deep vein thrombosis. Honestly! Anyone would think she'd been soldered to the seat.

'Yes,' I reply, equally enthused, 'it is!'

I furtively look behind me at the car. One filthy maroon Kia Sportage packed to the gills. Suitcases, clothes, countless carrier bags. Not to mention a 15-kilogram sack of organic dog food, several baskets of canine paraphernalia and two hairy salivating hounds leaping and barking hysterically in the cramped rear of the car.

'C'mon, boys! Out you get,' I shrill, gingerly opening the back door. One crack of the outside world and they recognise the promise of freedom, each throwing 6 stone of weight against the door, causing it to fly open, wind me in the stomach and send me hurtling into a rather posh BMW (which now has a slight dent, courtesy of my bottom).

I grab the dog leads while Mother continues to admire the chateau. 'It's so beautiful,' she gushes, brushing down her black linen trousers, having forgotten about the threat of DVT and that we've spent the last hour bickering about driving directions, maps and the glaringly obvious factor that we passed the turning for the chateau, ohhhhh, at least five times.

Yes, the view of the chateau is deliciously perfect.

Unfortunately, at this precise moment of contemplation, Barney and Ambrose choose to squat down in front of the chateau to do their business. 'Oh God, carrier bags!' I wail, running back to the car to grab the poop-scoop equipment in order to attend to the smelly mess.

I ferret out plastic sacks and kitchen roll to clean up after my two Old English sheepdogs. In case you don't know the type, those are the ones in the Dulux paint adverts. Ginormous, high maintenance, and totally adorable.

As I scoop up, one tall, slim, elegant woman unfolds herself from a roughly hewn wooden side door. The Comtesse. Size 8, forty-five going on twenty-five, no doubt has a tribe of children and thinks a beauty regime is something to spoil the horses with.

French women.

'*Allô!* You must be Sam? *Oui?*'

I drop the bags heavily laden with foul-smelling stuff, wipe my hands on my grubby Gap T-shirt and stick out my hand.

'Yes! Divine house! So lovely to meet you!' I jabber. A shuffling next to me prompts me to introduce Mother.

'And this! This is my mum!' Mother says hello in the high-pitched voice that she reserves for people she doesn't know, but wants to impress.

Meanwhile, we're both given a gimlet-eyed inspection by the Comtesse; I'm not sure whether we pass or fail.

She's eyeing up our creased clothes, shiny faces and hair falling out of clasps: we probably fail.

'Come with me and I show you to your room.'

I attempt to snap on both dogs' leads but they are already off ga-thumping after the refined blonde lady. Mother and I look at each other.

'Bloody sort them out!' she hisses.

'Why don't you try?' I hiss back.

'*Oh la la! Adorable!*' Shrieks come from the kitchen. I grimace, wondering if Barney is standing on his hind legs edging along the counters, swiping at anything within paw's reach.

Mother and I slowly enter through the vast white double doors where, at a large wooden oak staircase, the Comtesse is waiting, drumming her fingers on the exquisitely carved balustrade.

'Come! Come!' She clicks her fingers and we both scuttle after her along endless passages. All the while, I can hear the distant thump and thwack of my dogs' paws as they acquaint themselves with every aspect of the chateau.

'It's OK, we 'ave many dogs come to stay 'ere,' the Comtesse reassures me, on seeing my pained expression.

At the very end of a gloomy corridor is a fairly ordinary-looking door. *Is this it?* I wonder to myself, having paid more euros than I care to think for the room, when a bed and breakfast would have done the job at half the price. Yet when the door opens, both Mother and I stare, slack-jawed, at the sheer opulence in front of us.

The suite is bigger than my first flat in London. A wet room (a 'shower in the tower', went the blurb), a separate bathroom with a sunken bath in the middle, not to mention the centrepiece; a four-poster bed with more swagging than at Versailles. Desks, televisions, sofas – even Mother and I could rub along harmoniously in such vast accommodations.

It's only then that I spy in the corner the daybed (translation: a mattress on an iron rack) with horsehair-style blankets.

Mother and I each eye both beds.

I hesitate. Disaster!

For Mother instantly collapses on what must surely have once been one of Marie Antoinette's places of repose. 'I'm *so* going to enjoy sleeping here tonight!'

Defeated, I trundle over to the cot bed and half-heartedly throw my handbag on it.

Finally the dogs burst into the room, sniffing, on the hunt for something to scoff no doubt.

'Well, I leave you, you want to eat wiz us?'

'Yes please!' we both cry in unison.

'*Bon,*' is the response. 'Drinks on the terrace when you want.'

After the dogs have been fed, watered and walked they are both snoring gently at my feet as we enjoy our first aperitif. The terrace, a gravelled area in front of the chateau, gives way to a landscape which is simply stunning; a freshwater lake with swans gliding idly past and paddocks either side with impossibly beautiful horses in them, gracefully shimmying and strutting through the grass. The sun, still shining, bounces off the creamy walls of the chateau. Way after 6 p.m. it is heavenly to sit outside. I know it's fairly warm because Mother has let her wrap fall from her shoulders.

'It's perfect, isn't it?'

We clink glasses.

I stare off into the distance.

'You're doing the right thing, you know,' her voice gently interrupts my thoughts.

'Am I?' *Am I?*

'Who gets invited to move to France by their French lover?'

'True, true,' I reply, a sliver of a smile fighting across my face.

'There was nothing left for you in the UK, you know,' Mother continues gently, 'not after everything that happened...'

'I know, I know!' I reply, willing the tears to stay at bay for once.

'Your friends... well, your real friends...' Mother sniffs. '... they'll always stay in touch, and your dad will come round to the idea.'

I recognise the start of yet another pep talk, one of many Mother has had on rotation over the last fourteen hours.

'I know, I know!' I agree. It's easier that way. It's like trying to wind up an Academy Award winner when she gets going with one of her speeches – best just to let her get it over with.

My final hours in England were grim. A 4 a.m. start in the dark, rain lashing down, a breakfast wrap at a service station, before finally boarding a grubby ferry. Even the dogs knew something was up; refusing (refusing!) to eat when we arrived at the docks. I kept looking for a 'sign'; from the heavens, from the spirit world, even a dishevelled feather would have done. Just something to make me realise I was right to close the door on my old life and open a new one in France.

Apart from getting hopelessly lost – several times – between Cherbourg and Le Mans (was that a sign, I'd wondered or – more alarmingly – a lack of one?) I'd received nothing.

'Is that your phone?' Mother nudges me as I scoop it out of my soft leather handbag.

'*Allô mon amour?*' booms the voice as I open the phone.

'*O-o-oui?*' I stutter.

'You arrive?'

'We arrive just!' I find myself flipping over into a clipped version of English that the French seem to prefer.

'Ah, zat is good.'

'*Ça va?*' I ask, one of the very few phrases in my French vocabulary right now.

'*Ouai, ouai...*'

A few stilted words between us and the conversation is over.

'Everything all right?' Mother peers at me.

'Yes!' I bleat. 'Of course!'

I am, of course, OK, aren't I? Why wouldn't I be? This is the start of my new life.

After another walk around the grounds with the dogs, who, annoyingly, are showing no signs of settling down for the evening, we climb the stairs and enter the suite. Mother, in holiday mode, has already laid out her outfit for the evening. I know my mother; having already eyed up the French mistress of the house, she has prepared not just a dress but accessories too (if I know her, she'll have a fascinator in her luggage somewhere, 'just in case').

'Bath, Sam?'

'Absolutely.'

I turn on the taps, tip in some bath oil and undress, pulling off dirty jeans and T-shirt, peeling off my bra and slipping off my underwear. I catch myself in the many mirrors in the bathroom.

At thirty-six years old, I am closer to forty than I am to thirty. I suck in my stomach and pull the excess skin on my thighs towards the back of my legs. If only my legs were like that, I think ruefully to myself, letting my squashy thighs fall.

One hour later we're in the drawing room where aperitifs re being served and Mother is already mingling with the other guests.

All British. All house hunting. All with dreams of a new life in France.

'Buying a house, you say?' Mother jumps straight into the conversation. 'Sam's moving in with a Frenchman!'

Lots of murmurs of approval shoot round the drinks party. To my horror I am thus deemed an expert at this living in France lark.

For the record: I am *no* authority on living in France.

'Where?' one of the couples eagerly asks.

'Where is it we're going again, Sam?' Mother's eyeballs swivel in my direction – I realise she wants me to help her out.

'In the Lot, the south-west.' I walk over, attempting to sound breezy and confident. 'Do you know the area?'

'Aye, we do, have friends there I think, right Bob?' The woman, whose name is Babs, strokes her husband's hand.

'It's a little village in the middle of nowhere really,' I continue.

'Such a romantic story,' Mother picks up now she's in her comfort zone again. 'This Frenchman has wooed her for the last six months. He's been to visit. Very charming. Different, though.' Everyone nods, knowing exactly what Mother means. 'Doesn't stop calling her, ran up a two-hundred-and-fifty-pound phone bill during one week – isn't that right, Sam?'

'That's right.' I smile awkwardly.

The Comtesse enters the drawing room; Mother is already draining her second aperitif.

'*Alors*, dinner is served.'

Six of us head towards the dining room.

The walls are all panelled in wood, thick blood-red curtains are at the windows. The table itself could seat twenty-five comfortably. As it is the six of us are in the middle section.

Mother and I immediately make a dive for the wine. 'It's been a long day, right Sam?' she says as she pours the silky red liquid into my fussily cut glass.

'Very long, Mum,' I agree, glugging a large mouthful.

'*Voilà*, your starters.' As the Comtesse arrives with little plates, from the distance I realise two things.

We are not going to be offered a menu to select from.

We will be dining on foie gras.

I, alas, have been a vegetarian ever since Morrissey declared meat is murder.

I am not one for making a fuss at meals. Those annoying vegetarians who kick off over everything? Not guilty. So I say nothing and slip the slice of foie gras onto Mother's plate. After a day dining on Red Bull and jelly babies she hoovers everything up in no time.

I am famished.

The next course is, for me, even worse: pigeon. Pigeon! I instantly visualise those poor disabled birds that hobble around Trafalgar Square.

The Comtesse is no fool.

'You don't like zat?' she asks when she clocks me accepting it without the same relish as everyone else at the table.

'I'm vegetarian,' I mutter. Everyone around the table stops and looks.

'Why you no tell me before?' *I thought there'd be a choice!* I want to wail, but don't.

'Sorry,' I mumble.

'Well, I 'ave nothing else.'

And so I pay forty euros for salad and potatoes. Lovely.

After dinner Mother and I retire to the drawing room and drink more wine.

Bob and Babs follow us.

'You must be so looking forward to seeing your fella,' Babs smiles.

'Yes,' I reply. 'Yes I am.' It's only then I realise I really am looking forward to seeing my 'fella'.

By 11 p.m. the Comtesse has been drained of her bottle of brandy, most of her coffee is still stewing in the pot and we're already onto the subject of 'the trouble with the French'. I'm not sure I really want to get involved in this conversation.

At some point Mother and I stagger up the staircase, trying to find each of the timer switches and then race to the next one before the previous light has been extinguished in the gloomy corridor. As I open the bedroom door, Barney – the fatter, greedier one of my dogs, who I can spy has turned over the bins looking for food – launches himself at us.

'Ugh! Barney, get off!' Mother roars.

It is well after midnight and most of the other occupants in the chateau appear to have turned in for the night. I open the heavy front door for the dogs' final pee and as they bound past me I take in the vast star-filled sky above me. Moths dance around a night light, an owl hoots and there is a rustle in a nearby hedge.

Is my Frenchman looking at the same night sky, I wonder?

Chapter One
TV Executive, Interrupted

Spring 2006

'Daisy, I'm so sorry darling.'

There is a pause and a sob.

'I'm sorry for taking heroin… for ruining your childhood.'

My bottom is perched on the edge of my chair in the TV studio gallery. I gulp from the sugar-free Red Bull next to me. I am scrutinising every shot on the twelve screens in front of me.

'Take the lights down!' I whisper into my mouthpiece.

Pearl Lowe, friend of Kate Moss, member of the infamous Primrose Hill set, reaches across to her daughter, Daisy Lowe.

'Give me close-ups of each of them!' I continue.

My eyes roam the studio set, captured from every angle on the monitors in front of me. What else, what else?

There!

'The hands, the hands, I need the hands too!' I shout, watching a tissue being ripped into shreds between Daisy's fingers, as one of the cameras zooms in to find the close-up shot.

A hush descends across Pearl, Daisy and the presenter.

I know it is The Moment.

Their hands find each other across the intimately lit studio set. Emotion crackles on every monitor in the studio gallery.

Daisy Lowe, daughter of Gavin Rossdale and Pearl Lowe, is facing up to the reality that her mum was addicted to heroin throughout her childhood.

She's hearing it on my show.

It's a pilot for an ITV talk show. I pitched it as Oprah meets Jeremy Kyle, hosted by a presenter who exudes wisdom and empathy.

'Ask Daisy,' I whisper into the microphone in front of me, 'what she wants to say to her mum.' The presenter, on hearing my words, repeats them. At the same time I am frantically motioning the director sitting next to me to instruct his cameras to move in for a two-shot close-up.

'Mum,' Daisy replies, breaking the spell over the studio, 'I know you love me, it's OK, I forgive you.' As they hug, the audience breaks into spontaneous applause.

Everyone claps in the gallery; the show is over.

I jump to my feet, having had no sleep for the last thirty-six hours. I'm giddy with excitement and exhaustion because it's my moment too.

My dream come true – my TV company's first show.

My all-female team has decamped to TV studios in Kent. I even have an ITV film crew following me: apparently I'm a perfect example of how to launch a TV company. *Eek!* I have been gliding around since 7 a.m., resplendent in grey skinny jeans, Joseph black top and a Marc Jacobs jacket; giving off the aura of being in control – to my team and the cameras.

I'm living the dream. *My dream!*

For the last sixteen years I have worked my ass off to fashion a career in television. In 2005 I put my money where my mouth is, remortgaging my home to release over £100,000. I launched a TV company where women would be treated like the supremely intelligent beings they are: 'powerful programming made by passionate people' was my company's mantra. I had the connections, I had the talent; I put *everything* on the line to make my dreams happen.

And now, in the spring of 2006, with two shows in the US and a series in the UK, along with the ITV pilot – it looks like dreams really do come true.

Two hours after the pilot has wrapped (after I've promised to have lunch with Pearl) my Mercedes convertible purrs to a halt and I'm parked up outside my house. I still pinch myself – I live in Richmond, one of London's poshest suburbs. I know how lucky I am. I grab my Chloé handbag, open my black wrought-iron gate and click-clack up the path. I can already see my significant others through the window. They're just back from their own day care too.

I open my front door and gently close it, walking into the cream haven that is home. Hues of butter, vanilla, biscuit and caramel tastefully dominate the walls, the fabric on the sofas, the stone masonry of the fireplace and the distressed wood of the bookcases (my books are all arranged by theme – mind, body and spirit by the fireplace, relationship books opposite the telephone seat, chick lit next to the sofa). With the flick of a switch, the lamps carefully positioned throughout the living room light the space just so. I never fail to appreciate this place: my sanctuary.

As I open the kitchen door, the two men in my life are stretching in the downward dog pose. Their tailless (nothing to do with me, honest) bottoms swoosh and oscillate wildly.

Barney and Ambrose.

The two hairy loves of my life.

'C'mon now, outside and make pee-pee for Mummy!' I sing-song in a high-pitched voice.

I teeter across the kitchen (we're still having problems with the occasional 'puddle') and let the dogs out into the back garden. I flick a switch, illuminating my recent garden furniture purchases from a local French antique shop (although judging by their prices, it would've been cheaper to go to France and fly each item back myself).

In bloom, my professionally maintained garden is white – jasmine lazily climbing the fence, bushes of white roses in the border beds fighting for space with other white flowers I couldn't tell you the name of. I smile to myself as I watch the dogs potter together; paws padding, nails tapping over the recently paved garden. But they didn't make me smile at first – oh no. There was a lawn before, but when the puppies arrived, the place turned into a complete mud bath. *Nightmare!* Mud all over the kitchen stone flagging, the sofas in the kitchen, the pristine paintwork. In the end it was simple; I had the garden entirely redesigned to accommodate the doggies.

As they continue to potter in the garden, I ease out the cork, my shoulders relaxing at the sound of the reassuring pop, pouring myself a well-deserved glass of Veuve Clicquot. It gives me an opportunity to reflect; I have everything I want.

But then, of course, things start to go wrong; very wrong.

As spring gives way to summer in 2006, the first crack occurs when there is a change of management at ITV. This is par for the course in television, but it means that my talk show pilot is blown out of the water in one sentence: 'I've got enough overweight blonde presenters on my hands right now, I don't need another one.'

Harsh? That's TV for you.

I'm not too worried; I've got another series in place with a major satellite channel. But there have been three different bosses since it was first green lit, and with every new creative voice comes another change in how we should make it – without an additional penny thrown in our direction. As my profits are used to shore up the series, terse calls from the bank increase. To say my cash flow is stretched is putting it mildly.

I also have two shows in the US about to start. A cause for celebration? Not a bit of it; a clash of egos between two trusted staff members in my UK office delays the delivery of our budget to the American network, which in turn holds up our first payment. I have no choice but to inject precious UK cash reserves into the US as start-up costs. While I tear my hair out worrying about finding more money, contract negotiations and, without wanting to sound too American, 'winning new business', other things start to go wrong.

My dream of a female team working harmoniously alongside each other?

It is disintegrating before my eyes.

My open-plan office makes the *The Devil Wears Prada* set-up seem like a much friendlier option. It is turning into a hormonally charged snake pit. How did that happen? Whatever they can argue about, they do – laptops, handbags, even fertility treatment. I am powerless to stop it; all of my energies are focussed on keeping my businesses afloat. I leave the staff problems to my right-hand woman, Jane.

Jane and I have been friends for ten years. Jane is adorable. She is faithful, immediately likeable, quietly meticulous. Unfortunately, while I thought I'd hired myself a Rottweiler-esque Sharon Osbourne, instead I find myself having to take up the slack of a Bambi-eyed Kim Kardashian.

At the end of my working day in the UK, LA starts. I have great hopes for the US business, having already hired yet another trusted friend, Heather, as my right-hand woman there. Heather and I have always been there for each other; I'd trust her with my life. Ballsy, gift of the gab, gorgeous bod (alas, this is mandatory in LA).

Yet conversations are on my radar that should not be.

'Sam,' my voicemail blares out at me, 'you're gonna have to sort this out. It's urgent!' There's a dramatic pause. I unintentionally roll my eyes, waiting to discover what it is this time. '*She's* threatening to walk.'

Oh God.

Knowing how difficult it is to keep good staff in LA (everyone has their eye on the next big gig), I treat this seriously and immediately talk to Jane, whose job it is to deal with personnel issues on both sides of the Atlantic. I'm painfully aware we are both regularly working late into the night to support our LA office.

'What's going on?' I ask.

'She wants the convertible,' is the nervous reply.

'What?' This is about a car? No one drives a convertible in LA! 'We don't have that kind of allowance in the budget. You know that,' I reply. Jane and I look at each other. Those watery eyes! My instinct is to put my arms around her and give her a hug; I know she doesn't want to play bad cop. I also have a sinking feeling our friendship is in a terminal decline.

'You have to tell her the rate *you* approve,' I say gently. 'Anything over, she must pay herself.'

One phone call later, Jane is predictably in tears. The hardened New York native refuses to back down over the hire car, slamming the phone down on Jane – no doubt she is playing to an audience in the LA office. The friend in me desperately wants to console Jane, but the boss in me worries about what's going on in LA. I put down the contract I need to discuss with our US lawyer and pick up the phone to Heather in LA.

'She really wants the car, babes,' she breezes.

'But how are we going to pay for it?' I, too, hate this part of my job.

'Can't we find it?' she asks innocently.

'No! You know we can't!' She knows every dollar that's not approved in the budget is a dollar I personally have to find. Our TV series in the UK is now so far over its budget that I have no choice but to look at what I can personally sell to pay our bills. No one else knows this but Jane and Heather. While I pay them the going rate, I pay myself nothing. I shouldn't have to tell them how important it is to keep our programme budgets on track.

It's lucky I'm an optimist; the satellite series is already on air, and there is talk of series two. In fact, I've already been given the unofficial news. *It's gonna happen.* We just need to get over this sticky phase, tighten our belts. Like most things in TV, it will be fine. I tell myself this constantly during those nights when, unable to sleep, I spend hour after hour staring into the darkness.

TV is an expensive game. My company's outgoings are twenty grand a month and I know I'm taking a risk investing everything I can get my hands on. I sell my two Mercedes, much of my beloved designer wardrobe, bespoke pieces of jewellery, even my eye-wateringly expensive handbags while I wait for the contract for the half-a-million-pound series that has already been verbally promised to me. All the noises I'm hearing from the executives at the channel are good. Of course the deal will be signed.

I spend the summer and autumn of 2006 jetting back and forth between London and LA, crisis-managing from one continent to the next. I live on painkillers to combat the excruciatingly painful sinus problems from all the flying. While I might be putting on a brave front, my body isn't. One of the few times I allow myself to cry is when I see masses and masses of my blonde hair swirl in the bathtub. My body, it would seem, is protesting; deploring the stress I'm placing it under.

It is December 2006 when I receive the call.

My mobile rings. No number; must be someone important, I think. In an open-plan office with several members of staff milling around me I get up and walk to the fortunately empty reception area. Is this the day when they finally confirm the series, when I finally get a decent night's sleep?

'Hi, Sam! How are you? It's Catherine!'

'I'm good!' Thinking, *get on with it*.

The silence that follows speaks volumes.

'Listen, I'll be brief – we've decided not to go ahead with the series.'

'Right!' I breeze. 'Fine! OK! That's fine, no problem!'

Inane pleasantries are exchanged between us. I finally end the call, the urge to vomit overwhelming me.

I calmly walk to the loos, waving away the runner who wants a signature for something. I close the door behind me and throw up.

It's over, it's all over.

With creditors antsy for cash, and frankly baying for my blood, my company is hurtling towards bankruptcy. I can no longer afford the rent on the office, let alone the mortgage on my house. I have no choice but to get out of London.

Skeleton staff are let go; telling my loyal colleagues that the company is folding is one of the most difficult conversations I've ever had to have. At the same time I tackle the hideous process of winding down the business. I'm gobsmacked when my inner circle of friends flee. Jane hits me with an industrial tribunal court summons and Heather sends increasingly abusive messages about unpaid expenses. I understand that they need to look after their own interests, but their immediate volte-face hurts more than anything else. To the media world, I attempt to tell some white lies to save face, explaining I'm moving home to be with my family through an illness. I needn't have bothered, though – the grapevine in TV does a far better job than any advert on prime time.

Christmas sees just me and my dad eyeing each other over boxes. Me – trying not to cry. Dad – resisting the urge to say, 'I feckin' told yee so.' Just eighteen years earlier he'd reluctantly moved me to London, to the tiny room in university halls of residence. I was full of hope for the glittering TV career. Even then he was the voice of doom about 'London people'. And now; I'm defeated, he's been proved correct – we're moving me back to the Midlands.

Mother is a friend, mentor and all-round interferer (she'd take that as a compliment), and I've spoken with her daily since my business started to wobble. She's so worried (I now know) that she wants to get me back home. Under her wing. Taking a mortgage holiday has bought me time. Time to find moneyed tenants for my beloved home in London and rent somewhere cheap in Birmingham.

Mother has already hustled my retired stepdad into locating a house. Ten minutes' drive from both my parents' homes. It is shabby on the outside and even worse on the inside; think stained and smelly carpets, yellowing, once-white walls. Student accommodation at its worst. But I can live there with my dogs and so I move in during January 2007.

Time alone is time to reflect. I have lost everything. That'll be my home, my business, even most of my friends. Oh, and I owe, deep breath, over £100,000 in tax repayments, on credit cards, bank guarantees and personal loans.

It is March when my company is officially put into liquidation. In my eyes I am something I never thought I would be.

A failure.

It is an unforgiving, bitterly cold evening when I'm crammed in a too-small tepid bath, listening to the drip, drip, drip of the faulty tap. A bath used to be my sanctuary! My fall from grace has even affected how I pamper myself.

Shame doesn't even begin to describe it.

Before, a Jo Malone scented bath, Aveda candle flickering, glass of Veuve Clicquot champagne and a glossy magazine would have been my treat.

Not anymore.

I've just pulled a Bic razor across my leg. (Me, who swore by waxes!) As the blood trickles into the water I think... *deep breath*... I think... *here goes*... about a deliberate pull to an artery and what it would do. Oh God. *I can't believe I'm even thinking like this...*

I wonder how long would it take?

To slip into unconsciousness and leave this world?

I'm shaking; part in desperate anguish, part utterly ashamed of myself and part in sheer disbelief that I can even entertain such thoughts.

I couldn't, though. Could I? Could I...

Just then the bathroom door crashes open.

I freeze.

It's Ambrose. Uninvited, he trots in, thinking he's all that, one of my Agent Provocateur bras inexplicably dangling from his mouth. I know the deal: I'm getting 'the look' because I'm late for walkies. He drops the bra into the bath and then begins lapping at the foamy bath water. The prospect of one ruined bra and him vomiting in approximately thirty seconds' time snaps me out of my morbid thoughts. As I pull his nose out, we stare at each other; he cocks his head to one side and starts licking at the tears running down my cheek.

Chapter Two

An Invitation to France

'I should have bloody known!' my mother berates herself.

'What?' I nervously ask.

'You're depressed!' she tells me, eyeing the dressing gown I have worn for the last few days, the bags under my eyes and my unkempt hair. She pulls out her mobile telephone at the same time.

Depressed? Me?

Within minutes Mother has terrorised the local medical centre receptionist into freeing up an appointment with the family GP. I am frog-marched in front of my doctor, with whom I complete an 'at-risk' checklist (without Mother in the room). I leave with sage advice about TV types, another appointment and a prescription for sleeping tablets and antidepressants.

After that I know my parents are on suicide watch. Calls come through from them several times a day.

'Are you feeling better yet?' Dad shouts down the phone in full-on Irish twang (think Father Ted – he also looks like a rotund version of him).

'No... The same...'

'Sam!' Dad roars. 'You're not going to do anything feckin' stupid, are you?'

Silence.

'Those feckin' bastards, if I could get my hands on them...'

'Dad! It's not their fault!' It's all my bloody fault...

'Anyway so, will I bring you round a sandwich at lunchtime?'

'OK then.'

Dad arrives with a meal big enough to make Nigella Lawson think twice about tackling it. For this is how my dad has always expressed his love – through obscene amounts of food.

Calls from Mother, however, go something like this:

'Taken your medication, then?'

'Errr, yes.'

'Sleep OK?' Mother expresses her love through being practical.

'Nooooo.'

'Still feel like wanting to kill yourself?' she asks briskly, running through her own checklist.

'Ummm...'

'Put the kettle on, I'm coming round.'

I start to call debt charities, I meet with Citizens Advice, I see a counsellor at my GP practice, desperate for a lifeline. The problem is, the experts I meet with are too interested in my old life, wanting to know who I met, who did I know off the telly?

The only useful professional help I receive is from my doctor, who insists on seeing me on a weekly basis. Without fail, during every visit I sob into his scratchy NHS hand towels. He listens to me moan about the television executives who shafted me, whinge about the celebrity friends who dropped me, mourn for my old lifestyle, and he patiently assures me the experience will change me for the better.

But how?

I'm not just depressed. I'm also, well – who am I?

To my shame, my ego has taken a fatal hit. There's an undeniable pleasure to be taken from drawling, 'Yah, I work in TV.' People's eyes *always* light up. So shallow, I know that now. But if I can't have that effect anymore, then what?

I'm no longer the TV producer. The woman with a purportedly glamorous life.

I am painfully aware that life as I have known it has changed forever.

It is late afternoon. I'm having one of *those* days. My hair hasn't been washed in over a week. Even worse, I look, well, minging is the only word that comes to mind. But you know what? I don't care. I'm completely numb inside as I sit hunched over my kitchen table.

I loathe myself for what I have allowed to happen.

The pills only help so much. They can't give me my old life back. They can't manifest the hundreds of thousands of pounds I patently need to start again.

It was such hard work to get that career in the first place. The thought of returning to TV? I just don't have the chutzpah anymore.

Mother is arriving soon; she has finally succeeded in persuading me to go out for the evening. We are going for a curry, nothing special.

I knew I shouldn't have agreed, because then it happens. We're onto the main course and a weird shaky feeling comes over me and I panic. This has *never* happened to me before.

All that's going around in my head is I don't deserve to be here. I don't deserve another chance. I blink back the tears and try to pull 'TV Sam' out of the hat (normally she dazzles in any situation). But I can't do it. She no longer exists.

I blindly rush to the loos where I huddle in a cubicle. A pain so deep inside me wants to escape, but I'm afraid to release it. I know I can't. I'm frightened if I do, I'll never stop crying, you see.

Mother's hawk eye flickers over me when I return and it's not long before the bill is paid and we're on our way home. When I put the key into the front door she reaches her arms around me. I stagger into the hallway where I slump into her embrace and bawl my eyes out. Stroking my hair for what seems like hours she tells me to let it all out.

'You didn't deserve this,' she whispers softly over and over again.

Didn't I? Did I? I don't know anymore.

In April, circumstances force me to face up to the real world. I don't read any correspondence without Mother being there. She's not taking any chances, and neither am I.

A card from my ex-husband. Oh God, I dread to think how he's heard about my downfall. He hopes I'm OK. He reiterates if anyone can bounce back, it's me. I don't think so. She looks at the card disdainfully. 'Well, *that* can go straight in the bin,' she announces, no doubt remembering her strained relationship with him. We got back together and separated so many times, it's not going to happen again. I've nothing left to give to him anymore – financially or emotionally.

A letter from The Insolvency Service outlining an interview I must attend, to explain my role in the company's demise. Just great, I need that like I need a hole in the head. Mother has always been there to catch me when I fall. So when she asks, 'Shall I come with you?', we both know this isn't a question.

An invitation to stay with Miriam, a former London neighbour, who runs an exercise retreat in France. I have known Miriam for a number of years. When I lived in London I attended her studio three times a week. We bonded outside of our teacher-student relationship over our mutual divorces. To celebrate her decree absolute I surprised her with dinner at a posh London private member club. We've witnessed each other's emotional bruises and helped each other rediscover our joie de vivre. Miriam wants me to help her with a demanding client, Nadia, whom I have met before. But things have changed since. I don't possess that jolly conviviality anymore.

'I don't know, Mum,' I wobble. Old Sam would have speed-dialled her personal travel advisor, Martin, to book the flight, reserved the hire car and have confirmed the *deets* with said friend in the time it took to drink a skinny latte.

'It'll do you good,' Mother decides. 'I'll pay.' It's sorted, then; I'm going.

Before I leave for France I reluctantly spend an agonising morning at The Insolvency Service being cross-examined for three hours about why my company has failed. The interviewer's line of questioning makes me feel like a complete imbecile. One who shouldn't have been in charge of a piggy bank, let alone a company account with a turnover of over half a million pounds.

As the interview progresses, I can sense Mother in turn cringing and pursing her lips at my financial ineptitude. It is a humiliating experience to go through. Even more so when your mother is hanging on every word.

To her credit, all she says at the end of the ordeal is, 'I think we both need a large drink after that.'

A couple of days later I'm at Birmingham Airport. The babysitting is starting right from the get-go. Nadia, Miriam's client, and I are deliberately scheduled to get the same flight.

I spy her strutting towards departures.

'Oh God, I cannot do this!' I wail, from the passenger seat of Mother's car.

'Yes. You. Can!' is Mother's firm response.

The last time I met this woman I had a global TV company. I had a life that even she aspired to have! What do I say to her now? I'm a loser, drugged up on antidepressants, and by the way don't leave any sharp objects lying around?

Will we have anything other than work to talk about? That's the first thing you always ask of each other in snazzy London bars and the like. 'So what do *you* do?' The answer will determine if someone moves on immediately, talks to you while keeping an eye out for someone higher up the food chain or decides you're 'hot', and therefore worth talking to.

Mother is giving me 'the pep talk'.

The talk that she has given me all my life – that I can do *anything* I want to do.

Oh, how I used to believe her!

But I'm not so sure anymore.

Fortunately, she's wrapping up.

'... because you needed to get some bloody clothes on and get out of that bloody house, that's why!' She then shoos me out of the car.

Over the last few months the one thing Mother has simply not allowed to happen (apart from the wee matter of me killing myself) is for me to let myself go. Even when I was refusing to budge from the house, she still dragged me out every six weeks to get my hair highlighted (and stumped up the cash for it). 'You might want to kill yourself,' was her opening gambit, 'but we've still got to keep your hair blonde. You'll thank me for it one day.'

'Remember, it's just a blip, Sam, this is all just a blip,' Mother trills as I stand on the pavement looking at her and then over to Nadia, the caramel vision with matching soft leather luggage, an expensive phone in one hand and Chanel-covered passport in the other.

'You have got your Valium with you, haven't you?' I can't stop shaking and her fighting talk gives way to motherly concern.

I end up taking some Valium for travelling, on the advice of Mother. I end up taking Valium before I do most things these days. Me – who used to ensure I stuck to the recommended dose of Rescue Remedy. Not anymore! Protection crystals jangle in my pocket and an aura spray is in my luggage; I'm taking no chances.

Nadia is a well-preserved fifty-something; expensive hairstyle, subtle 'work' to the face, an artificially whitened smile. I've forgotten how executive speak goes. The second she sees me she launches into her bitter battles at work, barely pausing for breath. As it is, the only words I manage to get in are 'Yes please' to the gin and tonics she orders (although she tuts about the fact that her preferred gin isn't available – this is Birmingham Airport Eurohub, I lightly remind her, not Heathrow's Virgin Atlantic upper class lounge).

Our destination is a tiny village in the south-west of France. I'll confess; your average rural French holiday (Camping! Cycling! Canoeing! Ugh!) isn't my idea of an indulgent minibreak.

Yet I have been two or three times before. Miriam is *very* persuasive, having enticed me with a free place to stay in exchange for proofreading her business plan, sourcing glamorous websites for inspiration for her own, passing on clientele advice and recommending her to all my media contacts.

But here's the bombshell; I was unexpectedly seduced by south-west France. Food has always featured prominently in my travels – as a child I remember gorging on crumbly soda bread smeared with butter on the obligatory annual holidays to Ireland. The (extortionately priced) crab cakes at The Ivy restaurant in Los Angeles really are perfection. Yet so is a 50 pence spicy vegetarian curry on Baga Beach in India. The lingering tastes of my favourite dishes are at the heart of all of my holiday memories. So it stands to reason my senses fell head over heels for a gastronomic area of France, even one that had never featured on my radar before.

Even now I can still smell the heady odour of freshly baked *pain d'ail* (garlic bread) infusing the air of the local *boulangerie*, I can still savour the locally produced runny *Cabécou* goat's cheese smeared over a hunk of *pain de campagne* straight from the oven, I can still taste drops of the raspberry-flavoured rosé on the tip of my tongue.

I'm savouring these memories as the plane makes its final descent. The river, La Dordogne, looms large, dominating the surrounding countryside. It is breathtakingly pretty and the view is well worth bagging a window seat for. There isn't just the river carving through the lush green countryside; there are also countless fairy-tale chateaux, their turrets in view from the plane, their over-sized swimming pools twinkling in the sun, and acres upon acres of vineyards thread across the landscape.

The plane finally comes to a juddering halt at Bergerac airport, a tiny terminal in the heart of the Dordogne. I gulp nervously. Get it together, Sam! The chance of me bumping into someone from my former life here? Zero. You'll get an idea of how unlikely it is when I tell you that the airport terminal is more like a regional coach station. LAX it is not.

Instead, we have arrived in expat land. There are bronzed British homeowners, leather-skinned retirees, waving furiously at their friends and relatives who've stepped off the flight. Love, anticipation, squeals of delight fill the air around us. The sun winks lazily behind a solitary cloud in the azure sky. Nadia and I smile at each other – our shoulders visibly relaxing. Our adventure is about to begin.

Suddenly Miriam is striding towards us, frosty pink lipstick freshly applied and a cotton vest straining across her ample chest.

Just under fifty years old, Miriam has undergone a transformation since she's arrived in France. She has lost weight, gone blonde and overhauled her wardrobe. In short, she looks amazing.

Miriam has always surrounded herself with fun people, influential movers and shakers, only ever those who can help her. When she told me I was her favourite client, I didn't connect this statement with the fact that I was also her most lucrative one. I can't help but worry whether she is already reassessing my worth.

'Nadia, you're in the front with me.' She pats at the seat after we've stuffed our belongings in the tiny boot.

'You all right in the back, Sam?' Miriam asks as she pulls a scrunchie around her hair, in preparation for the fact she always – come rain or shine – drives with the roof of her MX-5 down.

'No worries!' I grimace as I fold my legs beneath my chin.

As we drive along the imposing banks of the Dordogne, I lose myself in the enchanting landscape. It's impossible not to. Signs of spring and new beginnings are in evidence everywhere; Mother Nature's creativity is utterly in your face. Dainty blonde cowslips and glossy buttercups fight for space alongside every verge, fruit trees I wouldn't dare to guess the name of are rudely in full bloom, fields are blanketed in a haze of fuzzy yellow dandelions.

Tractor after tractor blocks the single-track roads that Miriam's MX-5 thunders along; after we eventually overtake we wave at the surprised farmers who share their seat with an obligatory yapping dog. They put-put along with a frustratingly unhurried yet steady rhythm.

Miriam, happiest in fifth gear, explains our rigid agenda. We are to spend the next few days exercising and eating together at strictly specific times, then socialising together in the evenings in Miriam's nearest village. 'But we need to get there by 7 p.m. at the latest,' she says pointedly, knowing Nadia and I are no strangers to the hairdryer, and would rather have bags over our heads than go out without make-up on.

When we eventually arrive at Miriam's beautiful pile, we are ushered to our en suite rooms with the efficiency of the Claridge's hotel staff. As I hurriedly unpack, with one eye on the time, I am afforded a brief moment to reflect on numerous things. I am *not* a Francophile. As for speaking the language, the only one I'm fluent in is telly speak. I used to be able to flog a multi-million-dollar series pretty much anywhere in the world. Try to reserve a room in French? To my continual frustration – not a chance. Which is why I am not looking forward to the 'socialising' part of this trip.

The Dordogne, then, even if I do adore the food, is perhaps not the most apt destination for me (well, the old me). There are zero private members' clubs, a distinct lack of chichi bars and absolutely no trendy eateries. Instead, the Dordogne is the ultimate destination for posh, picture-perfect English families to dispense their city bonuses and snap up the hundreds of *châteaux*, *manoirs* and *fermes* that the French can't be bothered to renovate.

Moreover, Cazals, where we are scheduled to drink and eat, is in a different *département*, the Lot, just south of the Dordogne. It is even less trendy than the 'doing-doing', as Miriam insists on calling it. The less expensive Lot is high, dry, arid and wild – retired cabbies mingle with ex-army types. With one of the lowest populations in Europe, it is dominated by forest after forest of chestnut trees, oak trees, pine trees. You're on first-name terms with a celebrity? Who cares? Land and its wood are considered the things to brag about here. You won't find a copy of *Heat* or *Grazia* on sale, either. Cazals is the village that time forgot – this is (sort of) a compliment, by the way.

The roses are beginning to bloom, emitting a scent that is Jo Malone perfect, and the cherry-red and fondant-pink geraniums are already on display. Being house-proud and ensuring you have kerb appeal is taken to another level here – everything is film-set ready. Think *Chocolat*, think *Charlotte Gray*. It is beautiful.

In terms of nightlife, though, it's minimal. There are two bars and a restaurant. That's it.

In one of the village bars, we are due to meet with a crowd of people Nadia and I have met before. In fact, a table is already reserved for our arrival.

We three climb out of the MX-5 and inspect each other's outfits. I hoick Miriam's vest down and tuck it into her jeans, before turning to Nadia, who demands to know if her lipstick has stained her teeth. I finally appraise my own outfit in the reflection of a shop window: I am not by any means a staggering beauty. In fact, I'm 5 foot 11, with shoulder-length highlighted blonde hair, a size 10 (on a good day). My boobs are too small and my hips are too large. It won't surprise you to know that in my former life, I spent hundreds of pounds each year on beauty treatments, thousands on private Pilates and yoga sessions (I never could shift those final 10 pounds), and hundreds of thousands on my attire. I have fallen back on one of those numerous outfits – for the security they offer as much as anything else. For the first time in what seems like an age I have made it through 24 hours without the need to retreat into the security of a dressing gown. Instead, outwardly at least, I appear to be acceptable company. I am wearing a long linen top over Capri pants with a pair of ballet pumps.

Miriam has spent the last few years strategically recruiting her entourage at the bar. She now rubs shoulders with a mix of moneyed expats and influential locals. She also has on speed dial a number of handsome male friends. One of them is already at the bar when we walk in. Pascal Rubinat – carpenter, Parisian, the sociable guy everyone loves. Predictably, when I met him last time, I gave him short sharp shrift.

He's waving. Oh God, he remembers us!

I am nervous about seeing Pascal. He knows what I did in my former life.

'Make way for zee little Frenchman!' Pascal booms as he heads in our direction, clutching several glasses and a bottle of rosé.

Nadia and I look at each other and smirk. He is definitely *not* a little Frenchman.

'I am just zee little man!' He smiles at two female sixty-something expats, who knock their husbands out of the way to let him through, each receiving a kiss in return.

'You are both very kind. *Merci*,' he tells them. They beam. Beam!

''Ow are you, Sam?' He greets me with a huge hug. Smelling delicious; a deep musky odour oozing out of his pores. Meanwhile, his face lightens with a smouldering smile as our eyes lock onto each other. I quickly turn away.

Nadia impatiently flutters back and forth, waiting for her greeting.

As they kiss each other, I do the 'checking out, but not checking him out' assessment out of the corner of my eye. I take in his muscular arms, broad chest. His long coltish legs encased in faded Levis with matching denim shirt open halfway. All set off by battered cowboy boots and a Gitane cigarette hanging at the edge of his mouth. He is perfect billboard material.

Several small tables have been pushed together on a skinny stretch of pavement outside the Bon Accueil bar secreted away from the square in Cazals. It's a pretty little lane, frequently closed off in the spring and summer, when tables spill into the tiny road.

Nadia, Miriam and I are with a group of locals and expats, making at least a dozen people. Everyone meets early in France, straight out of work, and the bars are full. Rosé, ordered by the bottle, is poured into seemingly bottomless glasses. The last of the sun's rays are dancing and sparkling off the golden honey-coloured buildings around us.

'Sam!' Pascal bellows. 'Sit 'ere!'

Eek!

He pats the seat next to him, wiping it down with a hand while the cigarette held between his lips drops ash on said chair. Yet I comply and make no comment about the ash. I'm out of my comfort zone. I shift my bottom, trying to get comfortable, as conversations unfurl in rapid-fire French around us; for all I know, they might as well be talking in Cantonese.

I'm nervous. Nervous and tongue-tied.

Suddenly there's a tap on my shoulder. I lean towards Pascal, expecting him to ask about (cringe) '*l'empire* building' I'd banged on about the last time I saw him.

'Sam?'

'*Oui?*' This is about the limit of my French.

'*Tu es très, très belle.*'

Yeah, yeah, I think, while part of me takes pleasure in the compliment.

As the magical hum of the French language continues around us, Pascal persists. 'I want take you away from 'ere.'

My immediate thought is, *What's Miriam been telling him, then?*

'Just you and me, Sam,' he continues, oblivious to the look of horror on my face.

Well, that just isn't going to happen.

I already know he is ten years older than me. Ten years! In my book that's a total non-starter.

'I want take you *en Corse*. Just you and me.' Corsica? I smile in that nervous way you do, not knowing what to say – hoping he'll stop talking to me.

Unfortunately, he takes my smile as a positive and *santés* my glass, winking and grinning triumphantly.

In the lull of conversation between us, Nadia and Miriam have been straining like a pair of meerkats on the sidelines, waiting to dive into conversation with him. With not a second to spare they begin to flirt and flutter at him in French.

Language prowess amongst the expats is practised with the same degree of determination and competition as any beauty pageant contest. It is dirty and it is fiercely fought. Being fluent in French is the expat equivalent of owning this season's wait-list Birkin handbag. If you're lucky enough to have it, you flaunt it at every opportunity. I cannot compete. It is as though Nadia and Miriam are the star turn on the red carpet and I – rejected and embarrassed – am abandoned on the 'wrong' side of the twisted red rope which protects their VIP status.

In the car on the journey home Nadia and Miriam cackle about Pascal 'being soft' on me.

I listen from my seat behind them, where they can't see me roll my eyes.

I'd *never* consider a Frenchman – would I?

Chapter Three

The Way of the Hot-blooded Frenchman

According to Miriam, weddings are rare in this part of rural France. I am assuming it's because most of the locals are on the more genteel side of forty. When one occurs it's accompanied by insane celebrations. Miriam has been invited, along with the rest of the village, to the wedding of a twenty-something couple. It will undoubtedly be a wild and long evening. Consequently I am to babysit and entertain Nadia.

We have a reservation at L'Auberge de la Place in Cazals. It is one room; quaint, old-fashioned and simply decorated. A family-run business which has been run by *maman* and now her son for the last twenty-five years; regulars have 'their' table, and don't need to be asked for their menu choices either. I am a pudding fan – *mousse au chocolat,* crème brûlée, *tarte aux noix* – and my addiction is well fed here. In the summer you can shamelessly indulge dining outdoors in the square surrounded by fragrant lavender and rosemary bushes.

Philippe, the owner, is one of the nicest men I have ever met. Whenever I have visited Miriam previously he has always been beyond welcoming to me. 'That's because you're under forty,'

Miriam had sniffed at the time, nodding to the octogenarians slurping at their soup.

His face lights up when he sees us. Instantly he stops what he's doing and strides across his busy restaurant.

'Sam! 'Ow are you?' He opens his arms; the embrace is obligatory.

Philippe shoos away the waitresses and personally seats us at our table. Within seconds a bottle of rosé is produced.

'Well, they're all falling over you here, aren't they?' Nadia observes.

'Oh Nadia, it's not like–' I look pointedly around the room at the various retired gentlemen dining on their own '– I'd ever consider a bloke over *here*,' I finish with a whisper, remembering Miriam's warnings that most French, while they don't bother to speak English, actually understand far more than you'd give them credit for.

'Of course, you're young. Well, not that young.' She pulls me up sharp. 'But I thought even you would have figured out by now when love finds you, you take it. In both hands.' I'm surprised. This doesn't sound like Nadia, the high-maintenance executive.

'I don't think so,' I murmur, wishing she'd drop it. But Nadia is like a dog with a bone.

'Look at me! American! I moved to the UK to be with my husband. You need to be more open to life's opportunities, Sam! I can see you fitting in well here.'

'Live out here? You must be joking!'

Fortunately for me, our food arrives, halting Nadia's efforts to persuade me of the viability of life in rural France. Nadia rubs her tummy. 'I think those exercises were a little too strenuous today, I don't know if I can stomach a full meal.'

I say nothing when she polishes off her plate of duck confit in record time. Mind you, I can talk; I make a mean fist of my exquisite yet calorie-laden meal of salmon in a cream sauce. When we have finished, Philippe asks if he can join us. He wants to practise his English.

He strides over, with the expression of a man on a mission.

'Uh-oh,' mutters Nadia.

'You know, Sam, you are like a ray of sunshine for me when you come in here!'

Oh God.

Nadia sprays her wine everywhere. 'Cool it, Philippe!' she splutters.

I don't blame her; she's looking way more elegant than I am. The compliments should be aimed at her.

Undeterred, Philippe continues, 'You light up my day when you walk into the restaurant.'

'Oh, Philippe!' Nadia puts her head in her hands. 'That won't work with someone like her,' she says, jabbing a hand in my direction.

I wish the ground would swallow me up. However, before I get ideas above my station, I remember this line of patter is not unusual. To my cost (St Tropez – don't ask) I already know a little bit about French men's seduction techniques.

They treat all women like goddesses. Undressing you with their eyes and shamelessly telling you how beautiful you are. If this happens to you, be warned; he will seduce you so successfully you will be willing to drop your knickers in a flash. But before you do so, just know that he'll deliver the exact same routine to the next woman that takes his fancy.

And this is why English women flourish when they arrive in France. French men flatter and flirt with them while their husbands would rather potter in the garden or sip *un demi* with their newfound expat friends. English men retire for a more gentle life in France, while English women rediscover their sexual prowess.

It's nearly midnight, yet Philippe continues to ply us with wine (I don't even want to think about how we'll get home) and 'practise his English' with us, when suddenly the restaurant door swings open.

'Ah-ha!' booms Pascal. 'Zis is where you are 'iding!'

In strolls the village walkin', talkin' sex god, along with Miriam and some others arriving from the wedding party.

Philippe pouts, Nadia giggles, I redden.

'Another table, I zink, yes?' Pascal asks. Although it isn't really a question. Within seconds he is picking up a heavy oak table as though it were a clutch bag and whopping it against our little table for two.

Philippe shyly scurries off to organise drinks, while Pascal, as subtle as a wrecking ball, is grinning and grabbing me in an embrace – sloshing out a glass of wine for himself at the same time.

I can't resist checking out his attire and, with all the commotion, hope I'm not noticed sizing him up; doing that thing out of the corner of my eye again. He is wearing a stiff white shirt, muscles taut, straining to get out of it. Below the waist; charcoal grey trousers, bulging in a place where, truthfully, I really shouldn't be looking. Horrors! He catches my gaze where it shouldn't be.

'Sam!' His glass crashes into mine. ''Ow are you?' He shoves himself closer to me in a bid to ensure everyone fits around the table. As there is a wall to the other side I have no choice but to absorb the pressure of his arm against mine.

It takes me by surprise, the touch of another person. As does the sudden zing of electricity that passes between us. I pull my arm quickly away.

'Sorry,' smiles Pascal.

'No! I mean, it's OK.'

Pascal asks the question I have managed to avoid until now. ''Ow eez business, Sam?'

Oh God.

At first I freeze, and then, well, I surprise myself. It's probably the wine that has loosened my tongue and while I brush over the worst of the last few months, I do find myself, in a rosé-fuelled haze, admittedly, explaining what happened to me.

When I finish, he says nothing. I wonder if I've given him too much information.

But then he takes my hand in his. 'You are *très fragile* I zink Sam, yes?' he asks softly.

I nod, tears springing to my eyes.

He doesn't say anything else as I discreetly pull myself together. I certainly don't want the others to see my tears.

Pascal glances at me. The sex god has gone. Instead, a kindness has softened his face, and he gives my hand a squeeze.

Oh God, please don't let me fall for him.

I've had sooo many disastrous relationships recently. After my divorce two years ago, I spent that much time in LA, I thought I'd give the American boy a try. What a mistake that was. On paper they look good: the sports car, the condo, the bodies to die for. But there's only one person that kind of guy can truly love – the one he sees in the mirror. As usual I discovered this far too late.

I toss and turn all night. Ruminating over the guys I've chosen in the past. I always attract the wrong 'uns.

Always.

Late April in south-west France is letting us into the secret of its appeal, proffering sultry temperatures in the mid eighties. At chez Miriam, an oak tree provides just the right amount of shade and the pool is glistening in the sun. Miriam has already 'had it up to here' with Nadia's complaints about her ailments. 'She shouldn't have bloody come, if she didn't want to put some effort in. It's taken me bloody ages to tailor today's yoga programme precisely for Madam's needs,' she retorts witheringly to Nadia's receding back as she limps off towards her bedroom.

This should offer us a rare moment to relax and sunbathe by the pool, but Miriam isn't one for silent contemplation. Fired up by Nadia, Miriam launches straight into her own complicated love life. Since she arrived in France, she has been enjoying an affair with a married man. Unfortunately, his wife has just found out.

It is a riveting 'he said, she said, then I said, then she hit me!' account of the last few months of her once smoking hot, now dying-in-the-embers affair.

'What did you do?' I ask, in awe at the wife having the sheer gall to turn up at Miriam's house.

'I bloody hit her back,' Miriam retorts.

'Are you OK?' I can see through the bravado, I know she's hurting. She nods silently. I don't do the 'How could you do that to another woman?' line. It's a fact of life; it happens every day. 'And now?' I ask gently.

'It's over,' is the unusually quiet reply.

'I think it's for the best,' I say diplomatically.

But Miriam is a survivor. 'There's also Elliot to tell you about,' she grins.

'Elliot? Noooo!'

Miriam then brings me right up to speed on a recent overnight stay involving a much-sought-after local. 'He wouldn't stay unless we were both naked, what could I do?' she squeals.

A comfortable silence descends over both of us, birds dive and skim along the surface of the swimming pool. A woodpecker is busy at work in the woods nearby.

Turning myself over, I settle down for a snooze. But it isn't to be.

'You know Pascal has a soft spot for you,' Miriam starts.

Here we go.

'Really?' I ask, watching a snake ease itself out from behind a pile of logs at the end of the pool.

'Always asking after you,' she emphasises, seemingly pondering the significance of Pascal's interest at the same time.

'He seems all right,' I hedge. The snake is now flicking its way along the wall.

'Did he tell you he has two grown-up children by his first wife?' Miriam nods to herself.

Another one with kids? I knew there'd be a catch.

'And then there's the child with the recent ex,' Miriam continues regardless, 'another beautiful boy.'

'Talk about an excess of baggage,' I splutter.

'Oh, yes.' Miriam looks up and pulls her sunglasses down to the end of her nose.

'Right!' I laugh. Who'd be insane enough to take all that on, I wonder, mentally crossing Pascal off my list.

'Beautiful children, though, he's got fabulous genes. Imagine what you and he could spawn together!' Miriam laughs so loudly that the snake freezes where it is.

I redden.

'Not that you'd consider him? Not even a *leetle* fling?' The snake continues, coming menacingly closer.

'Not in this lifetime,' I reply, thinking of all those kids. Kids! I can't even look after myself right now. I instinctively reach for a drop of Rescue Remedy and squirt a mist of aura protection spray around me.

The snake is way too close for comfort now. 'Miriam, did you know that there is a bloody great snake just inches away from me?'

'Darling, there are snakes everywhere in France.' She sits up, takes off her sunglasses and walks to the edge of the pool. 'And you'd better wise up to that.'

It's a couple of days before I'm due to return home, and Miriam and I plan to spend Sunday in Cazals. In Cazals, Sunday is *the* day of the week; and Miriam should know, she's not one to miss a social 'do'. It is market day and full of people in their Sunday best; buying, gossiping, drinking. The tables from both of the two village bars and L'Auberge spill out onto the pavements and into the local square. Unsurprisingly, the population swells to five times its three hundred residents.

The air is thick with gossip; expat women, beautifully dressed in shades of tangerine, fuchsia and sunshine yellow, confidentially exchange their news. At the same time, they knowledgably fill the well-worn wicker baskets on their arms with seasonal products they can effortlessly rustle up into something divine. To me, they epitomise the French dream. Meanwhile their French equivalent, typically rake thin and more often than not puffing on ciggie after ciggie, is also encased in an exquisitely tailored outfit. She glides from stall to stall expertly selecting the very best each trader has to offer. Both sets of women have talents I clearly don't possess; how on earth would someone like me ever fit in?

It isn't long, though, before I'm lost in an assault of the senses. I weaken at the stall devoted to different types of honey (I can never resist a sample of my favourite type). Another booth overflows with punnets of plump ripe strawberries, an elegant woman of a certain age enticing you to try 'just one'. Then there is the attractive man taking orders for his spit-roast chickens (be quick! – they're all reserved before 10 a.m.), and pheromones radiate from the head-over-heels-in-lust couple selling foie gras, subconsciously drawing you to their goods – even the heady scent of for-sale spring flowers in bloom practically beg you to swoon at their odour.

Miriam cuts through the hypnotic effect.

'Pascal has offered to take us for lunch,' she says.

She has to drop Nadia off at the local train station (Nadia is racing back to London for a 'very important meeting' – I remember the fear they can instil).

'Would you like to wait here with him or come with me?'

I redden, thinking, *ohhh awkward*.

'He's still my friend, you know.'

'I know, I know.'

The thought of being on my own with a Frenchman for an hour fills me with more horror than being wedged in the back of an MX-5 convertible bumping along the notoriously bad Dordogne roads in the fierce midday sun.

'I'll come with you.'

An hour later Pascal is seated at his table at L'Auberge de la Place. Philippe smiles from his counter, before rushing over at the same time as Pascal leaps up to greet us.

'Ah-ha!' booms Pascal, as everyone turns to see who he's talking to. 'You arrive!'

Rosé is already on the table, our meals are already ordered.

'Ees no problem for you 'ere, Sam!' He winks. I smart at this. The cheek!

I am already marked down as *zee végétarienne* (yes, one of those really annoying ones who eat fish). Miriam has gone on about it often enough. I've heard 'very fussy, you know' whispered in my direction more than once.

Pascal and Miriam both devour a plate of steak (rare) with French fries while I discreetly pick off the duck gizzards from my supposedly meat-free goat's cheese salad. I know better than to try to explain what being a vegetarian really means. This area of France is famed for its gastronomic meat-centric delights – foie gras, *canard, cassoulet*. Someone only has to suggest a serving of tripe and everyone swoons at the delicacy it's supposed to be. South-west France isn't a natural home for vegetarians.

While we're finishing our lunch, we are invited for afternoon drinks at Pascal's house. It is a spur of a moment thing – the sort of thing the French love, apparently. Normally I don't do spontaneity. Before, my weekends would be rigidly mapped out, with brunch, lunch and afternoon dates scheduled weeks in advance. I'm not even sure why we're going, to be honest. Even Miriam cautions in a whisper, 'You won't like it there, Sam, he keeps his dog outside.'

Horrified, I think of my own pooches that share my bed and have the run of my house.

'It'll be on a chain as well, you know,' Miriam continues, while I stare bug-eyed in alarm at the very idea!

But it is the first time I'll get to see inside an authentic French home, as opposed to an expat version of one, and curiosity gets the better of me.

'You come wiz me, yes?' Pascal opens the passenger door for me and I, taken aback, slide into the front seat.

The journey from Cazals to his house, in the next village along, is ten minutes by car. He offers to take us there and return us to our car afterwards.

We drive along a winding hilltop road. The Lot is made up of high land and valleys and we are at the highest point. The road either side falls away to undulating countryside, criss-crossed with fat bustling hedgerows. In the distance pockets of thick woodland dominate the skyline. There are no pylons, no factories, no office blocks. It is simply stunning. Pascal drives slowly, which surprises me; I already had him down as an overgrown boy racer.

His head constantly darts from left to right. But there's a reason for this; he's sharing with us the secrets of his neighbourhood. He shows us teeny-tiny red squirrels ('There is one near my 'ouse, I promise you I talk wiz 'im every day,' he explains in all seriousness), a rabbit ('Zey come back now, before we 'ave none for many years') and a young deer that eyes us up suspiciously before darting into the safety of the wood, flashing us her creamy tail ('She ees beautiful, no? If I 'ave my gun, bam! She make twenty kilos in zee freezer').

Errr, right.

The single-track road approaching Pascal's house twists and turns, and we drive past a well ('You can still drink from it, I zink,' Pascal asserts). There is a farm to the left and meadows to the right populated by cattle that stop and stare. Fat pine trees are sprinkled everywhere and in the distance I spy a well-preserved village that time forgot, perched on a hill. I'm stunned when we arrive, for Pascal's house is chocolate-box perfect.

'Une maison en pierre' is how an estate agent would describe it; a house made out of vanilla-coloured stone. It has espresso-brown shutters framing every window. An exterior staircase leads to a shaded terrace where there are potted geraniums tumbling idly down. In the middle of the terrace is an authentically distressed table with a bowl of lilacs on it, their soft scent inviting us in. To say I'm gobsmacked is putting it mildly. Some mismatched chairs are hastily arranged and within minutes a jug of rosé and short stubby glasses are found.

At first I am uncomfortable. I know Miriam well, but not that well. I barely know Pascal. Am I insane? What if I have a panic attack again?

I'm suddenly aware of a wet nose nudging my calf. I jump, Pascal grins, while his teeny-tiny hunting dog, Elsea, jumps into my lap and promptly falls asleep. She is a scruffy black and grey Jagdterrier with biscuit-coloured paws. Bred specifically to hunt *sanglier*, wild boar, she smells of the countryside, and her coat is full of brambles – she is adorable.

Since declaring me *fragile* Pascal constantly asks if I am OK. When we're seated on the terrace, and with Miriam in the loo, he gives me another reassuring squeeze to the shoulder. *There's that zing again.*

The afternoon passes by quickly. Pascal is a talker, as is Miriam, and I am happy to be a spectator to their banter. It isn't long before Pascal tells us about his life with his ex-partner and why it failed. He doesn't spare any detail. I don't know why, but his frank admission (with Miriam translating much of it) makes me feel better about myself and my situation. Stuff happens to everyone.

As Pascal talks I can't resist taking in his appearance once more. His face is set off by dark, dark chocolate-brown eyes. He has closely cropped black hair with tiny flecks of silver, a prominent nose with a beauty spot next to it. He has one of those famous French moustaches, which takes up half his face. He tells us he is half Catalan, which explains the dark Latino features.

As the sun begins its descent, its rays flood the terrace with a golden glow, and I experience a moment in time when I feel OK about myself. I rub little Elsea's ears, she sighs contently and for the first time I feel all right. Those sunset chill-out bars all over the world are there for a reason. Contemplate, meditate, chill – call it what you will – but it works. I am afforded the opportunity to reflect, in a haze of rosé, admittedly, but it affects me profoundly. For the first time I think to the future. I find a feeling I thought I'd lost forever.

Hope.

On my final evening, Pascal arrives for dinner chez Miriam, along with other friends from Miriam's crowd, and as usual he sits next to me. I nudge Miriam at the sight of Elliot; she flashes warning eyes. I translate this as meaning – 'subject off limits'. As there are eight of us drinking and eating with Miriam's bed and breakfast clients, my gesture goes unnoticed. The men take over the cuisine (which is just as well as I – surprise, surprise – don't do cooking) and a scrumptious dish is rustled up from virtually nothing.

At some point in the evening Pascal brushes my hand. At first I think he's checking to see if I'm OK, but when he holds it for longer than five seconds I shoot upright and gently release my hand.

Everything else in my life is broken; I just can't risk my heart too. It's all I have right now.

Sometime later Pascal makes a move to leave. I awkwardly follow him to say goodbye. I don't expect I'll ever see him again, unless I visit Miriam. In the hallway he is pulling on his muddy, steel-toecapped workman boots. Suddenly he stops.

'Sam?' He gently takes hold of my shoulders with his large hands and pulls me close towards him. He looks at me intensely, those chocolate-brown eyes penetrating my soul. 'I wish to 'ave met you ten years before. Then I never, ever let you go.'

He then kisses me on each cheek and is gone.

During the night I toss and turn; sleep eludes me. Dragging myself out of bed, I open the French windows and take in the chalky moon waxing towards its full stature. The waxing moon; according to tradition this is the phase of the lunar calendar that is ripe with new possibilities.

Have I made a mistake in letting him go, I wonder?

I return to the UK the following day, and I receive a reminder that I haven't been forgotten about in France after all.

Texts, from a certain Frenchman.

Chapter Four

Reality Bites

When I walk through passport control at Birmingham airport, it isn't just my suitcase waiting for me on the carousel. Depression is also there. It's all too ready to give that feeling of Hope I experienced a swift kick up the derriere and send it hurtling back on the return flight to France.

Depression is smug and confident it's back for the long haul; its jabbering inside my head is louder than Gok Wan in a roomful of naked women. The upshot of its mockery is how could I ever have had the gumption to think anyone could be interested in me?

Remember, Depression kindly harks on at me on repeat mode: I had it all. I lost it all. It was All My Fault.

Before I miserably slot the key into the lock of my rental I hear the ping of a text message. A smile fleetingly passes across my lips when I realise who the message is from; it is Pascal asking if I arrived home safely. I look at it and Depression instructs me to delete it.

He is a kind and lovely man. But his idyllic Gallic world is not for me.

Later that afternoon, I collect my dogs from the local kennels. On our return, we wander into the garden where, to my horror, I am greeted by several large rats sauntering back and forth through the hedges at the edge of the lawn. I'm convinced they size me up, appear to shrug nonchalantly at each other and continue their game of tag. I look at them and then haul the dogs inside, bolt the door and shut the curtains.

The next forty-eight hours I spend in my dressing gown being tormented by Depression. I'm being rigorously chastised for having the gall to assume I'd managed to give it the slip while away. So the bad dreams, broken sleep and morbid thoughts have returned with a vengeance.

Mother pops in irritatingly often, notching up several visits daily. She cross-examines me on the status of my thoughts with the subtlety of a sumo wrestler. Yet even she is unsettled by those moments when we are together and I suddenly go 'all spacey' as she likes to call it.

'You're spacey, you're spacing out, YOU'RE SPACING OUT, SAM.'

She stares at me as though I'm something off one of those Channel Five human freakery documentaries – half scared and yet fascinated by me at the same time.

Mother doesn't like those occasions – neither do I, if I'm honest.

Desperate, I can only assume, for something to get me out of this mood, she announces she has an idea.

'Why don't you invite Madeleine over for the weekend?'

'Good grief,' I splutter, pushing back a greasy fold of hair behind my ear. 'Why on earth would I do that?' Honestly! I can't think of a more inappropriate idea.

Madeleine is my ten-year-old niece and goddaughter. We have an unbreakable bond. For me it is based on the fact that I was fortunate enough to be the first person to witness her entrance into this world. I held the hand of my sister as she gave birth to Madeleine – I saw Maddy take her first breath. For that reason, then, I don't want her to see me like this. I'm worried my bleakness will scare her.

'Invite her and that little friend of hers,' Mother continues, making herself another cup of herbal tea, pushing Barney out of the way as she flops into a chair at the scrubbed pine kitchen table. Mother is referring to Tani, Maddy's joined-at-the-hip best friend.

'You think?' I'm not convinced and I pull my dressing gown further around me for protection.

'You need someone to drag you out of this mood,' Mother announces, pulling a biscuit out of the packet in the middle of the kitchen table, while shoving Barney's paw off her knee. 'Besides they can help you clean up that bloody garden of yours.'

Luckily, Maddy and Tani are beyond delighted to stay for a weekend. Both are at the age where the highlight of their social life is Brownies. The surly attitude of adolescence has yet to kick in; which means that instead they are bossy, opinionated and a right pair of busybodies. This is rather good news for me. They turn up reminiscent of mini Kirstie Allsopps, decked out in gardening attire and, unprompted, set about dividing up the garden into areas to be tackled.

Maddy is tall and slim with endless legs, chocolate-brown eyes and long wavy dark brown hair. She is the image of her father, with the slenderness of her mum, my younger sister Fiona. Tani is the complete opposite: short, blonde, blue eyes.

Both are giggly little chatterboxes – I can't help but smile listening to their banter.

'Are you sure you don't mind?' I ask, popping a baseball hat on each of their heads as the sun begins to blaze.

The garden is twice as wide as it is long. The bottom of the garden – the rats' residence – backs onto a field, and Barney has unfortunately found a hole in the fence to fit his portly frame through. My task today is to locate and cut back the areas where the rats are coming in and to block up their passageways.

The girls are on what is known in our family as poop patrol.

'I like helping,' Tani announces. 'We're supposed to do a good deed each day.'

Noting the puzzled look on my face, Maddy explains. 'Brownies, Auntie Sam. It's the Brownies' motto.'

I watch, gobsmacked, as each girl takes a black plastic bag and, with gloves, proceeds to scoop up dog poop, leaves and anything else which shouldn't be on the lawn, while I hack at the hedging in order to oust the rats from their current dwelling.

'We love helping, don't we Maddy?' says Tani. Maddy, bottom in the air, bent over scooping up turds, shouts yes.

'Are you sure you don't want any payment?' I ask, astonished. 'Not even some sweets?' I'm so used to having to pay people before they'll lift a finger to help me, I can't quite believe they're not even attempting to negotiate an hourly rate.

'It's a good deed, Sam.' Tani, about half my height, brushes her silky blonde hair out of her eyes. She puts down the bag she's holding and looks up at me. 'We're not here for money, we're here because we want to help you.'

I walk away before she sees the tears that well up in my eyes.

A couple of hours later numerous bags have been filled and disposed of. The rats' home has been inelegantly cut back; I have amateurishly blocked up the holes with some earth and thrown some poisonous pellets into the tunnels for good measure; and I have inexpertly tied netting across the fence, closing up Barney's bid for freedom.

When we finish we each wash down a Twix with a glass of lemonade.

'What do you think about going for a W?' I ask Maddy.

She eyes each dog, knowing that I can't say the actual word, for fear of an eight-pawed frenzy breaking out.

'Excellent idea!' Unfortunately, Ambrose has already cottoned on to exactly what the W letter stands for and starts to move his osteoarthritis-riddled bottom from side to side.

Maddy and Tani grab the long, red, robust leashes and clip them on. As Tani is lighter than both of the dogs I delicately offer to help her maintain control of Barney.

We exit the cottage and turn left past the garden centre, staggering a couple of hundred metres before being winched onto a country track. It's at this point we can breathe a sigh of relief. Barney and Ambrose's bottoms oscillate wildly, impatiently waiting to be unleashed. They both shoot off along the track, Maddy, Tani and I tagging along behind them.

With two ten-year-olds, there is no talk of television, debts or men in France. Or the most dreaded question of all: how are you *really*, Sam?

It is a welcome relief.

Instead, we debate and quiz each other with such passion and fervour that we'd give Jeremy Paxman a run for his money, on subjects such as favourite pizza toppings, handbag pooches versus real dogs and – which is the real social blight – to be in possession of straight or wavy hair.

On reaching the end of the track we totter down some makeshift steps and onto the Stratford-upon-Avon canal path, where we turn right and spot Barney and Ambrose in the distance. Barney is already barking at ducks that have astutely migrated to the opposite bank and Ambrose is dipping his nose into the coolness of the canal water. I screech at him to take his snout out. The canal path is extremely narrow; there is little room for error. Unfortunately, this is a fact I have discovered on countless occasions when each dog has toppled over into the murky canal waters, having to be heaved out by yours truly.

As we start along the path, on our left is the water perfectly reflecting the willow trees dipping into it and to our right is a Christmas tree farm. Everywhere we look there are signs of new beginnings: ducks and their ducklings proudly paddling along the canal (wisely far from Barney); new Christmas tree saplings shooting up towards the blue sky overhead; patches of bluebells haphazardly sprouting in pretty little clumps beneath trees – it is sublime.

Later that night we all snuggle down in my double bed: that's Maddy, Tani, Ambrose, Barney and me. Barney and Ambrose do, of course, have their own beds. Two beds downstairs in the hallway and then two beds next to mine. Each bed is kitted out with bespoke allergy-free mattresses, flown over from the United States during one of my many former business trips in what one colleague witheringly referred to as 'the coffin' suitcase. Where most TV executives take pride in travelling with a carry-on case only, I was always the woman holding my companions up with my check-in baggage. Even with such plush bedding, each dog prefers to hop up next to me.

In the early hours, both Maddy and I are awake. She slips into the nook of my arms and rests her head on my shoulder.

'It's been a lovely day, Auntie Sam,' she says.

'Yes,' I say with a smile, 'it has been, hasn't it?'

'You're not going back to London ever again, are you Auntie Sam?'

'No,' I reply wistfully, stroking her hair, 'I don't think I am.'

'So you'll be here forever?'

'It looks that way, doesn't it?'

'You'll always have me,' she replies with the wisdom of someone far older. 'Me, Barney and Ambrose. You don't need anyone else.'

'Not even a boyfriend?' I ask, thinking about another text message which I received from Pascal today.

'Definitely not a boyfriend, Auntie Sam. We don't need men. Whenever you need me I'll be here.'

'Thank you,' I reply, a grin spreading across my face. Barney has by now assumed his place guarding the bedroom door, loud snores emitting from his nose. Ambrose is soundly asleep on my feet. I continue to stroke Maddy's hair, grateful for her and Tani's presence. Just a couple of minutes later I hear her soft regular breath indicating sleep and gently click off the bedside light.

For once sleep arrives easily.

April dances into May, and Pascal continues to call me sporadically at home. A curious one-sided relationship appears to be developing. He is a quiet yet strong presence and has taken to leaving messages on my landline. I never know when he's going to call and as I avoid answering the phone, without fail, I miss his calls.

Messages on my voicemail go something like this:

'*Je pense à toi.*' Click.

Heavy breathing for several seconds and then, 'I 'ope you are OK.' Click.

'Sam.' A pause during which I think he must have replaced the receiver, and then, 'When you come again?' Click.

Confession time; I am scared stiff to return his calls. What do I say? How do I say it? There isn't just the glaringly obvious problem: I speak zero French and he speaks limited English. The other perfectly logical reason for me not returning his calls is the fact that I'm pretty dismal when it comes to relationships.

My twenties were spent chasing the wrong type of men; 'danger men' my friends and I excitedly labelled them. They were the guys who were emotionally unavailable, those who swore blind they loved me and then tried to cop off with my friends, then there were the ones who I simply lusted at from afar. In my thirties – apart from my embarrassingly brief eighteen-month marriage – I had equally disastrous love affairs (or, more often than not, none at all). Brutally honest feedback from friends confirmed my worst fears: I was too intimidating. I was always first to stand a round in a swish bar, it was perfectly clear I could look after myself, all too often I dictated the social events. As one friend remarked while settling herself into my Mercedes for a lift home after some showbiz bash, 'It would take a strong bloke not to be overawed by all this, Sam.'

That'll explain why I've been single since my divorce, then. I've never had the third date dilemma of 'Do I wear alluring underwear?' The extent of my dating life post-divorce didn't go any further than first-date base.

So this time, if anything is to happen, it would be a total first to feel chased, cherished and loved. In those rare moments when I've elbowed Depression out of the way I like to think I deserve better than the one-sided love affairs and almost-but-not-quite relationships I've settled for in the past. This time, if someone is interested, there's nothing to be frightened off by, is there?

One evening my sister Jo arrives armed with a stack of books on something called Cognitive Behavioural Therapy and some DVDs, including the box set of *Sex and the City*. I had asked for the DVDs – apparently humour is good at chasing away ugly thoughts. What I hadn't expected were the self-help guides.

'What are these for?' I ask, tentatively pointing at the tomes she has plonked onto the coffee table.

'They're good, Sam, try to read them. If you take anything out of them, just remember this: you are not your thoughts. What you're thinking right now isn't the real you.'

'Right,' I reply unconvincingly, flicking through one of the books which has blank pages for exercises – eek!

'You'll switch your way of thinking back again Sam – you've always been a glass half full girl.' She looks at me intently. Jo works in mental health and has undergone years of training in this area. 'This isn't you,' she says gently. 'These will help challenge how you're thinking.'

As I reach for a tissue Jo reaches for the bottle of wine that is sat on the table between us and discreetly tops up our glasses while I pull myself together.

'Remember our time there?' Jo asks, pointing to the *Sex and the City* DVD cover showing New York.

'How could I forget?' I smile, scrunching the tissue up into a ball.

Jo is a brilliant holiday companion. She's easy-going whether on the slopes, shopping or sunbathing. Another bonus is that she can drink any man, woman or beast under the table and still retain a perfect palette of make-up too.

'Any plans to go back to France?' she asks as we chink our glasses.

'No!' I reply. Jo already knows about Pascal's messages. She is very gifted at wheedling out of me all necessary information to confirm that, in her opinion, he is very interested.

'I think you should.'

'Why?' I ask, stunned.

'Why not?' She swirls her glass around in front of her and lays down the challenge. 'The old Sam would have.'

I bite my lip. My mind is suddenly flooded with images of the Lotois countryside and Pascal, but I can feel Depression struggling to elbow these thoughts out of the way.

Out of the blue, something occurs to me.

'Would you come with me?' Even as I ask her, I can already sense Depression retreating.

Jo grins and nods her head. 'You know I will,' she replies, and points to the DVDs. 'Now watch those and no more tears. You're the big sister I've always looked up to – don't let me down.'

That evening, fuelled by two glasses of rosé, no doubt, I decide to call Pascal.

I am nervous. So many of our face-to-face conversations have been successful because they have involved much gesticulating and eye contact; undoubtedly the sizzle of our connection when we are in close proximity has helped propel our mutual understanding too. Before I call, I prepare and research some stock phrases in French.

Here goes. I nervously take another slug of rosé and tap his digits.

'*Allô* Pascal?'

'*Bonjour mon bébé*!' he replies, as though it is the most natural thing in the world for me to be calling.

'*O-où est t-t-tu?*' I stutter. Jane Birkin, husky and panting, I am not.

'*Je chasse avec Elsea,*' he whispers. Hunting? It occurs to me that he seems to do a lot of this. So far, I have only witnessed the sexy man about the village side of him. The hunter is unknown territory to me.

I tell him I am thinking of returning with my sister at the end of May. That, just to be clear, I'll book a room at Miriam's *chambres d'hôtes*.

'Zat is good Sam, perfect. I wait you. *Bisous ma chérie.*'

As I replace the receiver I realise I'm rather looking forward to seeing him.

When I arrived in the Midlands I had optimistically turned the dining room of my rented house into an office.

And promptly left its door firmly shut.

I have been too frightened to tackle the onerous financial paperwork in there.

Another reason why I rarely go in there is because it houses the telephone. Debt collectors are calling daily. While I know it's my own fault that I'm in this financial disaster, they still frighten me with their threats that they will take what's left of what I own. What if, goes my irrational mind in the dead of night, they force me to sell my dogs?

'We need to tackle those debts soon, Sam,' Mother says one morning over a coffee. The coffee is from a low-cost supermarket. I have economised in ways I never thought possible. I have learnt that you don't pack your bags at the till in Aldi. Instead, as was firmly pointed out to me by the cashier and the septuagenarian behind me, you use the counter behind the till, if you're like me, and dawdle and dilly-dally over what to put in which carrier bag. I am so relieved Mother wasn't with me when I made that particularly gauche mistake.

'You're right, we should,' I reply uneasily, taking a sip from my coffee cup. 'We will.'

'When?' Mother probes.

'Soon,' I reply, shifting awkwardly.

'We should set a date and time.' She looks at me pointedly.

Oh God – I knew this was coming.

She never lets up. Who appointed her chivvy-in-chief?

I mumble a date and a time.

'Good, I'll be here, we'll sort it out together.'

On the morning Mother is due to help me tackle everything, I gingerly open the office door. I am greeted by towers of paperwork covering every surface of the floor.

I suck air in and blow it out slowly.

It is a good sign that I am entering the room and finally facing up to what this paperwork means.

The bad news is that I am in my dressing gown with my greasy hair pulled up in a topknot.

I realise if I am going to have any hope of tackling this properly, I need a sharp readjustment of my mental attitude.

So I retreat from the room and re-enter thirty minutes later. This time I am in a pair of smart jeans, ballet pumps, a cashmere top and my hair is freshly blow-dried. Inexplicably, I feel focused.

The reason Mother is pushing me to tackle goodness knows how many thousands of pounds of debts is that my beautiful house in London has just been sold. Within a week of going on the market it went to five sealed bids.

As of twenty-four hours ago there is a six-figure sum sitting in my bank account.

After the mortgage debt has been paid off, I am left with £100,000 to settle the rest of my personal debts. While running my television company I was advised not to take a salary. So of course I never did; this business error is primarily the reason I am up to my neck in arrears.

I have just enough funds to pay everything off. I don't, of course, have anything to live on afterwards, but I have been making a mean fist of selling off my belongings on eBay and eking out just enough money to get by.

'So,' Mother asks briskly, having waltzed in, slung her coat on the hall banister and placated both dogs with a pig's ear, 'which one shall we pay first?'

I pull out the household decorating invoice. The owner of the company has left me in tears on several occasions. I know he never believed me when I pleaded that payment was coming, instead choosing to shout at me down the telephone and write rather abusive letters to me instead. His invoice – a real person's bill – should be paid first.

And so we rattle through each and every scary piece of paper, paying off credit cards via the telephone. No one seemingly bats an eye, their voices perfectly neutral when I pay fifteen thousand pounds here, seventeen thousand pounds there. I dread to think how people who don't have the safety net of property to sell can reconcile these types of debts.

It is somewhat disconcerting to see over £100,000 disappear in the space of four hours. As I settle each and every bill, I mentally reassure myself that this means no more threatening calls, letters or emails from collection companies, bailiffs and the bank.

At the end of it Mother heads for the kitchen and, putting the kettle on, shouts out to me, 'You're free. Debt free.'

Five minutes later she returns. The floor is clear of the mountains of paperwork, the bills have been returned to their files. Handing me a mug of herbal tea, I see Mother looking at me sadly. I silently stab a guess at what that look means; she was always so proud of me with my over-inflated salary, posh job, jet-set lifestyle and elegant wardrobe.

'Yes,' I reply quietly, 'but what am I left with? I've got nothing.'

'You've got everything Sam – you've got your life, your future in your hands.'

I hug the mug into my chest and bite at my bottom lip, willing myself not to cry.

Yet just as one set of problems is almost out of the way, something else far more catastrophic occurs.

At first I don't recognise the shaking for what it is, the pool of urine on the floor or the jerking leg. Fortunately my mother and stepfather arrive at the same time as I'm staring open-mouthed, witnessing Ambrose in the middle of what appears to be an epileptic fit.

Mother's nursing training kicks in and she takes over, places her scarf under his head, putting all four paws in the recovery position and pulling his tongue out of the way.

I would happily trade places with my dog for him not to have to go through this. While my life has imploded, my dogs have remained my rock-solid friends.

My dogs, oh my dogs.

Barney; eternally happy, permanently in a good mood, a born show-off. Within a month of disembarking from his Virgin flight at LAX, Barney had 'arrived'. I'd booked both dogs into a swanky Hollywood training centre. Mother thought I was bonkers as she accompanied me on a trip to visit them while they underwent intensive training to walk 'correctly' on a leash (what a surprise, it failed).

'It's not the Birmingham Dogs Home, is it?' she muttered on seeing the manicured lawns, canine swimming pool and roses climbing over pergolas. The US TV network ABC produced a news item on the centre and, lo and behold, there was Barney trotting back and forth across the screen during prime-time television hogging the camera, for potential agents and casting directors to see.

He is also food obsessed. Obsessed! I cannot tell you how many bins he's up-ended and troughed through (his nose isn't for sniffing, it's primarily for knocking bin lids off).

Then there is Ambrose. Desperately small for an Old English sheepdog, he contracted kennel cough within the first week of coming to live with me, followed by a limp, then there was the un-descended testicle to remove. All within the first six months of his life – I was convinced he would not live past his first year.

He wasn't like other puppies; at puppy training classes he sat on my lap, refusing to budge. (Barney, on the other hand, was barred for disrupting the class.) His body is riddled with osteoarthritis. One dog-walker in Los Angeles told me off for buying him, claiming, 'You gotta sue the breeder – he's useless, take him back!' It was all I could do to stop myself from flinging one of Ambrose's favourite rugby balls at her head as she stalked out of the front door.

Ambrose has tolerated everything thrown his way. As many ailments as he has developed, I've discovered 'remedies' to combat them. Doggie reiki, massages with lavender oil, acupuncture and swimming lessons. When he's not having alternative therapies, it's a slew of vitamins and minerals (not to mention the mind-blowingly expensive conventional medicine); then there's the grooming. For both of them.

Unfortunately, Old English sheepdogs are the canine equivalent of a high-maintenance WAG. We are never out of the dog grooming salon. They are shampooed, clipped, plucked and blow-dried every six weeks without fail. The cost of their six-weekly haircut and blow-dry rivals mine at £65 a pop.

Yes, there was a time when their upkeep was in the region of ten grand a year. Insane.

To my absolute horror, there was 'talk' of getting rid of my dogs. Dad was arguing that I should move in with him and his family. He didn't know I could hear him confront Mother about it, one day when they crossed paths on the doorstep, during the time when they were checking up on me several times a day.

'She needs to be back in the fold,' reasoned Dad.

'The last thing she needs is to be living with you,' my Mother snapped.

'Do you trust her on her own?' he went on.

'She's thirty-six, not sixteen,' Mother replied, her voice laced with sarcasm. 'I think she can manage.'

'I thought she didn't have any money,' my dad shot back. 'How can she afford to feed those bloody dogs? They eat more than me.'

'I highly doubt that,' came Mother's reply, pointedly staring at Dad's generous stomach.

I covered my mouth, desperately trying to prevent the nervous laughter that wanted to spring forth.

'Don't you realise those dogs are keeping her alive right now?' Mother continued.

The idea was jettisoned. On a temporary reprieve, if I know my father.

Mother was right, though, my dogs do maintain my foothold on this planet.

'My boys', as I know them, have travelled and lived everywhere with me. Hollywood, London – there was no way they weren't coming to Birmingham with me. So while I'm slumming it at Aldi, the boys are still on their organic high-maintenance food (translation: expensive) which I have couriered in fortnightly from Wales.

But they have been the reason for me to live; for that, they are worth their weight in gold.

During the nights when I couldn't sleep, I'd whisper to them, 'We're getting through it, boys, we're getting through it.' They would look at me and offer assurance; plonk a hairy wet chin on my lap, generously plaster wet kisses on my hands and even place their paws on my shoulders offering up hugs.

On those nights when just getting to the next minute was a struggle, I always knew they would never leave me. So it's beyond unfair for my poor beleaguered Ambrose to have developed epilepsy. But why? There is talk of tumours at the veterinary clinic where they are investigating his condition. I lose weight, unable to eat or sleep, while tests are carried out.

For the rest of May, I read all the websites, I swot as much as I can on the subject, I become quite the little expert on what can cause epileptic fits in dogs. All the while I'm researching the causes of canine epilepsy, I keep one ear finely tuned, listening out for the rattle of the collar and the all-too-familiar banging on the floor as his body hits the ground and I grab a pillow to protect his head.

Ultimately, nothing and no one can prepare you for the sudden jerking movements, the urine squirting all around the room while you try to insert Valium into your best friend's bottom, shoving poop out of the way at the same time, and wait for the fit to subside – soothing him all the while. It's a horrible, soul-destroying experience for you and for him.

I pray in front of my Buddha statues, light candles in my local church and sign Ambrose's name on dozens of Internet prayer sites in the hope that he will be OK. My local vets even arrange for Ambrose to be admitted to a veterinary hospital specialising in this condition. He is an in-patient for five days, during which time numerous tests are carried out to establish whether or not there is a more sinister, underlying condition, such as a tumour, causing the fits. Yet after his stay his consultant confirms that there isn't a tumour, it is epilepsy. I also give thanks that I kept up the payments for pet insurance. The bill for this little phase of treatment for Ambrose is running into thousands and thousands of pounds.

Chapter Five

Un Retour en France

Hideously early flight? Check.

Trying to remain upright in horizontal rain waiting for a shuttle while the umbrella inevitably turns inside out? Double check.

Battling through the airport terminal with countless hen and stag parties? Triple check.

My sister Jo sensibly stayed with me the night before our weekend to France. Well, it would have been a wise move if we'd made it to bed before midnight. We groggily set out for East Midlands Airport at 4.30 a.m. in my recently purchased car. It is a far cry from the glamour of a Mercedes convertible. Instead it is a car for which Mother beat down the price with the mortifying words hollered across the showroom, 'She's just been made bankrupt, give her a break, someone's got to.'

Jo and I haven't been on holiday together since *that* trip to New York, ten years ago. On New Year's Day we hurtled around an ice rink in Central Park, predictably hungover yet joyously happy. Jo sported a leopard-skin coat with purple ear warmers firmly in place as her hair flew behind her. I, meanwhile, was stuffed into leather trousers and a cheeky jumper with a not-so-subtle cleavage hole. Jo is now a married woman with a daughter, so holidays together have all but been consigned to the memory bank.

Jo has inherited Mother's Rubenesque figure with cleavage-length glossy red hair, and is in possession of impeccable fashion sense. Officially she is a senior manager within a high-security forensic unit. What that means in reality is, she assesses those who truly are dangerous and certifiably crazy or, even more sinister, pretending to be in order to avoid imprisonment for some heinous crime they've committed. So, down-to-earth Jo listening to my woes at this point in my life is no bad thing. I consider myself lucky to be able to offload my thoughts on someone with her expertise, who can put my troubles into perspective.

We trundle through the security line, taking off anything that is likely to set off the alarm system.

'How are things?'

'Oh, you know, some days are good, some days are still like I want to kill myself.' She looks momentarily alarmed. Minutes earlier she had laughed about the airport's security measures, and explained just how dangerous broken plastic cutlery is when used against the skin. I dread to think how she knows this and try to block this information from remaining somewhere in my brain to be used by my vulnerable self at a later date.

When we make it through security we sit down, each nursing a coffee before our flight is ready to board.

'Do you still feel guilty about letting everyone down?' Jo correctly identifies the main reason behind those suicidal thoughts which won't fully withdraw. I still cannot shake my massive guilt complex concerning those who relied on me for work.

I nod, lips wobbling.

'Well, don't!' Jo shakes her head furiously before continuing steadily, 'I've told you. They are all adults, equally responsible too.' Jo explains this with a reasonable degree of authority. 'They knew what was going on, Sam.'

We board the plane and each pull out a magazine – which neither of us open. Jo continues to gently probe me on my state of mind, while offering sensible advice. I confess more, mumbling what ifs, as yet more caffeine greases my vocal chords. Predictably I end up crying. Jo remains entirely unflustered, and wordlessly hands me a tissue.

Jo has always been of the opinion I think too much. I've always been guilty of over-thinking things, apparently.

When I finish snuffling she looks at my face.

'Take this and go to the loos,' she whispers kindly.

In my hand is a stick of Pout crème blusher in pink.

In the dim lighting of the plane's 'powder room', I try my best to make myself look decent. I rub the stick into my cheeks, careful to ensure I don't look like Aunt Sally afterwards. Surprisingly, it makes me feel better and I finally stop crying.

I've got to snap out of this, I berate myself irritably. While Depression is finally receding, the leaky tears that have replaced it can fall without warning at any time.

The final descent into Bergerac airport is a bumpy one. The plane is buffeted by the wind and rain. It seems pointless to enthuse to Jo that this really is a *un petit bijou* of a place.

Finally slotted into a titchy Twingo, and with the windscreen wipers on full speed, condensation in the car doesn't allow me to point out the endless vineyards and the Dordogne River. Predictably, within half an hour of leaving the airport – the

st time I am driving in this part of France – we are lost. We
have no choice but to pull into a supermarket to load up on
maps of the Dordogne and the Lot. Within the minutes it has
taken me to map out our route, Jo has managed to drop €50
on beauty items. She is nothing if not my sister.

The detour, the inclement weather and my hopeless driving
mean that we will arrive much later than anticipated into
Cazals, where we are due to meet with Miriam for lunch. We
have already telephoned at various stages en route to explain
we are late. As I am driving, Jo makes the calls.

'We're running late. Sorry!'

The roads are narrow and windy. I feel foolish for admitting
it but they are also unrecognisable in the rain.

'Now we're in a wood. Where? No idea. Sorry!'

The testy response from the other end of the line makes
Jo's eyebrows shoot into her hairline as she pulls the phone
away from her ear. Life isn't as laidback as I might have led
her to believe in these parts. Putting her hand over the phone
she diplomatically says, 'They might have to order and start
without us.'

Suddenly I see a sign for Miriam's house.

'Tell Miriam we're twenty minutes away. And tell her
sorry!' I enthuse, at last feeling relieved and confident that
following the two maps joined together has seen us through
the final miles to our destination.

As we pull into the car park opposite L'Auberge de la Place,
Jo clocks the restaurant and lets out a sigh of relief.

Inside and out of the rain we shake off our coats and
Philippe scoots them away, not before kissing each of us on
both cheeks and announcing to Jo that he is *enchanté* to

meet her. Seeing Miriam holding court at a large table with two highfalutin clients, we wave enthusiastically and edge towards them. We're instantly seated and within what seems like seconds have glasses of rosé thrust into our hands. Jo beams, while relief washes over me. I can't help but remember the previous time I was with Miriam. I'm relieved that I managed to squirrel away enough from last month's eBay sales for us to be here as paying guests.

Jo is delighted by the attention Philippe showers on us: do we have enough to drink, are we OK, do we need anything else? She struggles not to laugh when Miriam loudly announces that Pascal has already phoned her, explaining that he wants to see Jo and me that evening. Over the course of our meal Miriam delights in bringing her guests and Jo up to speed on the Pascal situation – both of whom declare it The Most Romantic Thing Ever. I meanwhile squirm with embarrassment.

After everyone else has eventually polished off a delicious lunch of *steak frites*, I have gobbled up a rather tasty dish of salmon in cream sauce, and all of us swooned over the crème brûlée, we head back to chez Miriam. The rain is unrelenting and I mentally erase thoughts of walks in the countryside, exchanging them for the prospect of curling up with a book in front of a toasty log fire.

Much to my surprise, however, both Jo and I fall asleep not long after we have unpacked. I am woken by the sound of my phone ringing.

It is Pascal.

'*Bonjour ma chérie. Ça va?*'

Pascal wants to confirm his date.

Unfortunately, I'm not *ça va* at all. I'm experiencing fierce stomach cramps and awkwardly explain that I'll call him later on to confirm this evening's rendezvous. I fling the phone at Jo and rush to the loo – which is where I remain for the rest of the afternoon.

Not wanting to be a holiday bore, a couple of hours later I head with Jo to the cosy and inviting lounge where Miriam and her guests are already enjoying an aperitif. I opt for a glass of water, while Jo settles into a comfy armchair and signals yes please to a glass of rosé. I anxiously look at my watch: 5.30 p.m. I have just stopped vomiting – if I can last an hour, then I want nothing more than to introduce Jo to Pascal and make an evening of it.

It is gradually dawning on me that in spite of all she said at lunch Miriam is less than thrilled about the possibility of my romance with Pascal. Unbeknown to me, Pascal has been updating Miriam on every voicemail message, text and conversation (the one!) that we have had. Pascal might well have handed Miriam a loaded gun, for over our aperitifs, while my stomach is still vociferously complaining, she fires several well-targeted bullets at me. Her mission is perfectly clear; to kill any whiff of romance.

Miriam's Theory on why a relationship with Pascal won't work goes something like this. He smokes all the time and his hands smell. I am a vegetarian, he is a hunter. He has killed more animals than I've had hot dinners (my stomach heaves in agreement at this point). He loves motorbikes and ZZ Top, I detest both mode of transport and musical preference. How, she concludes, could a relationship pan out with such a man; one who lives in France?

'But I really, really want it to work for you, Sam!' she tr.
with a smile at the end of her diatribe, in front of her noddin₃
audience. Does she? Doesn't she? Should I allow her to ride
roughshod over my hopes?

As if on cue, I suddenly race back to the bathroom and
hurl up the liquid contents of my tummy quick smart. Five
minutes later and I am shivering in the bedroom chair. Jo
tenderly wraps a blanket round my shoulders just as my
phone rings.

It is Pascal. Fortunately the word for vomit is a similar one
in French.

We arrange to meet the following day at Francette's Le Bon
Accueil bar. From there he will take Jo and me to his house for
lunch.

A couple of hours later and Jo and I are in bed.

I writhe in agony for much of the night, pondering whether
I suffered an adverse reaction to lunch or whether, as I really
suspect, it's just nerves.

The following morning, we're wakened by the sound of water
gushing down the drainpipe next to our room. Rain thumps
noisily against the window and clatters on the roof overhead.
Jo sighs and throws her sunscreen and sunglasses back into her
suitcase. I mouth sorry and we prepare ourselves for our first
exercise class and head into the studio.

I am feeling much improved after a decent night's sleep. The
French air has infused itself throughout my body once more,
allowing me to sleep soundly through the night.

We spend an hour and a half in the studio, chiefly working on several rounds of sun salutations. Jo takes to it instantly, although the irony isn't lost on her; the 'sun' is utterly non-existent.

As lunch beckons, Jo and I sprint to the Twingo and I cautiously drive through the Lotois countryside. Even in the rain, it is a sight to behold. The road twists and turns through fields left to grow into flower-filled meadows. Caramel-coloured cattle gather together under trees while their young scamper through their long curvy legs.

I gently squeeze the brake as the Twingo makes its final descent into the village. It is a bank holiday and so the blinds are down at *la boulangerie, le boucherie* and *le tabac*. The one place that is open is the Bon Accueil. We open the door into the steamy bar, where regulars occupy the half dozen tables or are perched on stools at the bar. Naturally there is the predictable fug of cigarette smoke to wade through.

I almost miss Pascal.

There are no sexy jeans and shirt this time.

Instead he is in head-to-toe camouflage clothing; that's T-shirt, trousers, jacket and a hat.

Jo stifles the urge to laugh, while Pascal and I nervously greet each other. A Gitane cigarette is alight in the ashtray. I'd forgotten that he is never without one hanging off his lip or burning dangerously on an inappropriate ledge. The only sign of nervousness is his bouncing knee.

'*Allô* Jo!' Pascal embraces Jo in a bear hug.

'*Bonjour!*' Jo nods with a smile, eyes casting everywhere about him, absorbing every single detail to report back to the Grand Inquisitor, Mother.

'You like to drink rosé too?' Pascal asks, having already ordered one for me. Jo nods eagerly.

Pascal waves behind my head. I spin around to look at who he is beckoning over.

At a table there is a young boy, with a peaked cap jauntily positioned on his too-long hair and a computer game console which appears to be welded to his hands.

'Antonio!' The cap is still the only thing we can see of Antonio, who doesn't respond. He is, it would appear, concentrating intensely on the game he is playing.

'ANTONIO!' Pascal roars a second time.

'Antonio' pushes his chair back and saunters towards Pascal. My mind turns and I instantly realise that this is Pascal's youngest son. He pulls himself up to full height, which is just about our chest region, and says *bonjour* and kisses each of us on our cheeks. Pascal watches our exchange closely, before signalling to Antonio that he can return to his game.

Pascal, it would appear, is in a flap. He has yet to buy food to prepare lunch for us. This is no easy feat on a bank holiday when all of the shops are closed. But, like most people in rural France, he knows *someone* and before we've had a chance to chirrup *santé* and clink glasses, he's gone. I crane my neck out of the entrance of the bar to see Pascal knocking on the door of the firmly closed *épicerie*.

With Pascal gone, Jo suggests we sit down with Antonio.

I stare at her bug-eyed. What do you say to a ten year old?

My sister is well versed in dealing with children so is instantly able to start name-checking computer games and films. Jo easily strikes up a franglais conversation about what games he likes. She confidently chatters away, fag in one hand and a permanently topped up glass of vino in the other.

As they chat I use this as an opportunity to check him out. I notice for a kid he's cute; tall, brown eyes and big smile.

During the Jo-instigated banter with Antonio, Pascal has returned and hovered around us on at least three occasions, ostensibly to verify what a vegetarian actually eats. When he eventually realises that no, it really doesn't mean I can eat chicken, he makes several more trips between bar and *épicerie*. Jo giggles at the bags spilling over with lettuce, celery and carrots. 'This is all for you, you know,' she whispers.

All the while Antonio politely responds to Pascal's '*Ça va?*' as he shoots back and forth across the square.

I can't help wondering if Antonio knows who I am. What have I been described as? Love interest? Or simply a friend? Does he know or even care why his papa is going all out to entertain two British women? Unfortunately, all this thinking has turned into senseless stressing, which of course sends me into an internal panic. I know perfectly well that this is the weekend that has the potential to change things between us.

With bags of fresh produce and several bottles of wine safely stowed in the boot of Pascal's car, we're finally on the road to his home. The journey, even in the permanent drizzle, is beautiful. The car leaves Cazals behind and mounts a winding road to pass through the village centre of Gindou and then continue along *le causse*, a high flat piece of the geographical landscape which dominates this part of the Lot. The fields and valleys that dip away on each side of the road are intermittently broken up by quaint *'mas'*, stone farm houses proudly standing guard over fields of chickens, vegetable crops and ancient pieces of farming machinery.

Gindou village is blink-and-you'll-miss-it tiny. Yet it is still defiantly picturesque, built in the same buttery, honey stone that typifies the houses in the area. There is a church, a *mairie* (or town hall) and one main street. Most of the 350 residents are part of a rich tapestry of families who have owned the surrounding countryside for generations. Pascal's home is tucked away towards the very commune limits of Gindou in one of the numerous rural lanes.

When we arrive, the house is as beautiful as I remember. Elsea, too, is there to greet us like a long-lost friend, excitedly bobbing back and forth on the stairs outside of the house. This time I notice *la grange*, a barn so enormous it could comfortably house a family of ten. The chalky off-white outer walls are as pretty as the main house. Honeysuckle blossom hugs the crumbly brickwork, scenting the air with its unique sweetness.

We make ourselves comfortable at a large oak farmhouse table, which dominates the living room, and almost instantly Pascal serves us both another glass of wine. We are subtly positioned to avoid Pascal and Antonio's places. I am seated at the right-hand side of Pascal's place at the head of the table.

Jo slides her camera out of her bag and suggests a couple of 'impromptu' snaps. Looking at me from behind the lens she mouths 'your new family', with a knowing wink. Unsurprisingly, I look startled in each and every photo.

I make a fresh attempt at bonding with Antonio. Unfortunately, I make the colossal mistake of asking him if he would like to play a game together.

'*Ouai!*' comes the excited reply.

Great, I think, recalling a rusty command of Monopoly, while he ploughs through cupboards, before asking Pascal for a lighter.

A lighter?

Antonio then walks towards the tall window and turns the oval-shaped handle before pulling open the delicate wooden frame. As the rain splutters in, I cautiously pull my jacket around me, while peering over at the window sill. There he places three red objects, each no bigger than a matchbox. Jo shoots me a pointed look and urges me to peer in closer, mouthing 'Take a bloody interest'.

As Antonio lights each of them I am still none the wiser as to what's about to happen.

Within seconds it is crystal clear. Unfortunately, my reaction – a loud and unmitigated squeal – is the desired response for Antonio. Our game is this: he lights a firecracker and I shriek the house down.

For the next fifteen minutes we 'play' with firecrackers. I sit as casually as I can, allowing Antonio the opportunity to ignite what is essentially gunpowder within close proximity.

Pascal, Antonio and Jo (traitor) all laugh in synchronicity as I predictably shudder and screech hysterically in response to the loud bangs around me. Fortunately, there are only six (six!) of the little red stress inducers.

God almighty, I think to myself. Are all French kids like this?

Pascal smiles, presumably at how well we're bonding.

Jo, between copious amounts of rosé, fails dismally to hide the fact she is snorting with laughter.

When they are, I assume, all finally dispersed with, I take myself off to the loo – down a little hallway away from the living room. I'm hoping to catch my breath in all honesty. It's only when I'm locked in the tiny confined space that I realise I have miscalculated the number of firecrackers. In mid pee, I watch aghast as a tiny red object slowly rolls beneath the door.

Bang! I nearly fall off the seat, bumping my head on the loo-paper holder.

I yelp and have to stop myself from howling various curses in the bloody kid's direction. When I have finally composed myself, I peek out of the loo door and, thank you God, don't find another fizzing firecracker. Instead I spy Pascal waiting for me. I assume he is there to check if I'm OK. I assume wrong.

Without warning he takes me in his arms. He is big and he is gruff, yet his kisses are as soft and light as a butterfly on the petal of a meadow flower. Nestled in his arms, I realise I am utterly smitten.

Jo and I watch, hawk-eyed, as Pascal and Antonio set the table for lunch. They each have their own knife, *un couteau*. They aren't just used for hunting or for assistance with everyday tasks; they also, it would appear, opt for them over traditional table knives. Antonio's is a chunky, dangerous-looking camouflage knife. Pascal's is a frankly terrifying 7-inch blade that, I learn, goes everywhere with him and is an essential tool in his trade as a carpenter.

Jo and I cannot resist handling them, but as we awkwardly attempt to open them, Pascal insists we stop. 'Zey are not a toy!' For the first time, his steeliness shows through.

'*Regardez!*'

We both giggle and receive a 'look'. We instantly stop.

'Open *le couteau comme ça*,' he demonstrates. '*Voilà!*' And then asks us both to try.

Jo opens her one perfectly. I try, not so perfectly.

'You are dead if you play wiz zee blade,' Pascal continues, warming to his theme, as he draws his thumb across the base of his throat.

'It ees really zee best to *fais attention, chérie.*' He finishes, looking at me.

As we eat a salad composed of lettuce, tuna, sweetcorn, tomatoes and at least a dozen other types of vegetables (it is surprisingly good), Pascal tells us of the last meal he prepared for some English friends. At one point during the meal one man remarked on the presence of a deer in the back garden (which is, technically speaking, a forest).

Poor deer. There it was one moment, at one with nature, being admired. Unfortunately, Pascal's friend Alberto deposed of it within seconds. Half an hour later, courtesy of Pascal, it was bagged up and distributed to all of the guests present.

Until now I have only witnessed the brooding, sexy side of Pascal. Not the deer hunter, who has more knives and sharp implements in his kitchen than your average serial killer. I see a deer and think Bambi. Pascal sees a deer and calculates how many meals it will make.

I know – I should be appalled. Yet if I'm completely honest with myself, there is something raw, sexy and real about

Pascal. It is the combination of these qualities I find utterly irresistible.

Jo and I spend our final day chez Miriam. Yet we won't be spending the final night together. For I have taken the plunge and accepted an invitation from Pascal to stay at his house. Jo wisely declines Pascal's offer to sleep in Antonio's bottom bunk bed. Instead, she has assured me she is perfectly capable of hanging out with Miriam and the other clients. Miriam dismisses the invitation as a 'good shag' for one night only. The cheek! I don't want to jinx what's happening between Pascal and me, but I'd like to think it's more than a one-night stand.

Pascal collects me and drives me to his house. I can tell he is nervous (more so than I am); his hands are shaking when he eventually opens the door to his home. For the first time it is just the two of us. Antonio has been packed off to his mother's house. He takes my coat and places it on a chair. Outside, the rain is unrelenting and has cast a misty hue around the house. It is as though we're all alone in the world.

The living room is chilly and when I shiver, no longer afforded the protection of my coat, Pascal instantly sets about lighting a fire. Within minutes, logs of chestnut wood lazily burn in the grate, gently crackling and throwing a soft glow around the living room. We are sat together on a sofa in front of the fire, there are mere millimetres between us. I feel the heat rising from his skin. Pascal offers me a glass of champagne from the bottle he has thoughtfully laid out in front of us. I inelegantly take a gulp from the glass and then place it on the coffee table. As I sit back Pascal gathers me into his arms. He holds me with such tenderness. He begins to stroke my face, before softly placing kisses on my neck, my cheeks, my eyelids; such gestures of tenderness are all the more profound in this macho-macho man.

We talk for hours; he is so different to the metrosexual type of man I normally find myself with. Yes, Pascal is older, but he's also wiser and has positively lived a life, and courageously faced head on what the universe has thrown at him. He eventually pieces together the puzzle of my life, slotting together the information I gave him during my last visit. This time I tell him everything. When he finally understands the full extent of my problems, his response is simple: '*Je te protège tout le temps.*' I'll always protect you.

The following morning, the alarm clock rudely awakens us at 6 a.m. 'You come again when?' is the first thing Pascal asks, before kissing me *bonjour*.

On the drive back to Miriam's, we excitedly discuss when I might return to see him again. For the first time in my life, I don't have work, I don't have a boss to answer to, I can visit Pascal when I please. We eventually agree for two weeks' time, the middle of June. It's an understatement to say we are both fizzing with happiness.

We stop and buy croissants in Cazals. When we are comfortably reseated in the car, Pascal proclaims, 'Everyone will now know you are *ma femme* [my woman].' Whoa, I think to myself, news doesn't spread that quickly. Yet when we arrive at Miriam's she tuts in response to the gesture of the croissants. 'Now everyone will know you are an item.'

On the plane home, I ask Jo, 'How was it with Miriam last night?'

'Well, you know, she really, really wanted me to know just how totally, utterly happy she is for you and Pascal.'

'Really?' Maybe I'd got her wrong.

'Sam, grow up! You and I know exactly what she means. She's really, really pissed off with you. Tread carefully around that one. She's going to cause you a lot of problems.'

chapter Six

Falling in Love

Before I've unpacked my suitcase I dig out a card to send to Miriam. I'm one of those annoyingly organised types of women who always have a hoard of cards on stand-by – birthday cards, sympathy notes, thank-you extravaganzas, sorry-to-hear-you're-unwell cards. I carefully select one and, having made a cup of chamomile tea, plonk myself down at the pine table in the kitchen of my rental cottage and mull over what to write.

Before I haltingly put pen to card, I thoroughly interrogate myself; have I been careless in neglecting Miriam? Am I treading on her elegantly painted toes? What advice would an agony aunt dispense with when it comes to the delicate matter of rather liking a friend's platonic male chum? On inspection, I find my behaviour wanting. I chastise myself; perhaps it was graceless to indulge in a night of passion with Pascal, leaving Miriam to entertain Jo.

I feel a fool for not realising that while she might not have any romantic inclinations towards Pascal, she wants to guard her friendship. I don't blame her; as I've discovered, Pascal is a good listener and charming company. I'd wager I'm guilty of overlooking Miriam's feelings – and she doesn't like it. If Jo's feminine intuition is correct, then I need to tread very cautiously.

So I painstakingly compose (after countless false starts) conciliatory prose which would make Kofi Annan proud. Please know I won't interfere in your friendship with Pascal, I implore. Please be happy for me, I plead.

I don't write, but perhaps I should have, that this *matters* to me. For once in my romantic life this liaison with Pascal feels right. Ecstatic doesn't begin to describe how I'd feel if this love affair rocketed off, sizzling into the sky, rather than fizzing on the ground before it's had a chance to launch. Which is usually the story of my life.

Three days later I receive a call from Miriam; *of course I'm happy for you*, she reassures me. I silently chastise myself for overreacting. I sit on the floor of my now pristine office and twist the cord of the receiver nervously around my fingers while she informs me that Pascal is currently the object of village gossip. It is also reported, she tells me, that he is only ever spotted with a huge smile on his face. This, according to Miriam, is worthy of a front page splash on *Le Figaro*.

'Are you really returning later this June?' she asks.

'Errr, yes… I am,' I say hesitantly.

There is a brooding silence down the line.

I take a deep breath before continuing, 'I'm going to stay with Pascal this time, though… You know, just to see if this could perhaps, errr, lead to something…' I trail off. I don't want to betray any more of the intimacies that have passed between Pascal and me, but at the same time I want to keep her in the picture. She deserves that much.

'Right, well,' comes the clipped reply. 'I trust I'll see you?'

'Of course!'

Before I replace the receiver, she says something I wonder if I really heard, or whether it was my paranoid mind playing tricks on me.

'I hope you've got a bloody dictionary.'

If I'm to make a go of things with Pascal, then clearly I'm on my own.

In-between reacting to Ambrose's epileptic fits – I'm working with the vets to get the right level of medication in his system – and more weekend sleepovers with Maddy, I am bombarded with calls, emails and texts. While Miriam probably wouldn't want to hear this, I adore being courted by a Frenchman.

Yet the reality is – as Miriam accurately predicted – I struggle with even basic French. It is acutely mortifying. Even to receive a message such as, *'Je te veux dans mes bras'* sends me scurrying to WHSmith to purchase a dictionary in order to decipher the simple fact that he wants to hold me in his arms.

To reply to a simple message such as *'Je pense à toi très fort'* takes an onerous half an hour to translate and then compose a suitably charming response – in French.

And on reading and not understanding, *'Je t'envoie un énorme bisou'*, I put my head in my hands. Why, oh why didn't I pay more attention at school? I smugly assumed I'd only need an understanding of the English language...

'Go on, Sam! Describe him for me!'

Staring out from the mirror in front of me is my hairdresser, Andrew, who is winding my just-highlighted hair onto large old-fashioned rollers.

'You'll need a bit of bounce,' he'd reasoned, after fingering my too-fine hair, when I'd entered the salon two hours earlier. Trailing behind me was a bulging suitcase and handbag bursting with a variety of magazines.

In three hours' time I will once more be checking in at Birmingham Airport, where I will then go on to wait nervously to board my flight to Bergerac.

'We-e-ell, he's tall, Latin-looking…'

'Yes, yes, I know what he looks like,' Andrew interrupts, 'your mum's told me all that already.'

Mother! I think to myself, crossly.

'What else can I tell you…?' I ask out loud, trailing off as I struggle to pull some other character traits from my memory bank. In truth, I don't know *that* much more about Pascal. I know his son is called Antonio, as opposed to Antoine, because he is fiercely proud of his Catalan roots. But beyond that? Not a great deal more. I'm a smidgen uncomfortable to confess that's what I'm hoping to discover on this next visit.

'Well,' demands Andrew, a tad impatiently, 'does he have any hobbies?'

'Hobbies? Hmm… well… he likes hunting.' I instantly visualise that rather alarming camouflage outfit he wore to meet Jo and me.

'He owns guns – not that I've seen any yet!' I add quickly. Only those knives, I think silently. They fit in perfectly in rural

France, but there is an entirely different set of social norms in a sophisticated Solihull hair salon.

At the mention of guns, Andrew's antenna is already twitching. Bug-eyed, he stares at me in the mirror.

'Guns? Hunting? Sam! You live to shop,' he reasons, looking at the dress I'd arrived in. For the record it was a rare new purchase: a pistachio green with fuchsia-pink flowers tea dress, cut just above the knee, with a darling little bow at the back. Chic, pretty, prefect for tea on the lawn; in other words, definitely not a dress to hunt in.

'Oh, Andrew,' I breezily reply, batting away the trifling detail that hunting is a sport practised by generations of Pascal's family, 'I'll cure him of that.'

Perhaps unsurprisingly, Andrew doesn't look convinced.

With my hair perfectly coiffed, I am smoothing down the very same dress as the little plane judders to a standstill at Bergerac airport. I peek out of the tiny window towards the squat airport arrivals building. Just next to it, friends and family gather, eagerly peering through the airport security fencing, hoping to catch the first glimpse of their loved ones.

A smile spreads across my face.

He's there!

I spy him standing proudly, unmistakable amidst the sea of expats, gazing in the direction of the plane, in his denim jeans and cowboy boots. A blue cotton shirt is sexily open halfway. His wraparound sunglasses are firmly in place to protect him from the intensity of the late afternoon sun.

My stomach performs an unintentional somersault.

I instantly jump up (banging my head on the overhead locker) and yank my oversized bag from the space above me. Impatiently waiting to disembark, I fuss with my drooping curls, attempt to smooth out the creases of my dress and wipe at the corners of my eyes where my liquid eyeliner is already gathering.

At the top of the steps I pause, look to the left and immediately clock Pascal. A grin dances across his lips and he waves. My heart flips! I can feel the pull of his allure already.

Ten minutes later I am walking towards him. He scoops me in his arms, oblivious to the clucks and stares of everyone around us, and envelops me in his warm embrace.

'*Bonjour mon amour,*' he whispers huskily into my ear, squashing my curls in the process. Not that I care. I am literally quivering in his presence.

'*Ça va?*' I giggle in response.

Inexplicably, instead of the carefully prepared image of a sophisticated thirty-six-year-old woman I'd hoped to present, I – at best – resemble a self-conscious teenager.

'I take zat for you, *chérie.*' Pascal effortlessly swings my weekend bag onto his shoulder and weaves his free arm around my waist.

Together, we are a walking endorsement for the phrase 'absence makes the heart grow fonder'. As we amble towards the car park, we cannot stop touching each other. At the same time we exchange coquettish smiles and we haltingly talk over one another in a series of incomplete franglais phrases.

The magical spell isn't even broken when we stop at a rather tired-looking white Citroën van.

'Errr, *où est le* Mercedes, Pascal?' I ask, staring at what must be a work vehicle, replete with several sets of ladders strapped to the roof and, having peered through a side window, a cacophony of tools haphazardly piled on top of each other in the rear.

'I 'ave a leetle accident in zee Mercedes,' he casually explains as he opens the rear doors, hastily pushing aside a tool box which tries to escape, while tossing my holdall in there at the same time.

I smile encouragingly when he leans over to open the passenger door. I don't flinch when he pats the seat, even though enough dust to fill the Sahara Desert escapes from it. Instead, I gingerly position myself – for the first time in my life – inside a little white van.

Eventually, we join a chain of cars leaving the airport. Instead of taking the turning Miriam usually takes, Pascal's indicator signifies we're going in a different direction; a little-known route, foreign to most expats. For me, it doesn't matter which direction the little Citroën points towards – I'm already lost in more ways than one.

'Sam!'

'Gurghhh? What?'

When my eyes reluctantly open they automatically flick to the electronic alarm clock on Pascal's side of the bed where his head was nestled next to me when we eventually got to sleep. I can just about make out 5.30 a.m. blinking back at me. Sensibly, then, I instinctively turn over with the express intention of returning to sleep.

'Sam! *Non!* Nooo sleeping. *Allez! On y va!*' I gingerly lift my head from the long French pillow bolster I've slept on for the last five hours.

More sex! I think to myself. Gosh, what's he like…! Insatiab–

'Sam! *Allez!*' Worried, and with coquettish thoughts receding from my mind, I pull myself up onto my elbows and I glance around the darkened bedroom. The wooden shutters are tightly fastened, allowing just flashes of dawn to peep under and over the cappuccino-coloured wood. At the end of the bed stands Pascal, staring down at me.

He is fully dressed.

In camouflage.

Apparently, Pascal has an entirely different leisure pursuit on his mind.

'*Chéri,*' I rasp, 'what is it?'

'Come! We go 'unt, Sam!'

Hunt? Me?

At that precise second a pair of camouflage trousers sails across the room, landing on my lap. They are swiftly followed by an army-green T-shirt, and a mucky brown fleece top.

'You 'ave *baskets?*' Pascal asks, meaning do I have a pair of trainers with me. I think of the rose-pink Converse I popped in my luggage as an afterthought. They'll have to do.

'Umm, yes.' I disentangle myself from the bed sheets, not wanting to be christened a party pooper. I eventually locate my black Myla bra, daintily covered in rosebuds, I dig a matching pair of panties out of my Mary Poppins-esque holdall and hurriedly pull the hunting clothes on over them. I try not to inhale the scent of the rustic clothing; it's fair to say 'freshly laundered' doesn't instantly spring to mind.

'*Allez*, Sam!' Pascal booms from the corridor which connects the bedroom to the living room. I frantically pull my hair into a ponytail and, on catching a glimpse of myself in the mirror, I shudder with embarrassment.

What a sight!

I look horrendous in a pair of too-small trousers – which must belong to Antonio – along with the over-sized T-shirt and fleece. On-trend I am not. Head bowed, I walk into the living room where Pascal is waiting for me. Elsea is pogoing up and down with excitement.

'*Génial!*' Pascal enthuses when I enter. No, not great. Not a great look *at all* I think to myself.

'You don't wash?' Pascal asks me with a look of concern on his face.

Shit! I think, guiltily, is it that obvious?

'I just...' I begin to motion the actions of a baby wipe pulled across my face, when Pascal interrupts me.

'No, zat is good.' He approaches me and begins to circle me, inhaling deeply as he does so.

'No nice smells, Sam, no perfume. *Bon!*'

As we walk to the Citroën van, Pascal explains that the first rule of hunting is smell. An animal can detect perfume, even laundry detergent, miles away. It is their biggest clue that man – the enemy – is on their territory. He pushes his scarf under my nose and I want to gag; it absolutely honks and could do with a bloody good wash.

'I never wash it, Sam.' Pascal looks at me in all seriousness. 'Ever.'

By now we are both in the van; the sun is already winkling its way above the distant village of Thédirac, its rays painting the Lotois countryside in a silky palette of pinks, oranges and reds. The sky is cloudless, distant planes streak across the sky, heralding the start of another beautiful day. Pascal fires up the engine, the radio kicks in and Brigitte Bardot sings about her home in St Tropez. Before I have chance to close my door, Elsea springs in and nestles into my lap.

'*On y va!*' Pascal grins at me, he lights a Gitane cigarette and the Citroën nosily complains as he shifts the gearstick into reverse.

Within ten minutes we are in the middle of one of the innumerable woods which characterise this little corner of France. Chestnut trees mingle tightly with pine trees, their branches hugging each other securely. The little van staggers and stalls as we make our way into the heart of the woodland. There are no roads to speak of, only barely discernible tracks. Pascal has already gestured to me to wind my window down. Immediately Elsea pokes her head out, sniffing the air, little brown eyes darting left and right, alert – I'm guessing – for prey. By now the van is puttering along in second gear as Pascal also scans the thick green scenery around us.

Suddenly there is a rustle in a clump of shaded fern nearby; it is the hunting equivalent of calling 999.

'*Allez*, Elsea!' Before Pascal has finished saying her name she has shot out of the passenger window. I give a pathetic little shriek as she lands and shoots off chasing whatever it was that caused the leaves to stir.

'*Allez*, Sam, *Allez!*'

I jump out and follow Pascal, who is walking purposefully in the direction that Elsea streaked off. Her yipping in the distance dictates our direction. After several minutes Pascal stops and turns me around.

'Is beautiful, no?' I take in the immense woodland, peppered only by blink-and-you'll-miss-them single-file paths. Pascal assures me that these have been created by animals that dwell in dense forests such as this one.

'Do you see zee animals, Sam?' he asks softly.

I look around me. I spy hundreds of trees, fallen branches, crumbling stone huts which once would have been used by shepherds. On the lush forest floor there are enormous pine cones, a bed of leaves and... errr, that's it.

'I don't see anything,' I murmur earnestly to Pascal. I keep the disappointment out of my voice, because I'd secretly hoped we'd see *something* this morning.

Pascal looks at me and shakes his head.

'*Viens!*' He pulls me towards him. 'See zat?' he whispers. I follow his gaze and to my utter astonishment I spy an owl sitting proudly on the branch of a tree. I'm convinced I'd cast my eye over that very spot just seconds earlier and seen nothing.

'Over zere!' Again I follow the direction of his pointed finger and see what Pascal tells me is *une poule-faisane* – a female pheasant – huddled under a fan of fern leaves. She is sitting on a nest, explains Pascal, who moves in closer to confirm his guess – that she is protecting her future offspring. The pheasant, none too pleased at being spotted, rewards Pascal with several rather angry clucks. Pascal wisely moves us away.

He points out wood pigeons, shows me deer droppings and reveals several entrances to a well-established badger set. It is magical, the forest really is alive.

While we wait for Elsea to return, Pascal explains why he doesn't have a hunting rifle with him today (not, I hasten to add, that I wanted him armed). The *chasse* season is closed. Even so, Pascal will only hunt if there is an overpopulation of an animal species; he doesn't shoot indiscriminately; he won't hunt when females are pregnant. While I still harbour doubts about hunting on principle, I feel rather ashamed that I'd lazily assumed all hunters had an 'if I spot an animal, then I'll shoot it' attitude and paid scant regard to the stability of the countryside's animal population.

While we don't see boar, deer or stag – a fact Pascal puts down to my Belisha beacon footwear which broadcasts where we are – I do see why Pascal only ever talks to me about hunting in the same breath as his love for nature.

'What do we do,' I ask, 'if Elsea doesn't come back?' I'm keenly aware that my tummy is rumbling and that we have spent over two hours in the forest. Since Elsea shot off, excuse the pun, we have seen neither hide nor hair of her.

'I leave zis 'ere,' Pascal says, patting his scarf. 'She know my smell and she stay 'ere until I come back. Maybe one day or two day later.'

Pascal roars out Elsea's name one final time. Just as we turn to leave, there is a rustle and a black ball of fluff shoots through the dense greenery. Elsea slows her pace down, and within moments she has fallen into pace with us and is skipping alongside as we return to the van.

Pascal looks at me and says, 'She is very intelligent. She understands the countryside, Sam.'

I, on the other hand, have got a lot to learn.

That lunchtime we drive to Cazals for an aperitif. The village square is buzzing. Pascal's colleagues – electricians, carpenters, builders – are all taking coffee or a glass of rosé on the little pavement terrace in front of the Café de Paris. It is the other bar in Cazals, and one that is widely referred to as the workers' establishment. This does not diminish its status in any way, it simply means it's where the local *artisans* (the skilled tradesmen) go to socialise, exchange news and – dare I say it – gossip.

While Pascal catches up with colleagues I wander over to the *tabac* to buy a postcard for my grandmother. Ever since I started to travel the world, I have always sent her news of where I am.

What on earth will my eighty-something grandmother make of my latest escapade, I wonder.

And then I remember; she too left Dublin to seek love in Britain. Somehow, I ponder, she'll be rather proud of this latest leap of faith.

Later on Pascal announces he has a surprise for me. We are going out for dinner.

We are to dine at a restaurant called L'Auberge Sans Frontière and it is, Pascal tells me, one of his favourite eateries. It's far, he warns me. At over half an hour's drive away, I realise this means that it might as well be on the moon. Curiously, and rather quaintly, most of Pascal's colleagues and neighbours haven't even been to Paris, much less left the borders of France.

We leave just before the sun sets. The drive to the restaurant is fast, exhilarating and akin, I imagine, to a Formula 1 race track. The Lot is principally made up of hills and valleys – where you choose to live can mean your daily temperature differs by as much as five degrees – and the road network has had to fashion itself to the unyielding landscape. This means that there are lots of scary hairpin bends and sudden steep drops. Yet the view more than makes up for it; we pass countless pretty hamlets, ancient churches, farmsteads still thriving in this agriculturally rich area.

Pascal is warmly received when we arrive. *Une bise* is planted on each of his cheeks within seconds of passing over the threshold. Pascal is cooed over and congratulated when it becomes clear we are dining *à deux*. I am afforded the same welcome by owners Jean-Christophe and his wife Patricia. Jean-Christophe, who cooks with a hirsute chap called Xavier, pours Pascal a welcoming slug of whiskey and I am offered a glass of Kir. A large satisfied-looking dog slowly heaves himself from in front of the bar, making way for us to perch on a stool. I already feel at home.

The family-run restaurant is tucked away in the village of Dégagnac, nestled in a tiny side street. The interior walls are creamy, rough-hewn stone. Copper pots adorn the walls and a glass refrigerator is already tempting me with home-made gateaux, brûlées and tarts.

As locals nurse glasses of pastis and pore over the daily newspaper, Pascal is gently interrogated by Patricia about who I am.

'*Ma femme!*' Pascal proudly announces that I'm his girlfriend. Oooooh!

I haltingly explain I am from England. Patricia politely listens to my faltering French, discreetly correcting me as I gradually introduce myself. She is tall and supermodel thin, and her alabaster-coloured face is framed with chocolate-brown, shoulder-length hair. She kindly explains that there are many *Anglais* in her village.

This doesn't surprise me. I already know that, roughly speaking, one in ten homes in the Lot is a second home. Brits, and also Belgians, Dutch and Parisians (who are considered foreign by the Lotois) have been seduced by the area. It seems as though everyone has fallen for the beautiful ancient properties.

We gorge on a divine meal. My generous plate of *coquilles St Jacques* is exquisite; plump, melt-in-the-mouth delicious scallops cooked in a mushroom sauce and garnished with vegetables and chipped potatoes. Pascal orders a *bavette*, a type of steak that is popular is this part of France.

'Are you 'appy, Sam?' Pascal asks me over an espresso when we have finished.

I glance around me; I don't understand a word that anyone says, I struggled to order my food and if anything were to happen to me then nobody knows where I am.

Yet I look across the table, at the handsome man before me, who is holding my hand. It occurs to me that he is always in physical contact with me; a thigh brushing against mine, holding my elbow, or a palm gently resting in the small of my back. I realise that while this man, this country and these people are utterly foreign to me, I am indeed blissfully happy and so I reply in his language as best I can:

'*Oui, mon amour. Je suis heureuse.*'

His face breaks into an enormous smile.

'An 'appier man than me don't exist right now.'

chapter Seven

The Rehearsal

As I am officially unemployable, the highlight of each day back in Birmingham is walking the dogs. Before, our outings together were hastily tacked onto the start and end of each day. Up before dawn, we joined the other alpha females, striding with their dogs along the Thames towpath. I could usually be spotted in suspect gym gear (typically a hotchpotch of colours and layers flung on over my pyjamas), roaring at Ambrose each time he scarpered in terror on hearing an approaching Tube train thundering towards us, if I had mistimed our approach to a railway bridge. Then in the evenings we would be kicking around Kew Green under an inky black sky, inevitably at pub closing time. I would – through gritted teeth – implore Barney to poop so I could bag it, toss it and bed us down for the night.

Now that such walks are the focus of each day, I'm *really* getting to know my dogs. Barney – the fat, greedy one – is sensitive to smells and sneezes profusely at anything alien to him. Even when we're at home I've taken to gently stroking his black muzzle, tickling his weak spot, and he will softly paw at me to stop. Meanwhile, when we're out, Ambrose bunny-hops enthusiastically, his weak back legs favouring the left, then he'll stop and look around to check I'm still there, before repeating the whole process thirty seconds later. I never noticed before just how much he relies on me.

On each walk we're more daring; we explore further and further along the canal. It isn't long before we've trotted around the entire perimeter of the Christmas tree farm which edges the waterway near the house we currently call home. Daring to venture off the canal path, we have tramped through fields, stooped under charming keystone bridges and said hello to countless boat owners. All the while I have one eye trained on Ambrose; looking out for the fall, the loss of bladder control, the juddering. Such occasions occur less and less. The anti-epileptic drugs just might be working. His fits, when they happen, are a weekly occurrence at most. Nonetheless, each night, before I sleep, I spend time meditating, channelling my thoughts and prayers towards his recovery.

My preoccupations, chiefly Pascal and Ambrose, have had a curiously positive effect on my psyche. My consultations with my GP have lessened to once a fortnight and, while I'm still knocking back the antidepressants and greedily ensuring I have 'just enough' in the medicine cabinet, I no longer sob my heart out during our appointments. Rather, I have started to reflect on the hollowness of my former career, the fact that I got caught up in the smoke and mirrors of such a superficial world. Those nights when I lie awake staring hollow-eyed at the alarm clock still occur, but they are few and far between.

Am I recovering? I'd like to think so.

What happens next? I have no idea who I am. When I look in the mirror I'm not familiar with the woman who stares back at me.

Mother tactfully suggests I turn my attention to the 'next step'.

'Workshops? Conferences?' trills Mother. 'Why not convert the garage, Sam? Anything's possible!' These are the inane brainstorming sessions Mother attempts to have with me.

'Ummm,' I ask tentatively, 'doing what?'

'Everyone needs media training these days,' she says.

'Me?'

'There's no one better than you,' she replies confidently.

I stare at her, aghast. Yet again she has rendered me speechless.

How I can launch myself as a motivational speaker in a Midlands lock-up garage is anyone's guess. It's hardly the Institute of Directors, is it?

The number of friends I still see from my old life can be counted on one hand. One is very practical, the other is supremely spiritual. The latter suggests I take time out to connect with who I am and what my journey on earth is. She sends me books on how to be a Warrior Woman. She also presses on me incantations from archangels who will, she reassures me, protect and guide me at all times.

The practical friend tells me to get my sorry ass back down to London, pronto. She thinks it's a crime I'm not embracing my talents. She urges me to take a fat cat salaried position with the requisite expense account. She reminds me that New York and Los Angeles are always waiting for me – she tells me in no uncertain terms that I'll be greeted with open arms.

While their opinions on my new life are wildly different, what they are unanimous on is that they are extremely suspicious of my Frenchman. They are convinced my dalliance is a Bad Idea.

Oh dear.

Am I about to make an idiot of myself all over again? They have both pessimistically predicted that the answer is a resounding yes.

Even my niece Madeleine thinks Pascal is 'bad news'.

I understand their fear, for if this doesn't work out, I'm not sure I'll be able to find my way back. I really will be trapped down the rabbit hole.

Nonetheless, like a bee to honey, I am drawn back to France again. Lust and love have successfully cast their spell, binding us together across the Channel.

It's July; the sun is shining, and the French countryside is achingly pretty, Pascal reassures me. Come, he urges me. Why not, indeed, for at this moment Pascal and I can find no fault in each other.

Of course, I go with guilt. My stepfather, Norman, and my dad are taking it in turns to look after the dogs. The advantage of being (whisper it) *ill* is that everyone is still rather keen on helping me. Dad has said surprisingly little about 'these fecking jaunts' to France. Perhaps more accurately, zero opinions have been expressed directly to me; however, I'd wager his opinion isn't one brimming with optimism. Whereas Norman, clearly coached by Mother, just diplomatically waves me off when I hand him over the dog rota, urging me to have a nice time.

What few people know is that this time my stay is a trial; a question lingers between us as heavy as the heads on the lavender which line one side of Pascal's house. Can we make it as a real couple?

It isn't a forty-eight-hour visit. This time it is for a buttock-clenchingly stressful, ordinary, run-of-the-mill week. I will learn what really occurs during Pascal's nine-to-five. He will

doubtless decide whether he can put up with me when w
not between the sheets. I'm the first to admit that the last st.
consisted largely of long sultry nights spent in bed or groaning
with pleasure over another delicious feast at a local *auberge*.

We've giddily got ahead of ourselves.

I have Mother's blessing. She reads the emails, overhears the
telephone conversations, hears the mobile phone signalling
another text message. Her caustic commentary, which was so
often, perhaps deservedly, meted out at the doomed love affairs
which dominated my past, is curiously absent.

When Pascal remarked that, within the space of a month, he
had spent over three hundred euros on mobile phone calls to
me, Mother, instead of shaking her head and clucking about the
waste of money, reacted girlishly, thrilled that such a romantic
gesture could be splurged on her daughter.

So then, the deal is this. Pascal will be working, Antonio is
now on school holiday and I am in charge – a French housewife.

Cooking, cleaning, keeping house.

Not speaking French is the least of my worries.

First, the good news. I swiftly discover that ten-year-old boys
like nothing more than to loll about in bed until 11 a.m. Result!
As Pascal arrives home at noon on the dot, this means I spend
roughly one hour with Antonio.

Who knew parenting could be so easy?

When he is finally, gingerly, prodded awake by yours truly on
the first day, it is with much huffing and puffing that he hauls
himself out of bed and into the living room.

is *not* a morning person.

This is my second encounter with Antonio. Since the firecracker episode, I have innocently pushed thoughts of him out of my mind. A ridiculously naïve thing to do, I know, not least because he lives one week in two with Pascal. If things are to work out between us, I need to find a way to fit into the daily humdrum of their lives. It's crystal clear that it won't be the other way around.

On discreet inspection of Antonio, I conclude a lot can happen in the space of two months in the lifecycle of a ten-year-old boy. He appears to have shot up. He is all legs and freckles and his face this time is framed with lots of thick brown curly hair.

During the hour we spend together I make him hot chocolate and toast for breakfast. When he has finished the crockery is, to my disbelief, left on the large farmhouse table. He then starts playing on a computer game. He does ask if it's OK, though – sort of. To my embarrassment he speaks better English than I do French. There is lots of pointing involved, while he tries to make me understand that he wants to play. I, predictably, meekly say yes. Although what would happen if I said no isn't something I want to find out. I know I should probably start as I mean to go on, but I'm so relieved there are no firecrackers to punctuate our time together that I figure it's easier to just let him get on with it.

Besides, having been left in control of house and child, I have something rather more pressing to contend with. For the first time in my life I am charged with gutting and cooking a chicken for lunch. After fifteen years in the expense-account world of television I know how to reserve a sought-after table at The Wolseley, but somewhere along the way I have forgotten to learn how to cook.

I stare anxiously at the chicken in front of me. The chicken, on the kitchen counter, steadily matches my apprehensive gaze. Fortunately, the chicken is dead. Unfortunately, it still boasts its head, feet and innards. I'm already running late; feebly I do the first thing that springs to mind. I phone Mother.

In fact, I call Mother repeatedly; it's just my luck that the one time I desperately need her advice she isn't home.

I am now really running late, having little under an hour to transform the bird into *la poule au pot*, the signature dish for a five-course meal I'd stupidly agreed to prepare. In Pascal's nine-to-five working life, lunch has to be on the table at 12.15 prompt. I don't let myself dwell on the fact that twelve months ago at that hour I wouldn't be slaving over a stove, I'd be click-clacking my way to one of London's glamorous haunts for a gossipy paid-for lunch.

As I replace the phone receiver for the umpteenth time, the chicken continues to stare at me. Hopelessly behind schedule, I squeeze my eyes shut and nervously ferret about inside the bird, before flinging its innards – replete with a yelp on my behalf – into the kitchen sink.

I cannot think of it as an animal, I remind myself, as I begin to hack at the feet and the neck. My stomach violently turns throughout this God-awful process. More than once I dash for the loo, where I retch into the toilet bowl.

Five minutes later it is on the stove. As I have no idea what the various seasonings on Pascal's spice rack are, on account of all the labelling being in French, I bravely sprinkle salt and grind some pepper over the bird before clumsily arranging it into a pot.

It is at this point that Pascal arrives home.

The air turns a French shade of blue when he realises I have absolutely no idea what I am doing.

'What you make with zat?' he roars.

'Errr, I'm not, umm, quite sure,' is my feeble reply.

'Too late to eat eet now,' he continues, barely pausing for breath, 'eet won't be ready for hours!'

I can't interject, because he continues with his rapid-fire complaints.

He takes the bird off the stove and inspects it closely. 'You no put oil on eet?'

'Errr.' *Merde!* I hadn't thought of oil.

He stares at me as though I am some sort of unpleasant smell in the kitchen.

''Ow eez eet you 'ave thirty-six years and you can't cook?' he hollers.

'Sorry,' I whimper. Now isn't the time to remind him that I am a vegetarian, one who wouldn't normally be expected to cook animals.

I try to ignore the fact that Antonio has been closely observing this interaction. He apes his father's gestures to a tee. They both shake their heads at me and regard me with a look of absolute contempt.

I am beyond embarrassed. The first meal I eventually serve for Pascal and Antonio is not one to remember. It is a shop-branded, ready-in-one-minute cheeseburger. But even they're not *'assez vite'*, according to Pascal. Because they were frozen, I took too long to zap them in the microwave.

Throughout the meal of revolting burgers he continues to grumble at me. I stare at my plate, picking at a pitiful-looking cheese sandwich. My culinary labours are declared *une catastrophe.* At the end of the meal, as I'm clearing away the table, Pascal whacks my bottom and roars *'Merci Madame Congélateur!'*

Both he and Antonio collapse in fits of laughter.

The cheek! As a result of my incompetence I have been christened Madame Congélateur (Mrs Freezer).

The end of each day is concluded by an *apéro* at Le Bon Accueil, run by the formidable Francette. A successful business run single-handedly by a woman. I can only guess at how hard she must work to keep her bar going seven days a week. Driving into Cazals to head to the bar swiftly becomes my favourite part of the day; without fail I receive a warm welcome from the elegant owner herself and, equally importantly, her clientele – which is mainly British.

This evening, a couple of nights into my stay, as usual, the half dozen tables which dot the pavement outside are faithfully populated from six o'clock onwards by couples and friends taking in a civil drink to mark the end of the day. Expats rub shoulders with *artisans* like Pascal. The atmosphere is convivial and warm, everyone visibly relaxes as the contents of their glasses are consumed. While the daily rhythm of life as a French housewife is alien to me, this part of the day I welcome with the enthusiasm of a long-lost friend.

There are two regulars who are already my favourites. They are sisters, Ann and Babs, who have lived in the village for ten years. They have fully embraced life in rural France, and their charming home is mischievously called Sans Souci (without worries). Both in their mid eighties, they implore me to pass by whenever I fancy a glass of rosé and a natter.

However, not everyone greets me like a long-lost friend.

Miriam arrives like clockwork at half past the hour; her late arrival, some murmur, is deliberately designed to make an 'entrance'. I have already seen her on numerous occasions since I arrived. She 'pops in' regularly and unannounced with her exercise clients. Each time she arrives just before lunch, even though I have gently suggested she phone beforehand – she has steadfastly ignored my requests. Rather than rocking the boat, I meekly serve her and her guests. They get to see how the 'locals' live, while I, exasperated, continue to cook Pascal and Antonio's lunch at the same time.

She makes *un tour* of Francette's clientele, planting a confident *bise* on every cheek she sees and exchanging a word with everyone. I am full of admiration for how she has so seamlessly integrated into village life. However, I have a sneaking suspicion she is about to inject some unnecessary brouhaha into my attempts at French family life.

When she has spoken with everyone in the bar (I subsequently discover that you cannot just arrive and select who you greet – it's everyone or no one here), she plonks herself down beside me and signals to Pascal that she'd like a glass of rosé.

Antonio and I are already sat convivially together. He sups a chocolate drink and I nurse a glass of rosé. Our communication can be best described as smiles, '*ça va*'s' and a general feeling of being at ease around each other. A storming result in my book.

Unfortunately, that feeling is a fleeting one – thanks to Miriam.

A butcher at the next table leans across, points at me, whispers something and almost immediately both he and Miriam hoot with laughter. I look on – blank-faced – as they then continue to chatter. I catch Antonio's eye; his face has reddened and he looks away quickly, the spell broken between us. Clearly he has understood – and the joke, it would appear, is on me.

When they have finished their exchange, Miriam turns to me, exasperated, and says, 'If you can't even understand when the local butcher is mocking you, then I really don't hold much hope for you here.'

'That's not fair!' I want to say, but I don't. Instead, I look away, willing the tears not to spill over.

Pascal catches my eye. He sees my troubled expression and, concerned, gets up from his bar stool. I discreetly shake my head, and so he sits back down and blows me a kiss instead.

Miriam goes on to explain that the butcher's crude pleasantry was something to do with the consumption of sausages. I redden at this as Antonio, who steadfastly ignores Miriam, also refuses to look me in the eye for the rest of the evening. I remind myself that for every Miriam and voice of doom underlining the unlikelihood of my romance with Pascal, there will be people like Ann and Babs who will welcome my arrival.

A couple at a table nearby distract us with news of their recent house purchase. It's a free-for-all here. I find it utterly charming that conversations can be struck up with people you didn't know when you arrived, but who offer the prospect of genuine friendship within the space of an hour. They have snapped up a bargain, which they're now in the process of carefully restoring to its former glory. They fully intend to while away the rest of their days here in what will be, they confidently predict, their rural idyll.

As the conversation unfolds Pascal continues to catch my eye, offering reassuring smiles and, when he refills my glass, a discreet squeeze of my hand. His silent complicity tells me all I need to know – he is always on my side.

As I listen to other stories of new lives forged in France, I try to forget that in my former professional life I made a television series for BBC1 that cast a pessimistic light on those who dared to buy property abroad. Even though just about everyone I meet has seen the programmes, it would appear that they are having the last laugh.

It is the halfway point in my stay, Pascal is at work and Antonio is at a friend's house. It is the first time I am alone in the little chocolate-box house that Pascal has called home for five years.

It is an ideal first opportunity to have an uninterrupted nose around.

The first thing I slowly come to understand is that it isn't a very large house. It's deceptive; it looks positively grand from outside, but every square metre must count. Houses here aren't afforded the luxury of the occasional dining room or a guest room. It's function first and foremost. Keeping up with the Joneses isn't something the rural French hold much sway by.

As is typical with many homes in this area, it is designed for those who work outdoors for much of their lives. A staircase runs up along the exterior of the house, to a covered terrace – ideal for shedding boots, Wellingtons and other outdoor garments. The actual living quarters are to be found on this first floor.

But first, I explore 'underneath' where, puzzlingly, a studio is located – replete with a grandiose double bedroom, a bathroom and kitchen. Next to it is a *cave* (cellar) that functions as a basement. Both quarters are clearly not in regular use; instead, each serves as a veritable Aladdin's cave to harbour furniture, treasures and clothing from yesteryear. It's fair to say that Pascal is a hoarder of eye-watering amounts of knick-knacks.

In the *cave* there are also copious traces of evidence that confirm that this is primarily a country home. Jar upon jar of an unidentifiable substance line one wall, a large saltbox takes pride of place on the floor, used apparently to cure the pigs that Pascal used to keep and then eat. I shudder at the thought of consuming an animal I've grown fond of. There are also chicken cages, sturdy baskets and machinery designed – I assume – to cut wood.

How on earth, I ask myself, can I take on all this?

Elsea skips alongside me the whole while, rootling about, unearthing a bone of I don't know what from a dark corner of the *cave*.

The house itself, spread out on the level above the clutter in the studio and the *cave*, is typically French. Excluding the loo, there are five petite rooms, festooned in elaborate wallpaper depicting country scenes. I take each room at a time, properly inspecting it, and every time the feeling is exactly the same. Without question each of them is dark, but I can't escape the feeling that each one is protecting its secrets from me.

I know that a girlfriend must have lived here at one time or other. There are clues to her former role as mistress of the house. A jar of sweets here, a fading bottle of perfume there, a long-forgotten romance novel – its pages yellowing – wedged underneath the bed.

I had recently asked Miriam about this person, but she had waved my question away, telling me to let sleeping dogs lie.

The kitchen is large and forbidding, with unwelcoming dark oak kitchen cupboards, and bleakly lit. There are knives of all sizes in racks, on wall hooks and in drawers. I don't even want to contemplate what some of them are used for. I have already been told off numerous times by Antonio for putting jars – of sugar, Nutella and honey – into the wrong cupboards.

The living room, accessed by a dimly lit hall, is large and central to Pascal and Antonio's life. I scrutinise it despairingly; there isn't a corner of it I could fashion into something I could call my own. I know, I know. I mustn't think like that yet, but with all of the computer games, cupboards full of hunting accessories and coat racks containing countless styles of camouflage jackets, I seriously wonder how on earth I could fit into this masculine household.

The bathroom – separate of course to the loo; a must, as I've discovered, in any French home – is functional, again with those gloomy brown cupboards and an acceptably sized, serviceable tub, with an ineffective shower overhead that reluctantly spurts out trickles of water.

The two bedrooms are woeful; one is small, the other even tinier. So far I have bitten my lip when asked what I think of the house. Truly? At risk of sounding like a snob, it's not what I'm used to. A bedroom for me is a sanctuary; a place to hide from the world, to indulge in mischief within the protection of its walls – *bien sûr* – but it is also a place which must be calm, warm and inviting. Pascal's bedroom is anything but. The room faces the north and it is bitingly cold, even in July. There is paper peeling off in the corners, and I shudder when I discover that, on closer inspection, what is behind the rotting paper is in fact mould.

Within the physical parameters of the room there is just enough space for a wardrobe, a chest of drawers and a double bed. The bed, which sags alarmingly in the middle, is an 'heirloom' from his grandmother's Parisian apartment. Consequently, I am reluctant to give it its true appraisal.

Behind a wafer-thin partition wall is Antonio's bedroom. He has a bunk bed and numerous pieces of furniture that also look suspiciously like family heirlooms.

Throughout the house the floor is tiled, each window is long and slim (like its former mistress?) and the dark wooden ceilings lend the house a sombre air.

Could I *truly* be happy here? I constantly ask myself.

Outside I fare little better.

Little Elsea skips alongside me as I take a leisurely stroll around the garden. Well, I say garden, when more accurately the land that comes with Pascal's home is a lot more grandiose than that.

I'm used to managing postage-stamp-sized gardens. I can just about cope with watering potted plants and expensive, pretty-to-look-at bamboo screeners. But this? This is nearly a hectare of land. At the rear of the house is an uneven lawn that is also home to a plum tree, a large unwieldy fig bush and a sprawling quince tree. A cherry tree dominates the entrance to the wooded area. Pascal has already assured me that all of the trees bear fruit, faithfully, every year. I can, he tells me proudly, eat and create dishes from all three of them. I smiled serenely at the time, while thinking 'help!' inside.

Beyond that the terrain extends into a thick pine forest. Its floor is dotted with fallen branches, a soft, springy bed of leaves cushions my feet as I explore and pine cones are scattered everywhere.

From the living room window I have already seen a hare and countless deer pass through this very same forest. Truly, it's idyllic here, but the thought of being responsible for the upkeep of house and garden every day, all year round? While I am already under the spell of Pascal and the Lot, I can't help but wonder what I'm getting myself into.

However, I must be doing something right.

For during the final night of my stay, we three dine at L'Auberge Sans Frontière. I am grateful for the chance to eat out. Pascal has warned me throughout the week that such expensive 'treats' will remain just that if we are to have a future together.

Picture the scene: dinner at our favourite restaurant, Pascal and I gazing into each other's eyes, the rosé perfectly chilled, our meals being prepared from scratch in L'Auberge's kitchen, Antonio not intruding, instead playing with his Nintendo. When suddenly Pascal turns to his son and they speak in rapid-fire French. I awkwardly interrupt, asking for a translation of what they're – animatedly, it must be said – discussing. Pascal has, apparently, asked Antonio if he'd be happy if I were to live with them.

I look from father to son. Pascal smiles encouragingly at Antonio, who shrugs and laughs.

'You want live wiz us?' Pascal asks.

I know I should probably say I'll think about it, while making the appropriate reassuring noises. But when has 'appropriate' ever been used to describe the path of true love? Instead, I reply with lust coursing through my veins and my heart thumping in my chest.

'Yes! Yes! Yes!'

We all laugh, Pascal and I kiss. He then announces to the bemused diners around us that I am moving to France. Patricia, on hearing our good news – *heavens, I'm moving to France!* – sends over glasses of Kir all round.

The rest of the evening passes by in a blur; Pascal doesn't let go of my hand, I lose myself in the steady gaze of those chocolate-brown eyes. He mouths to me, '*Je te protège tout le temps.*'

It is only later on that night, when I'm lying in bed against the contours of Pascal's taut muscled back, that I recall Antonio never actually said yes.

Chapter Eight

The Opposition

The dial tone starts its familiar trill. Unprepared, I jump, as it reminds me of the looming grown-up conversation I'm about to attempt to negotiate my way through.

In the next ninety seconds the course of my life is officially about to undergo yet another seismic shift.

As I listen to the authoritative ring tone, I nervously fidget with the handheld receiver, which slips and slides in my sweaty palms as I pace back and forth in the gloomy living room. The shutters are semi-closed to block out the late afternoon sun. The sobering light seems fitting for the conversation I am about to have.

If I say this out loud – to Mother, of all people – then there is absolutely no going back.

Pascal has left me alone to make The Call. He is taking Antonio to his mother's home, where he will spend the next seven days, before returning to live with his Papa once more.

Two different homes; it's not something I could put up with. It is an odd arrangement, to my mind, but one that, apparently, is considered very much the norm in France. Children of separated or divorced households benefit from the input of both parents in their upbringing this way, according to the French family law courts, that is. I'm not so sure. I watched

Antonio struggling towards the car, refusing his father's help, as he loaded in his luggage stuffed with clothes, toys and other mementoes important to his life, and couldn't help but think...

'Hello?' Mother's voice confidently booms down the line, cutting short all reflections on Antonio.

'Hello!' I reply, before adding somewhat unnecessarily, 'It's ahem, AHEM, me!' anxiously clearing my throat at the same time.

'Sam!' Mother's voice softens, she sounds genuinely cheery to hear from me. 'How are you?' There is a dramatic pause for the question she really wants to know the answer to, 'How are things?'

'Great!' I reply, nervously stalling for time. 'Just great!'

This isn't a satisfactory response for Mother. I can sense the peevishness and so I am rewarded with silence.

'Well, the thing is,' I start, not quite sure how to continue, 'Pascal has asked me to ummm move in with him...'

I leave the sentence hanging in the air, allowing Mother the opportunity to consider just what this means for her, for me, for my future.

A move to France. Living permanently in another country.

It's as though I can hear the reckoning taking place in her head: it is potentially the best thing that has ever happened to her daughter. Or, I think her calculations are surmising, runs the risk of being a rash, imprudent choice on her eldest's behalf – and she will be the one dealing with the fallout. Again.

'Did you say what I think you just said?' is all Mother can manage. So she *is* surprised at the curve ball I have neatly lobbed in her direction.

'Yes!' I genuinely can't think of anything else to say.

'So you've said yes, I take it?' She recovers quickly, does Mother.

'Well, I would like to.' I then ask, nervously, 'What do you, ummm, think?'

A heavy silence hangs between us. I know she is choosing her words carefully.

'There's nothing here for you,' she starts gently, 'so you might as well. What have you got to lose?'

I daren't say anything. *I think she's on board!* I push to one side for later inspection her on-the-nail assessment of my desperate status quo in the UK.

'You'd be mad not to!' she concludes. I can detect a smile – even if she is nearly a thousand miles away from me.

'Really?' A note of optimism pervades my voice.

'Yes, silly, of course!'

Relief floods through my veins. *I can do this!* With Mother on side, I know I can.

I explain to Mother that, if it's OK with her, and as long as Ambrose doesn't need me around, I'll be staying on for the weekend.

'They're fine! Stay!' she reassures me, cutting off any further questioning about Ambrose's state of health. 'Enjoy yourself!' she adds wryly.

I overhear Norman impatiently inquiring what's going on. Mother's hand is placed over the phone, not effectively enough, though, as I hear her announce I'm moving. There is, I notice, a satisfied note of I-told-you-so to Mother's voice.

Maybe she predicted this after all – she's a wily old fox, is Mother.

'Sam, don't worry about anything, leave your father to me.' I now sense barely contained excitement. 'I'll give those dogs of yours a big cuddle. Love you.'

With that, we ring off. I know that the proverbial bongo drums will be beating already, sounding out the latest instalment of my life in our little area of Birmingham.

Bugger! I'd forgotten about Dad and how he might take the news of the next stage of my haphazard life. Who am I kidding? I know full well how he will take it: badly. He has loved welcoming me back into the fold, mere minutes away from his watchful eye instead of hours away, hopelessly out of his reach, in 'bloody London'. He'll have a coronary when he learns that in the not-too-distant future I'll be the best part of a day away, living in a country where he'd struggle to order a pint, much less converse with my new beau.

Pascal.

I have learnt many things while living 'normally' with my French lover.

He is without question hot-headed, a demanding fusspot over his food, a traditionalist in the home, passionate in bed, dynamic and utterly charming in social situations.

I've never met anyone quite like him. He has completely entranced me.

At that moment I hear his little van grinding to a halt on the gravelled drive. I peek out of the window and watch Elsea leaping out, slowly followed by Pascal struggling to manoeuvre himself out of the awkward door frame. In his arms is a ginormous bunch of gladioli. They are startlingly tall and the blooms are a riot of colourful hues – sherbet shades of lemon, orange and pink heads are opening on the long green stems.

I unbolt the front door and race down the stairs to meet him.

'For you!' He beams when he sees me approach.

'*Merci mon chéri.*' I grin at him, overwhelmed at the sheer size of the bouquet and the extravagance of such a gesture.

He places them carefully on the staircase wall and I fall into his arms.

As we kiss, I excitedly interject, updating him on The Call. Elsea scampers feverishly around our feet, the sun's rays bouncing off the warm vanilla stone around us, preparing to set on what has turned out to be another perfect day in France.

Little wonder, then, that I choose not to notice the thunderclouds that are gathering on the horizon.

French village life in the summer months is rumoured to be lively and I, during my bonus weekend stay, am eager to embrace it fully. The prospect of a social life in the sunshine is the only excuse I need – well, that and Pascal on my arm.

The stars have aligned to give us a head start; Antonio's handover evening is Friday, which means we have the Saturday and Sunday all to ourselves. Suffice to say I'm off duty.

I'd forgotten that weekends really are respected in other countries. Work rarely encroaches on those precious forty-eight hours.

When we're not otherwise occupied – ahem – we're enjoying the sunshine in Cazals. In an attempt for me to get to know Pascal's colleagues, we while away Saturday morning drinking coffee on the pretty little terrace in front of the Café

de Paris. I adore listening to their easy banter, some of wh.
they take the time to explain to me in painfully drawn-ou
English.

I am also becoming acquainted with the village. Cazals
was originally a '*bastide* town'. Not in the English sense of
a town – there are no Starbucks or Carphone Warehouses
– in fact, most refer to it as a village. The walls no longer
exist to protect it; today it is based around a square. It is
a classic Lotois village. Buttery stone buildings dominate
with Périgord features (these are steep roofs which shoot
down and then jut out dramatically – think Chinese
pagodas without the frou-frou attachments). Every window
is framed with shutters in antique creams, pistachio greens
and Basque reds. There are six little routes into and out of
the village and the rest of the backstreets are arm-to-arm
wide, secreting away generations of families in immaculately
kept properties.

Once more we head to Cazals to visit the village market on
Sunday morning. I make an effort for Pascal; a pair of white
baggy linen trousers with a couple of skinny layered vests and
flat L. K. Bennett slip-ons.

The van pulls out onto the main road, which follows the
contours of the Lotois *causse*, and I examine Pascal as he
carefully shifts the van into fourth gear; we're pootling along
at a leisurely pace. Little wonder, as Pascal's mind isn't,
strictly speaking, on the road. He constantly looks left and
right for animals, pointing out their regular passageways that
cut through the French countryside. I listen, with rapturous
attention, as he explains the movements of the neighbourhood's
four-legged population. To the untrained eye the animal paths

n't actually appear to exist, but Pascal assures me that not only are they there, but that all animal species follow the same tracks – and will have done for centuries. These routes, according to Pascal, are determined by the subtle formation of the landscape. He explains that a *sanglier* (a wild boar) can easily cover 30 kilometres in the space of an evening and that a *chevreuil* (a deer) can initially outpace any dog, sprinting off at 14 kilometres per hour.

As we descend from *le causse* the van slows down and settles behind a line of other vehicles in front of us. We pass the oblong panel with its pretty red edging announcing we are in Cazals. Pascal respectfully drops his speed down to below 50 kilometres an hour. Even if the sign wasn't there, it's evident we're entering a much-loved and cared for village. Flowers spring up from each border of the road. Every colour of the rainbow is faithfully represented in their array of species. A large weeping willow dominates our entry, its languorous branches cut just so, perfectly in keeping with the village.

We pass numerous women confidently steering shopping trolleys along the single-file road into the village. A queue is already forming outside of the *boulangerie*. A cream-coloured Citroën 2CV ambles along in front of us, its owner trying, no doubt, to locate a parking space.

Pascal grumbles about the cars in front of us, crawling along like *'les escargots!'* He tells me that the number of stalls has tripled now that July is here. At this time of year there are vendors selling everything from locally fabricated goat's-milk soaps to traditional Breton striped tops, to organically produced honey. I'm giddy at the thought of it all! We eventually locate a little-used alleyway; a tiny *rue* neglected by everyone else and, with some deft manoeuvring on Pascal's part, the little van is stationary and tucked out of sight.

Together, hand-in-hand we join the throng of holidaymakers and Lotois locals heading for the main village square. Smartly dressed elderly couples and beautifully presented women armed with lists, all compete with younger families and their children – in their holiday outfits – who run excitedly back and forth. The market layout is nothing if not cunning and the prospect of fresh strawberries draws the attention of everyone at the well-positioned first stall.

We idly browse the market wares, leisurely taking in their produce. I am perfectly well aware that we probably seem like one of those annoying couples, all arms entwined, hips touching, high on love hormones.

I feel privileged to be in the company of Pascal, yet I try not to bask for too long in the rays of my good fortune. I'm scared that if I hold onto it too tightly, just as I have discovered when picking the scarlet poppies which dominate the fields here, that my luck – as the petals do – will slip through my fingers.

It takes time getting from one seller to the next. Pascal is well known and, it would seem, well liked by the many vendors.

There is the young man selling kitchen items who calls out to us and then, after nosily asking who I am, heartily pats Pascal on the back and congratulates him on his new life. He takes the time to repeat everything that he has just said to Pascal once again to me in English. I feel instantly guilty for having dismissed him as a nosy parker. It is such thoughtful gestures that reassure me I am doing the right thing.

As we move on further into the heart of the market, Pascal spies a distinguished looking farmer selling pots of pâté and jars of foie gras. He also boasts a superbly coiffed moustache, his whiskers curling out and pointing upwards in a rather cavalier fashion. On clocking Pascal, he waves excitedly in our direction, enticing us out of the unrelenting heat of the French sun and under the welcome shade of his stall's vast canopy. He speaks far too quickly for me to detect even the odd French word, and so I idly listen to the pair of them exchanging news. French men, it would seem, love to gossip just as much as their female counterparts.

Another stallholder proudly displaying what are labelled as cupcakes (which look suspiciously like fairy cakes) also steps out from behind his little stand. He takes Pascal's hand and pumps it up and down excitedly.

It is all *'Enchanté'* this and *'Je te présente ma femme'* that. I'm well versed in meeting people and making new acquaintances, but this flurry of introductions, both positive and genuine, takes me utterly by surprise.

As Pascal chats easily to a local *paysan* I am greeted by an expat. He charmingly introduces himself; his name is Nick and he tells me that he and his wife Jan have recently moved to the area full-time. He politely explains that he knows who I am and that he is also well acquainted with Pascal. Casually yet smartly dressed in light linen trousers and matching shirt, he has an easy confidence and warm manner that instantly puts me at ease. He affirms that I have made an excellent choice in Pascal.

I beam at this and reflect that, just maybe, moving here will be a good thing for me.

As I'm contemplating Nick's kind words, I spot Miriam weaving through the crowds. I wave in her direction and beckon her over. She looks right through me! Surely, I reassure myself, she can't have seen me. Otherwise why would she have ignored me?

When we have finally finished our tour of the market, we head for Le Bon Accueil and a glass of rosé. Pascal locates a table and, within minutes of popping our shopping on the floor and taking our first sip, he is greeted by one of the heads of the local French families who is sitting with his wife one table away from ours.

Pascal is professionally acquainted with Monsieur LeBlanc, and they both exchange pleasantries about their respective workloads. His wife, whippet thin with short, elegantly cut hair, leans across to introduce herself to me.

'I would like you to visit my 'ouse and eat wiz us,' she says in slow, but easy-to-understand English.

I'm astounded! I hadn't realised that I'd be so quickly accepted by the locals.

I turn to Pascal, who has overheard the invitation. He whispers in my ear, what you think? I see a flash of concern playing across his face. Or do I? Someone else distracts Pascal, offering to shake hands, and so I turn to Madame LeBlanc and nod affirmatively.

It is, I innocently assume, another one of those spur-of-the-moment lunches, a favourite pastime which the French so seem to love to surrender to, in order to while away a Sunday afternoon. By the time we have finished our glasses of rosé, Monsieur and Madame LeBlanc are long gone. I excitedly urge Pascal that we should go and find the van.

The first mistake I realise I have made is when, some fifteen minutes later, we make our way along the elegantly manicured drive. Just in front of us is a large, inviting pool, and Madame LeBlanc is already swimming in a too-tiny bikini. As she finishes a lap, I spot children playing with inflatable pool toys. We have brought a bottle of wine with us from the local grocery store, but what we certainly hadn't banked on is the need to bring swimming attire.

'*Viens*, Sam!' she calls out. Come into the pool? How on earth can I do that!

'*Désolée!*' I apologise.

'*Viens!*' She bats away my excuse.

I take in her other female guests, beautifully dressed in elegant sarongs and prettily coloured kaftans, clearly attired for a pool lunch, and wonder why she hadn't said anything.

I involuntarily clutch Pascal's hand, mentally taking in the outfit I am wearing. The long formal linen trousers and the layered vests. Suddenly I feel hot and bothered.

Is this a test? Or am I just being paranoid?

Pascal gently steers me away from the pool area and towards the cool shade of the terrace. There are twenty of us in total for lunch, the majority of whom, I'm pleased to discover, are sitting or standing in the shaded area, drinking aperitifs. I hear a melange of British and French accents and relief washes over me, knowing I will be able to, at the very least, converse with someone. Monsieur LeBlanc, already commandeering the barbecue, waves lazily in our direction.

It is then I receive the tap on my shoulder.

'Sam, darling,' Miriam cries. 'Fancy seeing you here!'

I am relieved to see Miriam and thoroughly reassured by her friendliness. I clutch her closely, planting a kiss on each of her cheeks. I feel daft for allowing paranoia to get the better of me earlier on. Of course she'd have said hello if she'd spotted me! As she greets Pascal, I can't help but notice that she has a man in attendance. He introduces himself as Martin.

'So are the rumours true?' Miriam asks, steely-eyed, sizing up the pair of us. It would appear, judging by the expression on her face, that she views us on a par with the odour that emanates from the local pig farm. 'A little birdie tells me you're moving in with Pascal!' This time her grilling is directed at me. The gentleman with Miriam is positively boggle-eyed at this nugget of news.

Bugger!

I had no idea our plans would spread so quickly. Why oh why hadn't we kept a lid on things today in the market? Miriam absolutely deserved to know this first.

'Errr, yes! Yes it is true,' I whimper, pathetically, before adding, 'I was going to ring you later.'

Miriam rewards me with a look that says she doesn't believe a bloody word of it. Rather than continuing with our conversation, she stalks off, Martin trailing after her.

Pascal gives my bottom a reassuring pat and, diplomatically saying nothing, remains faithfully by my side as we sip on our aperitifs.

I know it's not the done thing to use the loo in someone's home according to French etiquette, but I am desperate, and so go in search of the hostess to discreetly enquire where it is.

On entering the house I see Miriam in the kitchen with Madame LeBlanc. Both are huddled in a corner engrossed in an intense tête-à-tête.

Alarm bells instantly ring in my head. Feminine intuition tells me that the subject of the conversation is yours truly, and from the tone of their voices, I suspect that what they've got to say isn't particularly flattering, either. Embarrassed and flustered, I attempt to bid a hasty retreat out of the room, but fail miserably. Oh, how I wish I'd stuck to French etiquette.

'Sam!' Miriam cries. 'We were just talking about you!'

'You are moving 'ere?' Madame LeBlanc butts in, in an incredulous tone.

Talk about direct!

'Errr, yes, I am.'

'Why you do zat?'

Miriam smirks at the question, takes a step back and folds her arms as Madame LeBlanc moves toward me, getting into her stride.

'I love Pascal.' I shrug, not possessing the gumption to demand 'and by the way what bloody business is it of yours?'

'Pah!' She dramatically waves an arm in the air, instantly dismissing my feelings, before continuing, 'You don't even speak French!'

'Not a bloody word!' Miriam echoes in the background.

'You don't really know 'im.' Her hands continue to gesticulate wildly, ash flying in all directions from the cigarette held loosely in her hand.

'Silly girl!' Miriam adds.

It is a miserable half-hour during which both rather unkindly point out the vast differences between Pascal and me.

Admittedly, many of which I can't argue with.

'Enjoy zis fling,' Madame LeBlanc continues. 'But you don't need to live 'ere wiz 'im. Why you want live 'ere? Zis place ees not for you.'

Madame's diatribe is underlined by the vigorous nodding of Miriam's head in the background.

'You is *une femme d'affaires*,' she reasons. OK, this is definitely from Miriam – how else would Madame LeBlanc know I used to be a businesswoman?

'Pascal is just a carpenter. Zis man is not for you.'

I can't help but wonder whether this is truly Madame LeBlanc's opinion of my romance or whether Miriam has handed her a gun loaded with her own personal ammunition.

It is some time before I realise that Martin, the English gentleman who had accompanied Miriam, is with Pascal. Both are standing in the doorway to the kitchen looking on open-mouthed.

Madame LeBlanc shuts up immediately.

I wonder what, if anything, Pascal overheard.

Madame coos over both men, she refills their glasses and ushers them outside announcing (I think) that the meal is ready. This leaves just Miriam and me in the kitchen together.

As I turn to find Pascal she says, 'I don't know what you bloody think you're playing at, but I'll tell you this. I've worked bloody hard to fit in here. This is my village, this is my life. I wouldn't even want my daughter living on my patch so why the bloody hell would I want *you* here?'

The tears, which have rendered me watery-eyed and snuffle-nosed for the last half-hour, finally spill over. One big fat inelegant watery blob after another slides down my cheek.

Awkward and unwanted, I feel about as welcome as a WAG at a society ball. Madame LeBlanc and Miriam are the life and soul of the party, their beautiful bodies slide in and out of the pool on a regular basis – much to the appreciation of all of the men present. They flutter with their female friends and flirt with the male company.

I'm a bloody fool; why hadn't I realised they are joined-at-the-hip best friends? Madame LeBlanc doesn't want another English woman for a friend. I can only assume she's looking out for Miriam.

When I finally locate Pascal, he gives me a squeeze of the hand. I loathe myself for being pathetically grateful for his acknowledgment.

Martin, on witnessing my distress, walks past and whispers, 'It's extraordinary what jealousy will do to women, isn't it?'

I smile at him, quietly appreciative of his remark.

I silently curse myself for walking into what has all the markings of a cunningly laid trap.

'*Tu es faible*, Sam,' Pascal scolds me when we are finally alone, for being weak.

The victim role isn't a character the French strive to play in daily life.

''Ere you must be strong, Sam!' I know he's right. I smile at him, trying to project the image of a confident, strong woman – oh, how I wish old Sam were here. She would have given short shrift to the mocking words of Madam LeBlanc and Miriam.

Pascal watches me closely throughout the afternoon. I get the distinct impression he would prefer it if I upped the ante. What am I supposed to do? Push one of them into the pool? I have no idea how – or if – I should retaliate.

After a thoroughly successful week, I only have hours left with Pascal and our little love bubble is popped.

Miriam, it would appear, has declared war and so far she is comfortably winning.

Chapter Nine

Meeting the Rubinats

At the dinky little airport departure gate, I hug Pascal tightly to me, wrapping my arms inside the well-worn, smoke-infused denim jacket he wears constantly.

I detest goodbyes, but not as much as Pascal does. He was reluctant even to park up the Citroën van and accompany me into the tiny departure building.

I push aside the ominous words of Miriam. I try – yet fail – to keep them out of my mind as we exchange words of endearment. I can't help fretting about the future. Namely, do we have one?

We are so achingly different. Pascal is resolutely *un homme des bois*, a man of the woods, who would never consider urban living. I have only ever known a city lifestyle in London, Los Angeles, Birmingham. He thinks dining out is a 'treat'; for me, until now it has been a daily way of life. I am first and foremost expected to prepare his meals for him Every Single Day. How on earth will I cope with preparing and then cooking various parts of dead animals day in, day out? Even after only a week I have craved a Marks & Spencer pre-packaged salad box. I adore nice clothes and lots and lots of pampering. I have discovered – to my horror – that Pascal is happiest unwashed and in his pongy camouflage gear.

How can it possibly work? Is lust blinkering me to the realities of life in rural France with a man such as Pascal?

I catch his eye one last time before I pass through the point of no return. Pascal matches my gaze with those intense chocolate-brown eyes. He blows me a kiss and mouths, *'Je te protège tout le temps.'*

But will his protection be enough to shield us from the ill will of others? It is this type of senseless negativity that dominates my thoughts as I board the aircraft. I squish my bottom into one of the tiny plane's miniscule-proportioned seats. It isn't long before the first propeller starts to turn.

I need a sign, come on universe! Something needs to *happen*. I crave an omen. I close my eyes and meditate with all my being. I unashamedly place my cosmic order for something, anything, which will serve to reassure me that this tentative stab at a completely different life has some hope of working out. If cosmic ordering works for Noel Edmonds, then why on earth shouldn't this form of positive thinking work for me?

My rational brain, in trying to elbow out of the way the New Age nonsense, tells me not to be ridiculous. You make your own luck. Right?

I peer out of the tiny oval window and across the tarmac to the little fenced area where friends and family of my fellow passengers are waving them off. Of course, Pascal isn't there, already long gone I should imagine. No doubt Miriam is anxiously waiting his arrival, timing her appearance at Le Bon Accueil to catch him after he has finished work tomorrow, ready to continue her poisonous work against me.

Drop the negative thoughts, Sam!
You are the creator of your own life!

I might say it, but it doesn't feel like it.

The propeller continues to turn, but, it would appear, the other one is refusing to rotate with anything like the same amount of enthusiasm. Even though I'm no linguist when it comes to plane-speak, I can't help but notice that there are numerous flustered conversations taking place in the cockpit, the door of which is alarmingly open.

Within minutes there is an announcement over the tannoy. The plane is out of service.

What?

The next flight is tomorrow afternoon.

Tomorrow?

I am shunted along, sandwiched between two other anxious travellers, as we are shepherded off the plane.

The hostess has already reassured us that we will be accommodated in a local hotel for the evening with a food allowance (this has happened to me once before when the catch-all phrase 'engine problem' grounded a plane I was on in Spain – I know not to get excited about the prospect of either gourmand cuisine or a high thread count).

I think of my poor dogs and my, frankly, wanton neglect of them. I worry that Norman is already waiting patiently for me at the airport. Then of course there is Pascal, who has impressed on me the importance of calling him 'zee moment you 'ave landed'.

I forlornly yank my luggage off the manual push-it-yourself conveyor belt and head in the direction of the information desk.

As I walk through the automatic doors I am greeted by a rather tall, grinning Frenchman.

'*Mon amour!*' I shriek. 'How… why are you here? I don't understand.'

'I stay for just one drink,' he confesses with a cheeky smile breaking across his face, 'and I see your plane don't move. I say to myself it ees not normal and so I ask and zey tell me you stay for one more night.'

Words cannot describe how happy I am.

It's a sign!

This indication – which I know I will have to make a karmic payback for somewhere down the line – is one that I grab onto with both hands. It is all the reassurance I need to indicate that we are doing the right thing. One more night together is all that is needed to rediscover each other and rootle out the seeds of doubt that I'd stupidly allowed to be sown, courtesy of Miriam and her friend.

Twenty-four hours later, I discover that the universe has prepared another sign for me, except this one isn't such a welcome one.

I also learn why Mother and Norman were happy for me to stay on in France for the weekend.

My little rental cottage is flooded.

Inclement rain has fallen relentlessly for over a week, transforming the driveway in front of the garage, the footpath to the front door and the grassy area beneath my office window into the Birmingham equivalent of London Wetlands. Norman and Dad have had to don Wellington boots and wade through inches of dirty rainwater in order to look after my dogs. Not only that, but they have also been working round the clock to prevent water damage to the house.

My blood runs cold when I hear those words: water damage.

The house has a vast double-sized lock-up garage to the side. It has been the ideal storage space for all of my belongings. Furniture, decades-old paperwork, trinkets collected from around the world. In essence it is my life. Proof of my time spent on this planet over the last three and a half decades.

Except they have been destroyed.

All traces of my life up until now have gone – reduced to slimy, stained, foul-smelling, water-sodden goo.

I burst into tears when Dad wordlessly opens the garage door and I first take in the damage the heavy rains have wreaked, stealthily creeping in through the tiniest of cracks.

I have lost everything.

I shut the door behind me, until I am ready to face what it means.

I now have nothing in the UK. Is this what the universe had in mind when I placed my cosmic order?

The day after I return, Dad insists on helping me assess the damage. He is almost gleefully pessimistic about recovering any of my furniture.

We survey the mess and, after a call to the insurance company, photograph everything before stacking it to one side, for the inspection of an insurance assessor who will arrive at a later date.

I forlornly pick through first albums I bought, mementoes from far-flung holidays, souvenirs of my life in television: a

VHS copy of the first programme I produced, a certificate announcing an award I had won. All of it destroyed.

'The best place for it all is the local dump,' cuts in Dad, all practicality and zero sympathy. He goes on to explain that he has even discovered their opening hours. 'Best place for it all,' he repeats, kicking my eye-wateringly expensive, now sodden memory foam mattress. 'We'll get it all out of here in no time.'

'You're right, Dad.' I survey the 'fecking mess' one last time before we go inside for a cup of tea.

I fill the kettle and pop two teabags into a large cream teapot. Dad eases himself into one of my kitchen chairs and, after sneaking Barney a custard cream, helps himself to one too. He watches me as I pour milk into the mugs and set the sugar bowl on the table, and then cannot resist asking the question I know, *just know*, has been playing on his mind since he arrived.

'So you're really thinking about moving to France then, are you?'

'Umm, yes I think so, Dad.'

'But why? I thought you were happy here? We've got a nice routine going.'

It's true, we do have a 'nice routine' going. On those all-too-frequent days when I have been unable to get dressed, Dad would 'pop in' unannounced with some lunch for both of us. I know it probably goes against all medical advice for those suffering from depression, but he'd also arrive – bafflingly – with a four-pack of the latest trendy brand (which would always make me smile) of beer. He'd casually put them on the table and I'd wordlessly open one for each of us. We'd swig on a bottle each, while munching on a baguette freshly made by Dad.

The kettle pings and I wordlessly pour the steaming water into the teapot. Dad continues to slip Barney and now Ambrose custard creams – heavens! Will they interact with his meds? – as we eventually start on our tea. No wonder my dogs look as though they're putting on weight. When I mention this to Dad (thorny subject of 'the move' successfully changed) he starts to defend his biscuit rations to the dogs. It doesn't get very far, though; from what I can gather Barney is more a Hobnobs dog, whereas Ambrose prefers digestives.

Later that evening I call Pascal and explain what has happened. I learn another French word: *inondation*, a flood.

'Why you stay?' Pascal sounds incredulous. I am not sure whether he is referring to life in the UK in general, or whether he means why I am remaining in the house.

'You have nozink to keep you zere,' he reasons.

'Well, that's not true,' I begin, looking at the two fluffy dogs in front of me.

'*Viens!*' Pascal continues, 'I want you meet my family.'

Pascal is the eldest of four and every year the family reunite for a weekend get-together. Each of his sisters and brother live in the far-flung corners of France. Sibling attendance, according to Pascal, is obligatory. This summer they are meeting up near Limoges in the Limousin.

Help!

My family is feeling thoroughly guilty about the flood – they really shouldn't, it's not their fault – and so once more Mother urges me, 'follow your heart'.

I have neglected to tell Mother that just days earlier I had pleaded with the universe for a sign, something to suggest that a move to France is the appropriate next step. I hadn't quite anticipated that the results would be a faulty plane and all my belongings ruined. I know exactly what Mother would have to say if I ever revealed this to her: be careful what you wish for.

On the phone, later that evening, when I confirm that I can come, Pascal instructs me to pack carefully for a camping trip.

A camping trip?

I have never camped in my life!

By now, of course, it is too late to back out. I am determined to prove that I can fit into French rural life. So I listen, with a heavy heart, to Pascal explaining that we depart the day after I arrive. I have, embarrassingly, no idea where the Limousin is in relation to the Lot. I don't dare ask for an explanation of what a 'municipal camping site' is either or just where exactly Limoges, the nearest town, is located. I'm too excited at the prospect of being in Pascal's arms to bother myself with such minor fripperies.

So of course I pack as I see wisely: bikinis, suncream and books, as usual, take priority in my suitcase. My luggage, though, is even by my reckoning a little inappropriate for camping. I only possess a monogrammed Gucci set, ideal for making the right entrance at New York's busy-busy-busy JFK airport; will it, I wonder, be too much for camping?

I am intrigued at the prospect of meeting Pascal's mum and dad. His father is also a hunter. I have already discovered from Pascal that his family have practised this way of life for generations.

One sister, Veronique – who is just a year younger than Pascal – runs a bar and restaurant in a popular tourist town in Normandy. His youngest sister, Manuelle, is a dog breeder who lives in the Pyrenees, while his brother Carlos – just two years younger – lives in the Ardèche in the south of France where he runs a successful software company. All eminently capable human beings, I've no doubt. All likely, I fear, to be larger-than-life characters and extremely competent when it comes to camping.

When I arrive at Pascal's home, any ideas of a romantic evening are promptly scotched. We spend what seems like hours hunting through the *cave* attempting to; locate a tent, unearth a camping stove, stumble on deck chairs Pascal swears blind he has and, of course, I'm to keep an eye out for any other accessories that might assist us.

Pascal shoots me a look which suggests I've got a screw loose when I inquire whether he might have a spare mosquito net, perhaps some flares to keep insects away and, just maybe, a blow-up double mattress.

The expression on his face tells me that'll be a no, then.

It seems as though we have rather different ideas of what constitutes a successful camping trip.

In the early hours of the morning the van is finally loaded with just about everything Pascal assumes we'll need. I am relieved when he manages to slide a well-worn duvet in too, although its inclusion suggests we won't be glamping. As dawn breaks we point the car north, and join, on schedule, the A20 *autoroute*.

'It's all green and pretty,' I remark, as we drive over viaducts, through forests and spot chateaux perched high in the distance.

'Green iz not good,' Pascal replies ominously, 'eet mean eet rain a lot.'

Is it rude to confess, then, that a weekend camping in one of arguably France's wettest areas is perhaps not quite the first romantic holiday I had in mind for us?

After four hours on the motorway, shooting down tiny lanes, past fields dominated by the Limousin brown cattle and through picture-perfect villages, I am staggered to discover that there are twenty of us in total. Twenty! How on earth will I ever remember everyone's name, much less follow the conversation?

It gets worse; I am aghast to discover what municipal means. It is about as basic in terms of camping as you can get, just on the right side of camping *sauvage*. Camping 'in the wild' has been, thankfully, outlawed in most areas of France. The next step up is municipal camping; I discover that these are inexpensive, local authority-run campsites. There are no cooking facilities, an extremely primitive loo and nowhere to touch up your make-up. Glamping it most certainly isn't. We are to peg our tents around the perimeter of a lake, or *étang* as they are called in this part of central France. As there are just fifteen tent sites, we take the place over; as for entertainment, there is a beach, a stream and a copse.

Fortunately for me, our tent is whisked out of the little van within moments of arriving. Manuelle, Pascal's youngest sister, has three children – Miguel, Hugo and little Celine – who range in age from thirteen to seven. I am mortified to watch them erect our tent swiftly with ease and competence. I'm sure I must cut a rather pitiful figure, as I follow them handing out what I assume are tent pegs, and hold up other unidentifiable pieces of material, which they each calmly take and put in its proper place. Within half an hour the tent is erected.

While this has been happening, Pascal has been bonding with his brother and sisters. They are close, I can tell that much; there is much joking and leg-pulling, some of which I have no doubt is aimed at our unlikely coupling.

Pascal explains later that Veronique 'innocently' asked if he'd caught me in one of his hunting nets. I remember his large piece of camouflage netting in the *cave* and shudder at the very idea of being trapped inside of it! While Carlos, taking one look at my fully made-up face and painstakingly coiffed hair, enquired whether I would cope with the mosquitoes that dominate the area (Ha! Thank goodness for the bottle of lavender oil I bought with me).

Antonio is with his mother this week and won't get to play with his cousins. I watch them enthusiastically greet each other, jump onto the numerous bicycles that have also been thoughtfully transported here by someone, and head to the lake, where they fearlessly jump in.

I cannot begin to describe how out of my depth I feel.

I gravitate in the direction of Pascal's mother, Danielle. Pascal's parents have arrived at the camping site in *le camping-car*. It is a large swanky Winnebago that wouldn't look out of place on a film set for some hoity-toity A-lister – what I would trade to be sleeping in there! Danielle takes my hand and helps me into the vast mobile home and proudly gives me a tour. It boasts a double bed, shower room and loo, dining area, kitchenette and extremely plush armchairs. It's heaven! Unfortunately, we don't linger. Instead, she whisks me outside and shows me three tents she has also erected; one each for food, drink and then kitchen equipment.

She also points out the pieces of fish she has bought for me – installed in a cool box.

The woman has thought of everything.

I cringe when I remember my pathetic ferreting about the evening before, trying to locate luxury items to sustain *my* sojourn, while this sixty-something woman was packing electric lighting, coffee machines and grills. I know that I seriously need to up my game if I have a hope of emulating a modicum of Danielle's capability.

There is one surprising glimmer of hope for me; her name is Jane and she is the English wife of Carlos. Within seconds of being introduced I take an instant liking to her. Jane is elegant, yet laid-back, self-assured, but happy to let the family shine.

I can tell we are going to be friends.

I walk around the lake with her and she describes the character of each family member. It is immensely beneficial to get the low-down on everyone. I learn who the joker of the group is – her husband, Carlos – and that Manuelle has inherited her grandmother's healing abilities and it is she the

y turn to with aches and pains that refuse to heal with
entional medicine.

ne insists I call if I need any help with the family. She
hes off my fears about learning French: 'You'll start to
erstand things within a month of being here.'

ill I?

That evening we eat around a makeshift table, talking for hours
under a star-filled night sky. Lanterns, containing citronella to
ward off mosquitoes, have been erected in my vicinity. I am
grateful for such a thoughtful gesture that has been wordlessly
provided for my comfort.

The Rubinat family is *the* most competent family I have ever
met. It's camping but not as I had envisaged it. We eat a five-
course meal, and each dish is modified – without fanfare – to
accommodate my requirements. Vegetables are grilled in just
olive oil, rather than the animal fats that Danielle has brought
with her. Different types of shellfish have also been purchased
for my consumption only. I don't even mind the late-night,
inky-black stumbles to the loo.

Although I understand very little of the conversation, much
of which is banter by the sound of things, it's a pleasure to
witness the affection between such a close-knit family. Pascal
plays a pivotal role; everyone looks to him for reassurance,
for conviviality, for ensuring that the evening passes smoothly.
I'm reminded of just why I have fallen for him as each person's
face lights up when he turns his attention to them; sharing
a joke, refilling a glass or insisting that they have a second

helping. It surprises me to realise that I truly want to Make This Work.

Exhausted, I eventually slip off to bed. Naturally, Pascal accompanies me as I leave the table, asking if I mind if he stays up a little longer with everyone. How could I object? He leaves me with a torch and, waving him away, I boldly negotiate my way into the six-man tent that the children so efficiently erected.

Admittedly, it's a little big for the two of us. Much of the tent will remain empty. To keep as warm as possible we have commandeered one of the three internal zip-up pods. I have already prepared it with a duvet and some pillows.

As Pascal retreats I realise that the torch isn't quite as effective as I had imagined it to be. It is horror-movie dark in the tent, except for my underwhelming light source, which is about as useful as a Bic lighter. I ferret around in order to locate my pyjamas and, with much huffing and puffing, I eventually manage to get changed and under the duvet.

I'll say it again; it's dark. I am distracted from the murkiness by a cacophony of sound all around me; scratching, buzzing and even something moving outside.

I'm scared stiff.

I drench the duvet and pillows in lavender, praying that it wards off any mosquitoes.

The next morning when we wake, it's damp, cold and raining outside. However, I discover that's the least of my worries.

So much for mosquitoes disliking lavender, I think, as I survey the numerous bites on my arms and legs.

It gets worse; for my jeans have decided that today is the day they give up the strain of containing my derriere – I am thrown into an utter tizzy! The rip has resulted in a large split under one of my bottom cheeks.

Danielle looks wholly unperturbed when she views my Victoria's Secret knickers poking out of the ripped fabric, returning moments later with a sewing kit. Unfortunately, the tear is too large (either that or my bottom is) to repair. There is nothing for it – I have no choice but to sport a pair of Pascal's camouflage trousers.

While I shower in the municipal bathroom, I stop myself pining for the luxury of the Cheryl Cole (and Samantha Brick) favourite; the Sunset Marquis hotel. I pull on Pascal's trousers, all the while giving myself a stern talking to; those days are long gone.

However, our little camping trip could quite easily give a luxurious blow-out in Los Angeles a run for its money where the cuisine is concerned, I think, remembering last night's dinner. The food has been sublime. We ate barbecued tiger prawns last night. The impressively grand cooking fire was created by everyone mucking in (including myself!) to find kindling and wooden logs.

Maybe not a giant step for mankind, which has been, admittedly, onto this flaming 'magic' since the Stone Age. But a huge leap in the progress of the rural education of Miss Samantha Brick.

Sanglier, wild boar, is on the menu for this evening. It seems to be the norm to eat five-course meals twice a day and – *bien sûr* – each morning starts with a typically French breakfast of croissants and stonkingly strong coffee.

Pascal and I avoid the family walk, at his refusal, not mine – although I can't help but think he's looking out for me. Instead, we agree to take charge of the picnic to refresh the troops. We arrange to meet the family at a particular spot, without the aid of GPS or maps; Pascal – hunter that he is – takes it upon himself to faithfully follow the complicated directions his father, Antoine, has given him.

We eventually find our way, even though we have to confirm that we are on the right path with the advice of more than one local farmer. Our little van doesn't let us down and we finally arrive at one of the highest points of the Limousin. Pascal, in his element, binoculars glued to his face, doesn't relax until he spots his family walking towards us over the brow of a hill.

At last I'm in my element too! I confidently pass around the picnic items that Pascal and I had put together and brought with us. Each and every family member appreciatively accepts their baguette stuffed with ham and cheese – I feel like Julia Child! It might not be a swish and complicated five-course French meal served around a table – but it's a start.

I sense, although don't ask Pascal outright, that a family camping trip wouldn't be his number one idea of a holiday either. We're not hunting anything, he can't make all the decisions about the day's itinerary and he is missing Elsea. Nonetheless, Pascal subjects us to one more night of camping before we finally return to civilisation.

After breakfast we disassemble the tent; once again the children appear to help us – ahem. We pile the tent and our luggage into the van. Within seconds of closing the doors, Pascal's family have crowded around us to kiss us goodbye.

Veronique implores Pascal to 'pop' by and see her in Normandy. Carlos promises to send his big brother a piece of 'essential' software for his computer and Manuelle tells us that the route to her house is *très rapide* from where we live.

Jane squeezes my shoulders and whispers, 'Good luck, you know where I am if you need me.'

I smile at her, happy that I have found an ally.

The green fields, Limousin cattle and mosquito bites become a distant memory when we pass a sign welcoming us to the Lot.

After leaving the *autoroute*, as we snake along the Lotois roads, I can't help remembering what Pascal's sister, Veronique said to me, '*A la prochaine.*'

I ask Pascal what it means. 'She say to you see you next time, Sam.'

Really? I hope so.

Chapter Ten

Meeting My Family

While Pascal and I might be oceans apart when it comes to our life experiences, we are united on one crucial existential issue; we would unhesitatingly take a bullet for our families.

Antoine and Danielle, his parents, live less than forty minutes away from chez Pascal; a deliberate move on Pascal's part, in order to be at hand for his parents. The closeness of French families is something I'd always haughtily dismissed as nothing more than a cliché routinely trotted out in those bourgeois 'foreign' films – usually starring Gérard Depardieu.

Yet again I am mistaken, for what I have glimpsed so far in Pascal's village, amongst his artisan friends and on The Camping Trip, is that families are the bedrock of French society. It is patently obvious that Pascal, as the first-born son, is closer to no other male on this planet than his father. He rings him frequently, and their calls – from what I can glean – are to seek approval of each other's daily routines and to ensure 'Papa' is *en forme*. A stiff upper lip does not exist in a French household; tears, laughter and fist-banging-on-the-table approval are all regular gestures of familial love.

I've finally twigged that the camping trip was a metaphorical hoop I had to jump through. Could I fit in, was I game, was my character robust enough to establish a place within their intimate family set-up? Each of Pascal's siblings has enjoyed decades-long marital relationships. Sauntering into such a firmly established clan, I realise now, isn't to be taken lightly.

Even though I am quietly confident I can carve out a role in the family (although what it is, I'm not quite sure yet) I'm still dragging my inelegant size nines when it comes to setting a date to make The Move to France.

Before I commit myself wholly, I too need to know that he has – and wants to secure – a starring role in my quirky family set-up; there can be no blink-and-you'll-miss-him cameo bit-part or, perish the thought, him being cast as the villain. As far as my family life is concerned, I want Pascal playing opposite me as the hero.

A tough call – by my family's standards.

It's with little relish, then, that I announce to Pascal he is going to have to go through the exact same getting-to-know-you rigmarole with my family – without the damp tents.

I don't delight in the prospect of the Jane Austen-esque approval process from Mother, Dad and, above all else, my all-seeing sisters. Where previous suitors have been concerned, I'll be the first to admit, I've paid scant regard to family endorsements.

That'll be why such dalliances always ended in tears.

My harshest critics in life have been until now Mother and my two younger sisters – Jo and the beautiful yet sharp-tongued, hard-as-nails Fiona.

Dad will doubtless want to give Pascal 'the talk' – his finely honed speech that he has delivered more times than he's had hot toddies, what with having five daughters and all. 'The talk', which applies to any suitors of my two sisters and two half-sisters, is to treat us properly – or else. Whether Pascal will understand a word of it is another matter entirely.

I know I'm home and dry with Jo, who has already given her seal of approval. But will her opinion have changed now that Pascal is no longer a short-term, X-rated plaything, but potential uncle to her daughter Lola?

I *know* my family; they can easily give Simon Cowell a run for his money in the tell-it-like-it-is stakes, but they are also my biggest defenders. In the past (and usually after things have ended disastrously), if they've rewarded me with a forthright 'we told you so' lecture then it's annoyingly been for very good reason.

Their previous assessments, while brutal, have usually been spot on:

'Well, thank goodness for that,' was Mother's robust response when I nervously announced I was divorcing my first husband.

'Get a grip, Sam!' Fiona counselled when I phoned her in floods of tears one night about some wholly inappropriate bloke or other.

'An undeserving moron,' was Jo's disdainful conclusion on another chap I'd desperately tried to shoehorn into my life.

It's fair to say they don't do tea and sympathy.

Gallingly, their husbands have slotted into our family with ease – their decade-plus marital unions testimony to their successful choices. I have never been on the regular family holidays or partaken in the numerous Christmas gatherings – because my previous choices of men didn't want to, or simply didn't, fit in.

That's why I covet their approval of Pascal. I crave acceptance in my family as part of a couple. Heavens above, I'm nearly forty – I'd like to think I'll get something right as I enter my fifth decade, and not be forever regarded as the Flighty One.

My dynasty on the other side of the English Channel is an unusual set-up. My parents, both happily remarried, live in close proximity to each other. My dad and Norman (my second dad, really) can be found rubbing shoulders together on regular occasions; house moves, weddings and christenings, they're the ones usually putting the world to rights in the kitchen at some point during the proceedings, while steadily polishing off a not insubstantial amount of the alcohol on offer.

Dad has two daughters with my stepmum Debra, and as half-sisters go they are just as wilful and independent as my other sisters and me. One is in her mid teens; a mini-me, she's only interested in the high life – rural France does not cut it in her world. The other, in her late teens, has a better social life than the *TOWIE* cast put together. Their interest will be fleetingly piqued by Pascal's arrival. Debra, however, is already relishing the meeting with gusto, rehearsing her schoolgirl French on Molly, their haughtily disinterested sausage dog.

Dad has been in a total flap; all he knows of France is what he reads in *The Sun* and hears on talkSPORT. A dim view is putting it mildly. He is trying very hard to keep an open mind, but given that my father has only ever holidayed in one hotel whenever he dares to venture abroad – in the reassuringly anglophone resort of Magaluf – anything 'foreign' is deeply disconcerting for him.

Fiona, a deputy head teacher at a wildly successful independent primary school, is using this as an educational experience for Madeleine to trot out her French. Unfortunately, Madeleine is viewing the prospect of meeting Pascal with the same pleasure as meeting the wife of Brandon Flowers, the lead singer in her favourite band, The Killers; with deep displeasure. For this is the enemy: the foreign bloke who has the nerve to take her aunt away.

I know all this, because their lives are so entwined; speak to one and you've spoken to them all. Every home – that of my two sisters, Dad and Mother, is located within a couple of miles of each other. Every last one of them regularly pops in and out of each other's abodes, and everyone is fully up to speed with the minutiae of each other's lives. This set-up, Birmingham-based, has steadily continued for decades.

Unsurprisingly, then, my family is quietly panicky about the prospect of a foreigner – in the guise of a real-life Frenchman – trucking up and plucking me out of their fold.

I am in turn thrilled and terrified in equal measure at the prospect of Pascal's arrival in Birmingham.

Yet it is wincingly obvious from initial preparations that Pascal's entrée into a British city will be akin to the arrival of Crocodile Dundee in New York.

First off, there is the kerfuffle with the airline tickets.

Relatively straightforward for most inhabitants of the twenty-first century, maybe. Not, however, for those who dwell in certain areas of rural France.

'And you have Antonio's ticket, yes?' Pascal asks as I nimbly check us in online. As Pascal's isolated enclave has only been able to communicate with the rest of the world on the electronic superhighway for a matter of months, he viewed the Internet purchase of the airline tickets with grave suspicion. A palaver of meteoric proportions ensued when I insisted we use a credit card to secure the booking.

'But what if someone else try to use my card?' He worried continuously throughout the evening I'd found the tickets. His fears have been reignited with the printing of our boarding cards. It is with some exasperation that I mutter phrases such as 'website encryption' and eventually persuade him we need to think about packing the cases.

But this isn't without drama of near epic proportions either.

'You can't bring that!' I exclaim, in horror, when I clock one of his guns nestled in amongst his camouflage and green attire.

'I must 'ave somezing to protect you and Antonio,' he replies in all seriousness. 'I 'ate zee city. Too much people!'

'You'll end up in a British prison, Pascal,' I reason, 'and how can you protect us then?'

In the end we agree on a compromise and he packs his preferred knife with him. Heavens! My heart beats a little bit faster when he opens it, polishes the 7-inch blade and slides it lovingly into its bespoke leather case, before carefully zipping it into one of the internal pockets of a recently purchased suitcase. It is squished against two 5-litre boxes of Lotois wine we have purchased as gifts.

It is the first time Pascal has taken a plane. Both he and Antonio are adamant that they will each sit beside a window. By chance we have a row of seats to ourselves. It is akin to supervising the dogs when we're out on walks; placate one and the other uses it as an opportunity to misbehave and vice versa. Pascal insists on taking photographs, mainly, I note, of the wing, as opposed to the French countryside that shoots past beneath us. Antonio transforms into a human dustbin and consumes the Ryanair equivalent of a three-course meal at Michelin-starred prices.

The snob in me is mightily relieved there is no one to meet us as we stride through arrivals.

We certainly attract attention; Pascal struts through immigration in a large Harrison Ford-style brown leather hat – cocked to one side just so – he is wearing a hooded camouflage jacket, revealing tight Levi jeans and his familiar battered cowboy boots. Antonio takes up the rear wearing a fisherman's peaked cap, his long hair springing out in all directions.

I am the odd one out, not wearing any head apparel; instead, a rather worried expression is etched across my face.

The journey from the airport to my sister Fiona's house, where we are dining on our first evening, passes by in a flash. I had planned on pointing out some local landmarks; Sarehole Mill, the inspiration for Hobbiton in Tolkien's *The Hobbit*, for example, or perhaps, I'd naively thought, they'd be curious to see my first school.

But no.

Pascal and Antonio are not in the slightest bit interested in anything remotely cultural or relating to my childhood.

Rather, they are in awe of the cars they spot. Jaguars! Range Rovers! Aston Martins! They excitedly shout out each model they set their eyes on with an admiration and excitement I usually reserve for a trot around Harvey Nicks. They can't believe their eyes! In the Lot, they only ever pass Peugeots and Renaults (most of which have seen better days), alongside put-putting agricultural machinery.

After an hour and a half of this it feels as though I'm trapped in an episode of *Top Gear* – with no sign of the end credits.

Fiona lives in a well-to-do area of Birmingham. Even Channel 4's property guru Phil Spencer has talked in hallowed tones of the appeal of my sister's neighbourhood. But for a Frenchman used to his nearest neighbour living a comfortably distant half a mile away, my sister's terraced road is nothing short of nightmarish.

The curtains twitch in my sister's front room as I manoeuvre my car into a parking space. Fiona spots us and waves excitedly. Madeleine also clocks us getting out of the car – she, on the other hand, does *not* wave.

Meanwhile Pascal stops and, standing in the middle of the road, lights up a Gitane. With one eye closed for emphasis, he points purposefully at each of the large Victorian terraced homes – looking for all intents and purposes like a wannabe burglar sizing up his prospective swag.

'It's all 'ouse, 'ouse, 'ouse,' he declares, eyeing up, with Gallic contempt, the now bourgeois, turn-of-the-last-century terraced housing.

'*Mon Dieu!*' he cries. 'Antonio, look! Oh la, la... *regarde!*'

They both stand and stare upwards. Even I'm twitching nervously now.

'Look, Sam! Zey 'ave a bad roof. Iz ter-ri-ble!' I wince as he draws out the last word, emphasising each syllable in disgust. I hope that the owners of the 'bad roof' (which is missing tiles and flashing) aren't listening to this. My untrained eye only sees the cosmetic allure of the properties, all of which ooze kerb appeal: Farrow & Ball painted front doors, neatly manicured tubs of French lavender and chequer-board tiled pathways.

Antonio and his Papa linger in the road, marching up and down, and both gravely shake their heads.

'All zee cars too, Papa!' Antonio exclaims. 'Car, car, car, all on zee road.' His picky appraisal is delivered in English, doubtless for my benefit.

My sister, eyes on stalks at the window, mouths, 'What the bloody hell are they doing?'

'Ees too many people 'ere,' Pascal concludes, stubbing out his cigarette while effortlessly picking up one of the 5-litre boxes of wine from the boot.

Fiona rushes out, no doubt to pull us in before any of the other curtain twitchers clock that she's acquainted with the shady-looking foreigner eyeing up their property.

This time it's my turn to stop and stare.

What in God's name is Fiona wearing?

Her well-toned arms pull me into an embrace, her size 8 figure beautifully encased in a – wait for it – blue and white stripy Breton top and dark blue skinny jeans. She is also sporting a jaunty red scarf knotted at her neck and a slash of red lipstick has been expertly applied. 'I thought I'd make the effort,' she confides in my ear. 'It's appropriate, right?'

The pièce de résistance is a beret. She looks stunning, but she might as well have draped a string of onions round her neck and whacked a baguette under her arm.

'*Bonjour Pascal et Antonio*,' she cries, straightening her top. '*Bienvenue en Birmingham!*'

All delivered in perfect French. They are speechless, preferring instead to stare at her. Fiona remains resolutely nonplussed, and strides forward to kiss each of them delicately on both cheeks, in the correct way.

Madeleine, scowling in the doorway, is also wearing a Breton top and a neckerchief – also jauntily tied. Unfortunately, her scowl tells me that's where the similarities end.

'*Bonjour.*' She pouts. I know she is gunning for me, and is determined not to like Pascal.

She and Antonio exchange an awkward kiss.

Within minutes of entering, Pascal bonds with my sister's husband, also called Sam. Sam, tall, good-looking and (whisper it) a banker, makes a friend for life in Pascal when he offers him an extra-large gin and tonic. The pleasure on Pascal's face is palpable. He doesn't move from Sam's side for the rest of the evening, affording him a level of respect he usually reserves only for his family.

There is a tring on the doorbell, announcing the arrival of Jo, her husband Dave and their daughter Lola.

Four-year-old Lola proudly says '*Bonjour*' to Pascal and, when he bends down, she carefully plants a kiss on each of his cheeks. We all unashamedly melt at the sheer cuteness of my little niece's well-rehearsed (I later discover) gesture. Pascal swings her up on his shoulders and she wails excitedly. I see my sisters exchange a positive glance; good father material.

Big brownie point.

Aperitifs are passed around and soon everyone is at ease, effortlessly chatting away with Pascal and Antonio.

The only cultural snafu is when Fiona's other child, my teenage nephew Anthony, eyes up 'the' knife, which Pascal boldly slaps onto the dining table, ready to eat his meal. To say Anthony nearly suffers a seizure is putting it mildly.

'Whaaaaaat is that?' He points, spurting out his beer at the same time. 'Auntie Sam,' he says shaking his head when he's recovered, 'he can't take that out round here. Pascal,' Anthony starts slowly, speaking in Pascal's direction, 'you will get arrested with a knife like that in Birmingham.'

'*C'est vrai?*' Pascal asks, puzzled, opening the blade out while everyone looks on agog.

'Put it away!' I murmur furiously.

Anthony and Madeleine do not speak to each other; instead, they sit beside each other, relaxed in each other's presence, playing the same game on their respective Nintendo consoles.

It is a convivial evening, passing by in a whirl of jokes (mainly at my expense), thanks to my darling sisters and brothers-in-law, and alcohol propels it to finish in record speed.

Before we leave, we kiss everyone goodbye. Madeleine hangs back, with a moue mouth and a sulky air.

Pascal has already picked up on the negative vibes, aimed squarely in his direction.

'You want know 'ow I make a kiss in Catalan, Madeleine?'

Madeleine, her interest aroused, nods.

'Like zis,' he demonstrates, tapping his heart with his hand, then pressing a kiss onto his fingertips, before blowing in her direction.

'You try to make one to me?' he asks.

Madeleine, the focus of his undivided attention, tentatively repeats the gesture back to Pascal. When she has finished, she smiles shyly at him.

Magically, I think he might just have won her over.

Another brownie point.

Mother, on the other hand, does *not* need to be won over.

We dine at her house the following evening.

I am gobsmacked to discover she has set the dining room table so beautifully, Kirstie Allsopp would twitch with envy. She is even serving a five-course meal.

Pascal panics when I tell him this.

Earlier in the day, Pascal was determined to introduce Antonio to what he believes to be the epitome of a British meal: fish, chips and curry sauce. We sat in a chip shop just off Kings Heath high street, at a quarter to midday, impatiently waiting for the fryer to get hot enough to cook the battered cod that Pascal had positively lusted over ever since he arrived on English turf.

While Pascal charmed the chip shop staff, Antonio, looking distinctly unimpressed, asked if he could have a hamburger instead.

'Antonio!' I'd replied, thinking of the rite of passage that Pascal excitedly wanted to share with his son. 'Papa wants you to try.' Antonio rewarded me with a Gallic shrug and a 'pfff', before continuing to play with yet another Nintendo game.

Fair credit to the chip shop staff for not looking too surprised when, at Pascal's insistence, I took photo after photo of father and son as they tucked into their meal. Neither were they startled when Pascal asked if they could serve the fish and chips in the traditional paper wrapping even though, as we were eating in, it wasn't strictly speaking a takeaway.

Pascal had ordered large of everything, and I rather suspect he was regretting that choice when faced with the prospect of a five-course meal, courtesy of Mother.

Mother had already grilled me on Pascal's likes and dislikes, thoroughly interrogating me to ensure she knew precisely how the French like their roast beef cooked and just how she should prepare the potatoes.

Mother, in a formal frock, has also insisted Norman dress up for the evening. She deliberately sits herself opposite Pascal and focuses her laser-beam attention on him throughout the evening.

Norman has cunningly thought to set up one of his many computer games for Antonio, thus preventing Antonio from passing out with boredom at the dinner table. Unsurprisingly, Mother is utterly seduced by Pascal, who bewitches her throughout the meal.

It is an interesting spectacle to watch; he pours compliments over Mother and praises to the high heavens her cooking, a tactic (I assume) he has employed in order to eat as little as possible. Mother revels in such flattery and, in a bid to demonstrate her appreciation, after each course she slips yet more food onto his plate. It wouldn't be so bad if it was nouvelle cuisine, but this is traditional English fodder: hearty soup to start, then huge chunks of pâté, followed by a full English roast and all the (admittedly stodgy) trimmings. Then cheese and finally two types of dessert. There is little I can do to save him – he has to eat or else risk insulting my mother. I recognise her modus operandi; this is her moment in the spotlight, she is determined to prove that it isn't just the French who know how to cook.

'Have you set a date to go yet?' Mother asks as we walk out of the front door, another successful evening in the bag.

Result! I wink at Pascal, who lets out his belt by several notches, and professes to being perilously close to throwing up as we pull away.

The following lunchtime we ring on the doorbell of Dad's house.

Pascal has already been briefed that Dad is staunchly against The Move. With that in mind he arrives with a peace offering; a large bottle of an expensive malt whisky.

Dad, having no doubt already witnessed us parking in front of the house, is taking his own sweet time in opening the front door.

I squeeze Pascal's hand, and pretend not to notice that his large palm is shaking in my decidedly smaller one. I give him a rallying smile and ruffle Antonio's hair. *It's going to be fine,* I repeat over and over to myself.

I can hear Dad shuffling about in the hall, the front door still firmly closed – *dear God, what's he playing at?*

I hope, I grimace to myself, he has put some trousers on. When at home, Dad's leisurewear of choice is a pair of shorts, which can – horrors! – be mistaken for boxers.

I don't know what's keeping him. I have already given him a list of some basic French words to try to learn. Nothing taxing; just *bonjour*, *ça va*, to quell his nerves. He used to fall about laughing at the BBC comedy series *'Allo 'Allo!*, set in occupied France, retelling the well-worn one-liners over and over again.

Surely even he can manage those most rudimentary of French greetings?

Debra had replied, 'You're wasting your time, Sam,' on seeing the said list, when I emailed it to her to run through with him before we arrived, assuring me that the piece of paper it was printed out on would end up being used for noting down his lottery numbers.

She's proved right, when Dad finally opens the front door and booms, 'Welcome, Pascal!'

They shake hands, and Pascal replies, 'Ees really nice to meet you, Patrick.'

Dad turns his attention to Antonio, offering his hand too.

Antonio proudly steps up and shakes hands with Dad. The three men beam at each other.

Dad then casts me a Look, which I take to mean start translating *now*. Any need for interpretation, though, is pushed to one side the moment Dad clocks the whisky.

I certainly hadn't banked on whisky being an international beacon of communication all on its own, silently announcing on Pascal's behalf: 'Hello, I really respect you and love your daughter.'

Neither did I know that, as the bottle was passed over, it could prompt, from the recipient, another wordless response: 'Oh, you shouldn't have, and my favourite brand. Come in, come in. You'll fit right into this family.'

As this silent conversation passes between both Pascal and my father, it is evident that they are going to Get On. Already I can feel my pulse rate steadying.

Within minutes of entering the house, and having said hello to Debra, Sophie and Victoria, Antonio is installed in front of a *WWE* television show. He is mesmerised by the larger-than-life characters engaging in wrestling pantomime, and his gaze doesn't leave the screen.

Dad steers Pascal into the kitchen with the bottle of malt. I shudder, knowing that's where Dad holds most of his 'important' conversations, while Debra rolls her eyes at me. Molly the sausage dog alternately paws and yaps at the closed kitchen door, furious at being left out of the action.

I can only assume Pascal is being given 'the talk'; she's had a hard time, look after her, don't be like that feckin' useless ex of hers. Pascal, I imagine, is going to deliver the 'fragile' and 'protection' line.

The whisky was obviously a good one: I nearly fall off my chair when fifteen minutes later they both return to the living room, looking distinctly shiny-cheeked and with huge grins plastered over their faces.

'I've got some good news,' Dad booms. Antonio continues watching the television, Sophie and Victoria are respectively tapping into their phone and updating their status on Facebook – both look distinctly nonplussed.

Only Debra and I perk up, meerkat fashion, at the sound of Dad's announcement.

'Pascal has asked me if he can have Samantha's hand in marriage.' He pauses. Debra instantly reaches for a tissue, while both Dad and Pascal congratulate each other, before taking another leisurely swig from their glasses.

'I,' Dad proudly declares, 'have said yes!'

I, meanwhile, am staring open-mouthed, at the two men in front of me, as they congratulate each other.

I thought there was very little left in the world that could genuinely shock me; seems as though I'm wrong.

They've just spent the last quarter of an hour discussing *my* future. Without me present!

I sense my militant inner feminist has got her knickers in a twist over their unanimous male decision. Yet her views are thoroughly overpowered by the pink princess who also rubs along beside her. She is no pushover either; and she wants her happily ever after. So that's settled, then.

I'm getting *married?!*

On the day before Pascal and Antonio are due to fly back to France, there is one final meeting I reluctantly orchestrate, knowing that actually, fiancé or no fiancé, my future really does rest on this encounter going well.

It is the final confrontation that will dictate whether I really do get my happily ever after.

Pascal is obliged to meet Ambrose and Barney.

For the last two days, while we have toured Birmingham and met the family, I have opted to keep them at the local kennels. We have been staying in my rented cottage and, as we have been out most days, it seemed like the most logical option. My dogs are high maintenance and I want their meeting with Pascal to go as smoothly as possible. Their canine accommodation is a plush number, as Pascal sniffily notes when we drive into the beautifully maintained grounds, replete with cherubic water fountain and pots of begonias dotted about. It is as though we have arrived at a National Trust property, rather than the local kennels.

As we walk into the reception area, immediately Pascal eyes one of the staff walking towards us, struggling to control my

>-stone woofers. A red leash is gripped and straining in each hand, as the dogs come bounding down the path, bashing open the glass doors, and attempt a running jump at me.

'*Non!*' Pascal roars.

I jump out of my skin, Antonio shrugs and Pascal instantly whips the leads out of the kennel assistant's hands. He shortens both leashes, allowing them zero room for shenanigans as we walk out to the car.

I am dumbfounded.

Ambrose looks around and, if I'm not mistaken, glares at me. Barney ignores me, instead he sniffs at Pascal's pockets, expecting a treat.

I know my dogs are spoilt; organic food, filtered water, treats on demand.

They are my one indulgence.

Back at the house Pascal watches in horror as they bound from the hallway into the living room, before making a U-turn back into the hallway, from where they bolt into the kitchen and, paws on the counter, their black noses begin sniffing in the direction of the biscuit tin.

I am mortified; they are never normally quite this bad.

Pascal is horrified.

'In zee country, Sam,' he starts, struggling to control his temper, 'zey can't make what zey want in the 'ouse. Dogs 'ave a different life in zee country.'

'I know,' I reply in a small voice, 'I know.'

'*Hors des question*, Sam!' (without question) he finishes, a bit unnecessarily in my book.

Pascal has, throughout his life, owned and trained dozens of dogs; he has also educated unruly canines for friends. He regularly provides a 'last resort' training school for his sister Manuelle when she has a particularly awkward pooch. He is the Lotois dog whisperer.

Pascal, after I plead that they can't be locked outside, eventually restricts their access to the hallway. They have their beds, their toys and some water – *not* the run of the house.

Initially, I'm miffed by Pascal's blatant bossiness, but I think back to those times when they have sent Dad flying or, in their enthusiasm to say hello, have left scratch marks on Norman's arms and legs. Then there are the countless times they have ruined Mother's tights. They have, I fear, met their match. And not, painful as though it is to admit it, before time.

Pascal pointedly wags a finger at them, announcing that the kitchen is *'interdit'* (prohibited) and, after I have repeatedly assured Pascal they normally behave themselves, we go out in order to purchase Antonio a present. We had promised to buy a gift for him as a souvenir of his time in Birmingham – and it is something he doggedly holds us to.

On returning, a couple of hours later (inexplicably with a replica machine gun, rather than the toy model of the Birmingham Bullring I had my eye on), Pascal is appalled to discover that one of them has had an 'accident'. A rather large puddle, to be precise. Pascal will not accept for one moment that this is an unfortunate mishap. Rather, he believes that this is a dirty protest; they are jealous, apparently.

That evening Pascal puts *my babies* to sleep in the garage.

It is my turn to be horrified.

'There are no bad dogs, Sam,' Pascal warns, 'only bad owners.'

Pascal has outlined what others must surely say behind my back. Ambrose and Barney rule the roost – not me!

I have a sinking feeling about this. I *know* I overindulge them. How on earth will my dogs cope in France without their pampered lifestyle?

Chapter Eleven

The Move

I cannot *believe* I am doing this.

Moving to France!

It never occurs to me to question the long-term viability of our engagement and how feasible it is for two virtual strangers to live together – the actual time we've spent in each other's company, is only just, I realise, running into a month, all totted up.

Yet, I try to reason to myself, aren't onerous expressions such as 'viability' and 'feasible' usually applied to economic forecasts and – shudder – never for matters of the heart? I'm in love! I have the approval, I am certain, of the majority, if not all, of my family members – who needs mathematical equations?

If truth be told, my friends have done their own calculations and remain somewhat unconvinced about The Move. They believe that, statistically speaking, my love affair is doomed. Their theory is that my move isn't a permanent one, rather that it's some temporary flight of fancy.

'Mid-life crisis' and 'breakdown' are the phrases I've heard slip out from friends' mouths under the truth drug alcohol. Most of them assume I'll be back in London in twelve months' time, holding court in Soho House and talking up the tale of my brief, ill-thought-through sojourn in *la France profonde*. Either that or I'll have gallivanted off to live with some other riotously inappropriate gent – except the next stint will be in Bavaria or Bolivia, so the humourless rumours go.

I'd like to say that I brush off their sarky appraisals, but their comments hurt. My rule of thumb in friendships has always been this: no judgements. We all make enough cock-ups in our lives, without them being 'helpfully' speculated over by those who are supposed to be our nearest and dearest.

Dad and I speedily and proficiently pack up the contents of the rental house. Well, what's left of my worldly belongings, that is. We give away much of the furniture to friends of the family; there are many grateful homes for the beds, sofas and kitchen furniture. Dad rightly persuades me it's 'fecking ridiculous' to take all of it to France.

There really is no going back, then.

Not only am I homeless, I'm without fixtures and fittings.

I insist on taking what's left of my clothes; what I haven't had to flog to make ends meet. Neither will I be parted from my book collection. Well, those tomes that survived the flood. I know I should be travelling lightly, without painful reminders of my past. It is, I remind myself, as I um and ah over whether something should stay or go, a new chapter in my life. Yet I'm not brave enough to forgo mementoes, I need to hold onto something of my old life, to remind me who I was and what matters to me now. Such items – trinkets really – will assist me in carving out a little place of my own in that French house that, daunting as it seems right now, will soon be my home.

I already have the predictable, yet necessary, packets of Hobnobs and jars of Marmite stashed away in my main suitcase – the ultimate in comfort food in a country that dips butter-slathered bread into bowls of sweet steamy coffee and yet frowns on terms such as 'elevenses' and 'it's time for tea'.

To that end I also toss into a large cardboard box my collection of hearts: china, fabric, gingham material, lavender-scented ones, not to mention various other shabby chic ensembles. They'll rub along nicely by the camouflage, I smile ruefully to myself. Pascal has already promised that I can put these up – one in each room – to remind me of home.

I also (sneaky, I know!) buy in a supply of Barney and Ambrose's organic dog food. Not much, just six months' worth of provisions, while their delicate tummies get used to the French equivalent – whatever that might be. I shudder just thinking about it! I have already arranged for the sacks, along with my belongings, to be transported at a later date.

'Are yee sure you're doing the right thing?' Dad demands as we gaffer-tape boxes closed and I number them, as per the instructions from the removals firm.

'Of course,' I reassure him. 'You've met Pascal. Aren't you confident I'll be safe in his hands?'

'Well, yes, but...'

'Dad, don't worry,' I say, giving him a hug, before releasing him and looking him in the eye. 'I know I can come back if it doesn't work out.'

Shame on me; I cross my fingers behind my back as I say this. Returning to the UK, tail between my legs, *a failure again?*

That just isn't a possibility I can contemplate right now.

I have talked up the expat 'French dream' to the family. The countryside! Sweet rustic house! The permanent departure from my stressful TV career!

I haven't told anyone about Miriam's attempts to discourage my romance, or my uncertain place – for what it's worth – in the village.

'And you're sure Pascal is happy to take on these?' Dad demands, pointing to Barney and Ambrose who are in turn sniffing and pawing at the sacks of dog food.

'Get away from there!' I shriek, dreading the consequences of them 'accidentally' ripping the bags open. Immediately I feel guilty, I'm uprooting them *again*, so I toss them each a bribe; their favourite snack of pig's ear.

'Of course Pascal is happy to welcome all three of us – he knows without Barney and Ambrose there is no Sam,' I say with more certainty than I feel.

The evening before I leave I host a farewell dinner at an Italian restaurant in Moseley, a neighbouring suburb. The eatery is a family favourite where everyone can bring their own wine.

My sisters, their husbands, my nieces and nephew toast my future. Mother and Debra try not to cry and Norman retains a stiff upper lip.

'Thank you so much for all of your help,' I quiver, lips wobbling, desperately trying to hold it together.

They have been so generous to me during these last few months, far more so than I deserve. I feel unbelievably sad that I've been so fleetingly back in their lives, part of their family routine, watching Lola and Madeleine blossoming, and now I am leaving them again.

Dad, of course, has refused to attend my last supper. He initially tried to soft-soap me into believing that he couldn't leave Molly on her own. Molly is a perfectly independent, wily little hound. She's utterly content home alone, and wouldn't miss his company in the slightest. As long as she has full run of the living room and has, within the last four hours, been served her usual bowl of fresh chicken (lightly cooked, if you please).

When he realises that excuse won't wash, he delivers an 'I've got a bad tummy' yarn.

In any event, he doesn't show up, his empty chair at the table speaking volumes. I can't help but wonder if it's because he's annoyed with me for leaving (which makes me unbearably sad) or acutely upset (which tugs even more so at my heartstrings).

At the end of dinner, only Madeleine dares to vocalise her true feelings about my move.

'I don't want you to go,' she mumbles, when she stands up to put her coat on.

'Oh Madeleine, I'm sorry,' I say, blinking back the tears.

She folds her arms across her chest. The lump in my throat gets tighter and I notice she too has watery eyes.

I ask for a kiss and she stubbornly shakes her head.

I sadly watch as she holds my sister's hand and together they walk to their car. As I watch them retreat, it occurs to me that I don't know when I will see Madeleine again.

Suddenly she turns around. Looking me straight in the eye, she uses the Catalan gesture for a kiss that Pascal has taught her; hand on her heart, palm to her lips and then a kiss is blown in my direction.

I repeat the gesture back at her, as tears silently fall down my cheeks.

Less than twenty-four hours later, Mother and I are zipping along one of the countless French national roads we have traversed since disembarking the ferry. I have avoided the *autoroutes* in order to give Mother a glimpse of real France. We finally motor through one deserted French village after another ('Where is everyone?' Mother asks, genuinely perplexed), hopelessly lost and unable to find our pre-booked accommodation, a luxury night in a hotel.

After a beautiful, if at times testing, stay in the dog-friendly chateau, we leave the Loire Valley behind us and make for the territory of south-west France.

Pascal phones me at regular intervals, inquiring where we are, whether we're making safe progress, telling me he can't wait to see me.

I have given up asking Mother to map read.

'We're that bit closer to Toulouse, Sam,' is her sketchy conclusion, peering at *autoroute* panels, having binned the map hours ago. 'The kilometres are definitely getting lower.'

'*Merci madame le co-pilot,*' I reply sarcastically. Unnecessary, maybe, but I haven't the foggiest idea how to convert kilometres into just how many hours left we have to drive. So I am clueless when Pascal poses such questions.

When we finally arrive, I toot the horn enthusiastically. Pascal instantly appears on the terrace, a huge smile breaking across his face. He races down the stairs and helps us out of the car.

'*Mon amour,*' he cries into my hair, as I collapse into his arms. '*Je t'aime.*'

Before we do anything else Barney and Ambrose are released from the boot of the car. They leap out and, after a couple of minutes of sniffing, squatting and marking their territory, they collapse into their fluffed-up bed cushions, freshly prepared and awaiting their arrival on the terrace.

Elsea has watched all of this, animatedly trotting back and forth on the terrace wall. Clearly outraged at the unanticipated arrival of two hairy hounds, she intermittently growls and yaps at them both, voicing her utter indignation. I don't think she's clocked it yet; these aren't passing visitors, these are new recruits to her pack. Watching Barney and Ambrose settle into their beds, she follows us into the house, but not before turning on her four paws and treating them to another warning growl, as if to say, *'Attention vous deux, c'est moi la maîtresse ici.'* (Watch out you two, I'm in charge here.)

In the living room, Pascal fusses over Mother, pouring her a glass of rosé, settling her on the sofa and offering her some nibbles, which she ravenously accepts.

Then he insists I close my eyes and hold out my hands in front of me. I look at him mischievously. What's he planned, I wonder? Is it appropriate for Mother's eyes?

After something is placed softly in my hands, I slowly open my eyes. Carefully, I undo the beautifully wrapped package to reveal a rose-scented heart, in traditional French fabric – there is a message attached to it too: 'Welcome home Sam.'

I melt into his arms, whisper *'merci'*. I catch Mother's eye, she gives me the thumbs-up behind his back. When he releases me, I tell him I have a confession to make.

'I don't have a present for you, Pascal, I'm sorry.'

He looks at me tenderly before replying. 'You change your life, you change everyzink for me. Ees enough, Sam.'

This is Mother's first, fleeting visit to rural France, and I have a mere forty-eight hours to reassure her that I will fit in seamlessly here. It is the first week of September when we arrive for what she refers to as the 'handover' to Pascal.

With Mother in residence, then, it is not quite the romantic first night for Pascal and me; yet valuable, nonetheless, for strengthening family ties. We three sit easily together on the terrace until the early hours, with Barney and Ambrose snuggled against our feet, sipping glass after glass of perfectly chilled rosé. Elsea is keeping her distance, surveying each of my pooches with a gimlet eye. Mother and I listen attentively to Pascal's passionate reminiscences about the region he has called home for the last fifteen years; the chateaux he has restored, the magnificent stags he has trekked (not to kill, but to observe). I delight in watching Mother's face come girlishly alive. I so want her to be seduced, as I am, by the Lotois lifestyle.

She is seeing the Lot in one of her prettier moments; her flowers are still in bloom, her sun still sets shamelessly late, releasing her last burst of magnificent hues across the cloud-flecked skies, and her arid parched land which dominated the landscape throughout the scorching summer months has finally been rewarded with a silky swathe of lush green foliage.

Over the next few days I fully intend to enjoy, with Mother, the last breaths exhaled by the summer season. The tourists have already reluctantly vacated this magical area of the

Midi-Pyrénées, its gastronomic and picturesque pull releas
them back to their nine-to-five lives. Rural life is resuming it
regular rhythm. The family of farmers who labour on the land
that surrounds my new home are working feverishly, not just
harvesting its luscious green corn plants to feed their ducks
and chickens; they also mow late into the night the richly
grassed meadows, the bales of which are eventually parcelled
up ready to be used for their animals food supply during the
winter months.

Mother, who has only ever lived in Birmingham, is entranced
to witness the magical rhythms of rural life unfolding around
us. We walk with Barney and Ambrose, as they cautiously
acquaint themselves with the surrounding countryside. I
eagerly point out to her the numerous stone built *gariottes*,
tiny structures unique to this area with steep Quercy-style
roofs, typically round in form and with an opening, as opposed
to a door. These buildings were first fabricated centuries ago
to provide shelter for shepherds and those working the area's
vineyards. As I excitedly explain their use, I realise I've been
absorbing everything Pascal has told me on our jaunts in the
countryside. It hasn't all been al fresco sex...

Rural France isn't just picturesque; she also knows how to host
a party.

Nick, the expat who I met at Cazals market, has continued to
greet me, along with his pretty wife Jan. They kindly exchange
pleasantries with Pascal and me whenever we rub shoulders
in Le Bon Accueil. To celebrate their move to France, they

hosting a meal. Pascal and I have been invited, and the invitation has also been extended to Mother.

The event is being held in a restaurant, Le Poule au Pot, a family-run establishment in a neighbouring village. It is a glorious evening and we three have unashamedly grabbed the opportunity to dress up to the nines. Pascal is wearing a pair of tight faded jeans with a black linen shirt, the short sleeves casually rolled up to reveal his tantalisingly large biceps. The shirt is unbuttoned to mid chest; sexy as hell, he looks as though he has stepped out of the pages of a Jackie Collins novel. Mother dons a beautifully tailored fuchsia-pink dress and I wear a long floaty white halter-neck dress, the fabric of which is covered in flowers. Once more Pascal and I are night and day, the devil and the angel.

When we arrive, music is gently playing, and there is a terraced area outside where at least fifty people are already talking softly and sipping on flutes of Kir. I spot Ann and Babs, the elderly ladies who reside at Sans Souci, who greet me warmly with a kiss and implore me to visit them soon.

My blood runs cold when I spy Miriam, who has arrived with a party of French villagers. Our gazes inevitably lock onto each other. I turn away first, blushing, but not before I notice she is tugging at Madame LeBlanc's arm and pointing in my direction.

Pascal gravitates to the only French-speaking couple in attendance, the Dutch DJ and his French partner. I glance over to see him deep in lively conversation with them. I shrug, take Mother's arm and guide her outside on the terrace where I spy a vacant table. As I ease myself into a chair I relish the feeling of the last of the sun's rays on my skin.

We are introduced to couple after couple, all expats who have happily settled into life in the Lot. One such couple, Wendy and Steve, indulge in more than just small talk with us. I discover that Wendy teaches French and mentally file this information for later use. She declares that she regularly clocks French *artisans* propping up the local bars, before going on to conclude that from what she can see it is a wildly misogynistic society round our way. Mother, noticing my worried expression, wisely changes the course of conversation.

Unable to stop myself, I glance over at Pascal, straining to attract his attention. My efforts are futile, he is lost in conversation. My ego bruised, I fear he has abandoned us.

Eventually, we are asked to sit down. I haven't seen hide nor hair of Pascal for close to an hour. There have been zero reassurances to see if Mother and I are OK, neither have his eyes sought me out across the room.

We are seated with a party of lively Dutch people, and Mother is instantly trading jewellery compliments with a rather elegant Amsterdam-born woman. More than a little cross, I get up to find Pascal. I march over to where he is standing, with the DJ and the girlfriend. Without waiting to be introduced, I tug on his arm, saying, 'You come and sit with us?'

'*Bien sûr chérie,*' he replies, not even turning around.

'Now,' I say firmly. 'You're coming with me now.' The former TV boss courses through my veins and my bossy Type A character flashes to the fore.

It is a huge mistake on my part.

He turns to look at me.

'What you say?' His usually soft chocolate-brown eyes are flashing with inky black rage.

I pull myself up to my full height. 'I said now.'

I notice Jan, who is discreetly guiding the last stragglers towards their places, looking nervously in our direction out of the corner of her eye.

'No woman talk to me like zat!' Pascal spits before stalking out.

The restaurant momentarily falls silent.

Merde! I think to myself.

Miriam looks over, smirking squarely in my direction.

I want the ground to open up and swallow me whole.

Mother, boggle-eyed, furiously beckons me over. She wastes no time on niceties.

'Bloody go and get him,' she hisses, 'and drag him back in here if you have to.'

I nod, wordlessly.

'You are both behaving atrociously,' she whispers as I stalk off in his direction.

As I walk outside I can already hear Mother reassuring Jan, who checks if everything is OK.

The sun is setting and I can make out the silhouette of Pascal, my fiancé, leaning across the balcony, a Gitane lit between his fingers.

I silently walk up behind him and weave my arms around his waist.

'*Chéri?*' I begin.

He spins around.

'*Non! Sam, non!*' His body is taut and coiled, like an animal about to pounce.

I've never seen him like this before. I jump back, tears springing forth in my eyes.

'Pascal, please?'

After what seems like hours, his body finally relaxes, his shoulders drop and he opens his arms. I fall into them.

'I don't see you all evening,' I explain. 'Why weren't you with me?'

'I think you and your mummy want talk.' I can feel his body doing that Gallic shrug which serves to emphasise a point. 'Iz 'ard for me to talk in English all zee time.'

I try to make him understand that it's our first formal dinner invitation together as a couple. He might not know the language, but I don't know this country either. I need him by my side, not hidden in a corner.

I eventually encourage Pascal to hold my hand and accompany me inside. I spend the evening trying and failing to erase our first quarrel from my mind.

Mother must be wondering if she's in the Wild West as opposed to the south-west of France; for even she isn't immune to a showdown.

She visits the ladies' after we have eaten and, while washing her hands, she finds herself next to Miriam. Miriam holds her gaze squarely in the mirror. She has found her match in Mother, though, who easily meets her stare and says, 'It's Miriam, isn't it? Thank you so much for making my daughter feel so welcome here in France.'

With that, Mother turns on her heel, leaving Miriam gawping in the mirror.

Mother's plane isn't due to take off until Sunday afternoon. That leaves time for a thirty-minute tour of Cazals market.

Mother is a seasoned market browser, and this is more than enough time for her. We arrive mid-morning, and within minutes she has located and zoomed in on the stalls that have piqued her interest.

We purposefully avoid the elephant in the room, steering our conversation away from sticky issues and onto safer subjects such as presents; we eventually decide on pots of honey for my grandmother and a bottle of prune liqueur for Norman.

We sit down at the terrace at L'Auberge de la Place.

Philippe comes over to take our order, shooing away the waitress who covers the terrace.

Great, just what I need.

We exchange kisses and I introduce Mother.

''Ow iz it for you 'ere, Sam?'

'Good, Philippe, good.' Inside I am thinking please don't say you've heard about last night.

'Everything OK wiz Pascal?' he asks.

'Fine! Fine!' I trill.

'You want zee rosé, Sam?' I glance at my watch: just after eleven. Surely that's an acceptable hour? On a Sunday?

'Errr *oui, deux verres s'il te plaît*, Philippe,' I manage.

Philippe has barely trotted off before Mother starts.

'You're living in a bloody fish bowl here. If I'm not mistaken, he knows exactly what's gone on last night.'

I nod miserably.

'What were you thinking of?' Mother demands, before continuing without pause for breath, 'Poor Jan didn't know where to put herself.'

'I know...'

Philippe places both glasses on the table, and Mother buttons
while I struggle to get my purse out, but Philippe shakes his head
when I offer him a note. I reward him with a half-hearted smile.

'You and Pascal have got a lot of talking to do,' Mother
continues when Philippe is out of ear-wigging distance.

'I know…'

'You cannot let your temper get the better of you, Sam.
This is a small village,' she says, stating the bloody obvious.
'Everyone is going to be watching your every move.'

Understatement of the year, I think, groaning inwardly.

Less than an hour later we are en route to Bergerac airport. We
all barely exchange a word in the Kia. Before we set off I asked
Mother who she'd prefer to drive. Naturally, she simpered
'Pascal', smiling in his direction.

Traitor.

Pascal and I are speaking to each other, just. Last night's
debacle hasn't been forgotten exactly, more put in the pending
tray, for now.

Mother scoots through check-in and decides to head straight
to the departure lounge, pointedly saying she doesn't want to
hold us up.

Pascal goes to pay the car park ticket, leaving Mother and
me on our own. Tears well up in my eyes as, 'I *really* am on
my own' flashes through my mind, rapidly followed by, 'Please
don't leave me.'

Mother matches me tear for tear. She hugs me tightly; I can
sense she's reluctant to let me go.

'Sam,' she whispers, 'you've got to buckle down and make this work. After all,' she cautions ominously, 'it would appear many people are willing you to fail.'

Chapter Twelve

Daily Routine – Trying to Fit In

My September arrival coincides with an important time of year: *La Rentrée*.

It is the unofficial start of the year for France; children reluctantly return to *école* and *lycée*. They don't wear a school uniform. Even so, I note, they all look the same; with their back-breaking rucksacks and an obligatory, achingly trendy scarf swathed around their neck. The French workforce – equally sulkily – also return to their posts after, as is their wont, a luxurious August month off.

This means that Pascal is back to work too. He is *débordé*, deluged, with roofs to finish, countless *devis*, or estimates, to complete and prospective clients to visit.

Within hours of Mother leaving, Pascal asks me if I would like to go for a drive. I dreamily assume that this is a romantic gesture on his part. I even, naughty I know, allow myself to envisage a spot of al fresco make-up sex in the secluded countryside.

Nothing could be further from the truth.

My fiancé wants to take me on a tour of his current worksites. Self-employed, and working on his own, there are times, he explains, he will need me on site.

Heavens!

'If I forget an *outil*,' Pascal enlightens me as we walk towards the little white van, 'you must come *tout suite*!'

I don't know what most *outils*, or tools, are called in English, never mind in French, and so I make a mental note to order an English-French dictionary of building terms.

We climb into the van, Elsea jumping in first. I gingerly pat down the seat, removing dog hairs, sun-bleached receipts and an unwieldy tape measure. The van points its nose in a different direction than I'm used to; we drive through an idyllic little village, Les Arques, home to a regionally renowned restaurant, La Récréation. I spy Jan and Nick's house on the edge of the village; their garden is perfectly maintained and still bursting with flowers. The van follows the winding road downwards, in the direction of La Masse valley. The trees have yet to turn golden and lose their foliage; their leaves hide numerous chateaux, farmhouses and water mills.

La Masse valley is peppered with little villages – Les Junies, La Masse, Castelfranc – all beautifully maintained rural settlements. A drinking-water fountain takes pride of place in one village, in another a chateau dominates a stretch of the valley. As we drive, following the same route as the river La Masse, Pascal describes his next project.

'*Enfin*,' Pascal starts, 'I make zee roof at chez Alberto.'

Alberto, a *forestier*, is one of Pascal's close friends. Portuguese by background, though brought up in rural France, he is small, dark and solidly built.

'He take years to make zee 'ouse,' Pascal explains. 'Now he is ready for zee roof. Zat is my work.'

According to Pascal, Alberto is typical of many French *artisa*
who live in the countryside. They can't afford to buy a house o.
renovate the older properties that expats and other foreign buyers
have snapped up, and paid over the odds for. Such purchasing
power – so rumour has it – has priced the locals out of the market.
Instead, they work hard, they scrupulously save up every *centime*,
they barter and then eventually buy land and construct their
home as and when they have the spare funds to do so.

Alberto's land was purchased five years ago. To date, only
the floor and walls have been completed. Clearly Alberto isn't
someone to be rushed.

His wife Luisa has had to put up with living in a tiny two-
bedroom *gîte* during this time. The *gîte*, ideal for a two-week
holiday, isn't perhaps the des res in which to raise two young
sons, numerous animals and a dog. Nonetheless, it is Luisa who
holds the purse strings and has, I discover, been phoning Pascal
on the sly, coercing him to start work. She has negotiated a
price with my fiancé, for she is determined – come hell or high
water – to have a roof on her home before winter sets in.

When we finally arrive on site, I weigh up the shell of the
house, built in burnt-orange-coloured bricks, and struggle to
envisage its transformation into a home. It is then that I notice
that the family has etched each of their names into the concrete
floor, replete with dates, wobbly shaped hearts surrounding their
autographs. Hope and love pour out of their proclamations.
It fills me with indescribable pleasure that Pascal plays such a
crucial part in creating homes for such families.

isn't just Pascal's routine I have to get up to speed with. As Pascal shares custody of Antonio, every other week he lives with us. Pascal has a thirty-minute journey each morning in order to complete the work on Alberto's property – with Luisa chivvying them along, Pascal fears there will be no let up. No stolen afternoons together, and absolutely zero chance of him being able to ease me gently into life as a French housewife, one who will also be in loco parentis from the get-go.

Publicly I reassure Pascal that he isn't to worry; privately I'm terrified. To my shame, I used to pay people to cook and clean! As for Antonio's welfare, well, I also forked out for an army of helpers to assist me with the dogs.

I won't fib; the first month is brutal. At times I am convinced that I am trapped in a warped fairy tale – Cinderella in reverse. The glass slipper has already been sold on eBay to fund my voyage to France and now I'm in my proverbial threads in a kitchen I don't know my first way round.

I am up at 6 a.m. getting to grips with what constitutes a French breakfast, repeatedly coercing sleepy, moody males out of their beds and putting up with the dramas of numerous hungry animals. I discover there isn't just Elsea to care for, but also Caramel – Antonio's treasured *chat*. Caramel is a tetchy ginger tomcat. Like most of the male felines in France, he isn't neutered, reckons he's all that and makes more noise in trying to attract my attention than the three dogs combined.

I am akin to a short order chef, with my L-plates firmly in place; Antonio takes *chocolat chaud* and waffles smeared in a thick layer of Nutella, while Pascal wolfs down a bowl of milky, sugary coffee and toast dripping in jam and butter. I soon learn if I'm to have any hope of finishing my breakfast

then I must rise half an hour before they do. When both fat.
and son have eaten, I chivvy Antonio into dressing for schoo
while preparing a bag for Pascal; water, beer and clean hankies
are all essential items for his morning ahead.

Amidst this chaos the dogs are fed; their organic food is measured
and carefully poured into each of their bowls. I daren't translate
into French what 'organic' means – and neither do I reveal the
price of their food. Pascal would throw a wobbly if he knew our
animals were sitting down to the canine equivalent of a Michelin-
starred menu. At first Elsea turns her snout up at the hard, dried
balls of food, but after much drama, involving pushing said balls
around her dish with her little black nose, decides she rather likes
it. At Pascal's insistence, I mix in any leftovers from the night
before. At first I'm unconvinced – their delicate stomachs! Yet
Barney and Ambrose eagerly gobble up pasta, potatoes, any types
of veggies – without any nasty after-effects.

The school run is an awkward ten-minute drive. It starts
with me alternately hollering 'Antonio!' and honking the horn,
my blood pressure threatening to burst an artery; particularly
when I notice that his bedroom light is *still* on. Ten-year-old
boys, I discover, don't 'do' timekeeping.

Each morning is predictably identical.

'*Viens!*' I cry for the umpteenth time. '*Prêt?*' I manage,
picking up words from Pascal's vocabulary, when he finally
saunters towards me, where I am waiting in the car.

His chocolate-brown eyes warily regard me.

'*Ouai*, Sam.' Yeah, Sam, comes the reply.

Then either just as I'm reversing out of the drive, or just as
we've started to climb the hill towards the road along *le causse*,
Antonio will 'remember' something he has forgotten.

When we are eventually ensconced once more in the Kia – after a mad scramble to retrieve the dictionary, gym kit or whatever else has been mislaid – I silently concentrate very hard on the road in front of me, while Antonio – equally silently – concentrates very hard on the passing countryside.

Internally, I agonise over the social awkwardness between us. To be fair to the poor little sod, Pascal and I haven't exactly followed the step-parenting manuals when it comes to integrating me into their lives. In fact, one of those la-di-da family therapists would probably report us to the social services. The number of times Antonio and I have been in each other's company can be counted on one hand. We're virtual strangers; it's preposterous for anyone to assume that we can fall into an easy relationship overnight. Yet because we both happen to love the same man, I have to make it work between us – no matter what.

So when I holler and yell for him to get a bloody move on for school, what the poor kid really thinks of me is something I would rather not take a stab at.

When Antonio is deposited at school, the Kia cuts a swathe through the Lotois countryside, shooting along lanes and dangerously taking bends, so that I can return home to walk the dogs. On such walks Elsea never misses an opportunity to impose her 'top dog' status over Barney and Ambrose. Lording it over both of them, who are firmly on their leashes, she shoots off into hedgerows and disappears into forests for minutes on end, before sauntering back with a mysteriously triumphant look on her face. Ambrose, the scaredy-cat, is virtually glued to my side; alternately barking at the cows in the nearby field and quite literally jumping out of his skin when the donkey brays *bonjour* at us from a neighbouring field. He is as wholly uninterested in the local wildlife as he is in his new housemate Elsea. Barney, on the other hand, adores her. When she scampers off, he tries to follow her. When she deigns to walk with us, he matches her dainty trot step for step. Barney, it would appear, has fallen hard for a high-maintenance French woman, albeit one with four paws.

After the morning walk, I sweep the kitchen and living room with a large natural-fibre broom. I then wash and clean up after breakfast, before preparing lunch. Pascal, I am painfully aware, arrives at midday and insists on a five-course meal on the table within moments of his arrival. To say my meals are basic is a generous appraisal.

The first course is a doddle: *saucisse sèche*, which is housed in the *garde-manger*, a pretty looking contraption that is home to produce kept at room temperature. I just have to keep remembering to close it properly, to keep out the flies, which seem determined to feast on the same meals as us. Thinly sliced, the cold meat is served with *une flûte blanche*. This I must buy, fresh each day, mind, at the favoured *boulangerie* of his lordship. I boobed during my first week; arriving late and finding the bread sold out, or daring to go on Monday when it's closed. Don't get Pascal started on the day I tried (and failed) to fob him off with *une flûte blanche* bought from a different *boulangerie*. Anyone would think I'd attempted to forge the crown jewels.

The second course is a trickier affair. Any of the pitifully limited dishes I can semi-confidently turn my hand to, Pascal turns his nose up at. He doesn't 'do' anything that involves pesto, parmesan or rocket. He won't eat anything cold or anything that revolves around salad leaves. 'I'm not zee rabbit!' he has retorted more than once.

Predictably, then, I haven't taken the liberty to suggest we go veggie for one lunchtime.

Consequently, Pascal is usually served *un steak haché* with buttery pasta oozing in fats and carbohydrates to keep him going for the afternoon. *Un steak haché* – that's a beef burger to the rest of the world – is something I'd always assumed is casually cooked without much fanfare. Wrong. It's only ever prepared in a frying pan, sizzling in butter (the calories!) and only when the pan is piping hot. Each side of the patty of meat kisses the searing heat of the base for mere seconds before being served. The main course is mopped up with a hefty crust of the hallowed flute.

It is the third course that is Pascal's favourite – cheese. I discover Pascal prefers a selection – at room temperature – on the table to choose from; pungent goat's cheese, the whiffy blue variety and soft runny Camemberts are dairy temptations he cannot refuse. I note he artfully selects a portion of each, carving it and then teasing it onto his plate. He slowly, yet deliberately, savours each of their flavours on yet another hunk of bread. I watch and learn, for Pascal only ever eats them in their correct order; that is from tantalisingly mild to heart-stoppingly strong.

The penultimate course is dessert – this isn't as fattening as it might sound, thank heavens. I don't – mercifully – have to channel Mary Berry either. Rather, it's yoghurt or a piece of fruit. Rapidly followed by coffee as the final course.

Pascal merrily returns to work at 1.30 p.m. with zero idea of the sheer effort it has taken me to put all of this together.

Before I arrived he ate every lunchtime at L'Auberge de la Place along with his other *artisan* colleagues. At this precise moment I'd happily trade my first-born for that routine to continue. Ever the devoted girlfriend, without fail I wave him off and blow him a kiss. As soon as I can no longer hear the little van's engine, I collapse in a heap for approximately half an hour. In reality, after five minutes' rest, I restrain myself from jumping onto the Internet and wailing to Mother, via email, about the sheer bloody hard slog involved in my new life in France. Frankly, even if I wanted to carp on, there just isn't enough time.

Invariably, there is a ginormous clean-up after lunch; I haven't yet mastered the art of washing as you go. I walk the dogs again, attempting to quash any canine squabbles from breaking out. There is only ever one stick in the entire Midi-Pyrénées that all three of the dogs just so happen to covet at precisely the same moment. Barney invariably wins, his sheer girth ensuring all competition is flattened in his wake. He then proceeds to lord it over the other two.

When I return, Antonio is usually ready to be collected from school.

When the dogs and I lived in our swanky London suburb, we'd wave (well, I'd shake their paws) at the snooty little children who deigned to pass our house on their way to the local much-coveted prep school in their pompous little uniforms. Their even more unbearable yummy mummies were in a class of their own. Pert bottoms contained in Sweaty Betty leggings, blonde ponytails swishing; or, for those women who had to work, their hard aerobicised bodies were encased in the latest purchase from Selfridges.

These women are the only role models I have to steer me in the dress code for the school run.

Disaster!

Are they really to blame, though, when – stupidly, unthinkingly – I slide into a pair of jeans that have cost somewhere in the region of three figures. Likewise, a pair of wedges that would have Pascal yelping in disgust and me most likely twisting an ankle were I to receive an urgent call to arrive on a muddy building site with this chainsaw or that drill. In rural France, swanking about in my labels, I stick out like the proverbial sore thumb.

During my first painful week each day is the same; I *bonjour* the other mums at the gate. They, in turn, mutely gawp back at me. Towards the end of the week I eventually pluck up the courage to ask Antonio why everyone stares.

'You are *une femme de la ville*,' he responds. 'Your blonde hair, your heels, your diamonds...'

'Right,' I reply in a small voice, I think I get the picture.

Undeterred he finishes, '... You are not normal, Sam.'

When Pascal asks me how I'm getting on with Antonio, with the other women of Cazals, how can I say, 'It's really, really awkward, actually'?

Within weeks of arriving in France my first clothing purchase isn't something divine from Chanel (I wish – those days are long gone) or a racy pair of Louboutin *talons*. Instead, it is several fleeces and a pair of steel toecapped boots.

When we arrive home, after the social gaucheness of the school run, my work is far from finished. Practically all French school children eat *un goûter*, a snack of whatever they fancy, and then it's homework. Homework in France for children of Antonio's age is baffling; most of it seems consist of learning poetry – whatever the subject. Granted this is probably just my limited understanding of *les devoirs* – as homework is called – but we do seem to spend endless evenings reciting chapter and verse for virtually every subject.

The evening meal, if I'm canny enough, is concocted from whatever I've prepared at lunchtime. The three of us dine together at the farmhouse table that dominates the living room. It is civil, sociable and just about edible. Madame Congélateur is still relying on frozen 'help'. I notice Pascal struggling to hold his tongue when he clocks the ready-made contents of my shopping bags.

Antonio is in bed at 8.30 p.m. and we follow him an hour later. Funnily enough, I have no problem in falling asleep and maintaining my shut-eye.

A year previously I was living in another social sphere for weeks on end in LA. My mornings before work were spent in this yoga studio or that gym and dinner was invariably a hotly sought-after reservation at the latest sushi bar. If anyone had told me that in twelve months' time this would be my new life, I'd have thought they were bonkers.

Daily life in France is exhausting.

I'm not the only one having problems adjusting to the new set-up. Ambrose cannot tolerate being taken down several notches in my affections. Without question I am utterly at fault for allowing my little prince free reign until this point – spoilt, I know, is putting it mildly. His protests are nothing if not consistent. To Pascal's horror, he scratches at our door nightly, indignant that he is no longer allowed on the bed.

After a few weeks of getting to grips with my routine, I'm puzzled to discover that the laundry basket is by and large filled only with my things. Do the French wash their own underwear, I wonder? Is this yet another quirky French habit I've yet to discover? One morning at breakfast I decide to ask.

'Pascal? Antonio?' They both turn and look at me, a flash of annoyance sweeps across both their faces – I am, after all, disturbing French men during their crucial first meal of the day. 'Where are all your dirty clothes?'

'*Quoi?*' comes the nonplussed reply from both of them.

'You know,' I reply, 'your clothes, the dirty ones, that you've finished with at the end of each day?' I mime, sniffing my underarms, wrinkling my nose and waving my hand in front of my face. Antonio laughs, Pascal frowns.

'I wear zee same for two, three days a time, Sam,' Pascal replies, looking mystified. 'Why?'

I try not to gag while eyeing the pair of them. As it is morning, they are both in their T-shirts, socks and boxer shorts.

'And you?' I eyeball Antonio. 'Well?' I trust that at least he changes his underwear every day.

'The same to Papa.' He shrugs.

I just about stop myself from pursing my lips, folding my arms and unleashing a tirade about cleanliness and hygiene.

That evening I sit them both down and ask them to walk me through their bathroom routine and laundry habits. According to Antonio, he washes his face and teeth each morning and evening, 'If I remember.' He changes his clothes when they start to smell, apparently.

Pascal, far from being the role model he should be, is even worse. His face might get a scrub once a week, he can't remember the last time he used the shower, he gives himself a swill down as and when he thinks he merits one. If he forgets to brush his teeth, and they're looking somewhat yellow, he will use Cif – the kitchen cleaner – to scrub them. His socks and pants are given a thoroughly good wearing, sometimes for four days – he's nothing if not eco-minded. His T-shirts, just like his son's, are changed when they start to whiff.

I am aghast!

Does this mean it's true, then, I can't stop myself from thinking, what 'they' say about the French and their cleanliness?

I gently explain that I'd like to implement a 'change our T-shirt, socks and boxer shorts daily' rule.

The look on both of their faces tells me all I need to know – this is *not* going to be easy.

Pascal insists I am *têtue* – that's stubborn – for not letting the matter drop. I have already christened him *le tyrant* for refusing to take any of my 'helpful' suggestions on board.

We both, it would appear, want to be top dog.

The following morning, before either of them is awake, I tiptoe around their sleeping forms and swoop in on their dirty offending underwear, still lying in a puddle where they'd been dumped the night before. I scoop them up and plonk all of their clothes into the laundry basket.

In their places I lay out a clean, sweet-smelling set of freshly laundered garments; T-shirt, socks and boxers for each of them. I even soften the blow with a squirt of lavender water.

Thirty minutes later, you'd think the world had ended.

To say pandemonium breaks out is putting it mildly. In my opinion, they rather overreact, the grumbling – the '*putain*' this and the '*salope*' that – is not for a lady's ears so early in the morning.

When they eventually dawdle into the living room – where their individual breakfast orders await them – I can't help noticing how well turned out they both look.

Round one to me.

For the first month, I really don't have much thinking time. Before I'd arrived in France I'd pictured myself living *la vie française*, skipping along the lanes in flippy skirts and strappy tops (the reality is I wear neither, for fear of ticks and due to the fact that I am a magnet to any insect which happens to be in a 30-mile radius). I'd assumed I'd be drinking rosé on the terrace most evenings, and that I would adjust easily to running a French household.

What planet was I on?

Yet the reassuring, regular humdrum of domesticity gives me something to do with my time; which means that the opportunities for pitiful navel-gazing are few and far between. There are the inescapable moments when I grieve for my old life. Anything can trigger it off; finding an old business card of mine in a purse, an airline boarding card in the bottom of a handbag, watching planes soar across the sky on their to, so I convince myself, far-flung glamorous destinations, passengers all hugely successful in their own lives. I used to be one of those, I scold myself.

Pathetic, I know.

Such glimpses of my past are raw reminders of what I was and the sum total of me now – which by my own estimate isn't very much. The tears fall freely then.

During the weeks when Antonio isn't with us, inevitably my schedule slackens. Alas, it's at some stage in that time when depression and insomnia kick in again. It's during the hours of darkness when I learn the real meaning of love. Pascal lies awake with me night after night holding me in his arms, offering tender reassurances. On more than one occasion he softly suggests I can always go home if I think I've made a mistake.

I haven't made a mistake in moving to France to live with Pascal. I can do this.

Can't I?

chapter Thirteen

Nasty Surprises

Mother Nature is a wily old fox.

She isn't letting me go anywhere.

An enduring memory of my childhood is of scrunching through the large beech leaves that dominated the paths and roads during my walk to school. Hand-in-hand with Mother, I would listen carefully as she enlightened me about the meaning of autumn. Her explanation went that autumn wasn't a time for death, that the leaves falling, the bare – and to my eyes – sad trees wouldn't stay that way forever; rather, that it was about rest and renewal. For my seven-year-old self it was one of those life-affirming moments between mother and daughter that I will always treasure. It was then that she sowed the seed; that the end of one season heralds the start of another. It's only now, nearly thirty years later, that I'm finally beginning to understand what she wanted to convey to me.

It seems Mother Nature is perfectly well aware of this memory; she is taking full advantage of it in my current surroundings in order to soothe and reassure me about the supposed pickle I've found myself in this year.

For a Lotois autumn *is* breathtakingly beautiful, easily rivalling that of the famed North American New England colour extravaganza. It is a sumptuous spectacle to behold as

October slides towards winter; shades of sienna, amber, r
and sunset all jostling for the award of best hue in show. Mor
than once, while out on errands, I have been compelled to pull
over, extinguish the car engine and indulge my senses in the
display of colours around me. In emails home I struggle to
capture just how strikingly pretty my neighbourhood truly is.

Dog-walking takes another turn for the better too. I no
longer have to worry about insects and midges gorging on my
Anglo-Saxon blood. Rather, I dodge the conkers and acorns
that rain down as I crunch, crunch, crunch through the fallen
leaves in seemingly endless forests of chestnut and oak trees.
My walks each day are neither long nor adventurous; Pascal
has ensured I keep to a trail known to him and one on which,
he is confident, I cannot come to any danger.

It wasn't always the case. At first I'd set off, tramping
mindlessly across fields, with scant regard for the animals that
might be contained within them, never mind the electrified
fences that surround such fields. If the dogs weren't howling
with pain and fright after one electric shock after another, they
were yapping and excitedly running towards sheep and – even
worse – their tiny lambs. It was far from being a relaxing walk;
I'd return stressed and troubled for my animals and the four-
legged country residents we'd managed to upset.

No longer!

Today I turn left out of the house, walking down the
narrow road that rarely welcomes traffic on its ancient path.
The first house I come to is that of our neighbour Coco –
a retired security chief from Paris. I wave to him, and he
rewards me with a hearty *bonjour* in response. I then turn left
again, this time off-road and onto a dirt track. It's then the

…gs are unleashed, for rural trails signal canine liberty. The track is steep and uneven, marked out only by huge tractor tyre indentations in the crumbly soil. Even though there is no likelihood of passing cars, there are other hazards I am watchful for in our surroundings. The field to the left of the track is occupied by dozens of dairy cows – and occasionally a menacing bull. Most of the time, though, the cows simply moo a *salut* when we pass. Barney and Ambrose are not so well mannered.

Ambrose cowers away from them, while Barney (putting on a show for Elsea, no doubt) pompously barks, warning them in no uncertain terms to clear off.

To the right of the track, or *chemin*, is a wood of pine trees. I adore walking through this forest. The trees, which reach some 10 metres in height, offer – I soon discover – protection from the rain and the wind during some of the wilder weather patterns that can take the valley hostage for days at a time. The dogs love scampering in, out and around the tree trunks, dodging fallen branches, chasing after pine cones and sniffing around the entrances to the badger sets along the perimeter of the forest. I delight in the silence that the imposing trees afford, as I pad softly over the mossy carpet of the woodland floor – such walks never fail to still my mind and provide solace from my mithering thoughts.

Continuing along the track, it climbs steeply; I usually huff and puff, the muscles in my bottom reluctantly beginning to work overtime. To my shame, Elsea and my boys – even Ambrose – easily scamper ahead of me. The two shaggy sheepdogs always dart back in my direction, attempting to round me up. Their efforts are soon abandoned when they scoot off, enticed by a sudden noise in the forest or distracted by a distant scent I have no hope of getting a whiff of. Yet they always return for me; circling me, encouraging me onwards towards the summit of the by now vertical *chemin*. I am usually shamefully out of breath when we arrive at the hilltop. But the view when we reach it, goodness – it is stunning and never fails to take my breath away.

It's a vista which typifies this part of rural France: undulating fields separated by hedgerows and dry stone walls for as far as the eye can see. To my right there is the chocolate-box village of Thédirac in the distance, its cluster of stone built houses marked out along the skyline. I can just about make out smoke lazily escaping from their chimney pots. Directly in front of me is a hillside dominated by golden woods. To my left are yet more fields marked out by hedgerows, criss-crossed by abandoned vineyards and several apple trees which bear delicious tasting fruit. So high up, the wind invariably whips round me, my blonde hair a tangle of knots to be combed out later on.

I have yet to meet anyone on this walk – yet not for one second have I ever felt alone or afraid.

For just across the valley is home. I know I only have to call out and, if Pascal is there, he will come for me and rescue me, just as he has already done in ways perhaps neither he nor I will ever fully comprehend.

I find the succour of the woods, the staggering beauty of the view and the richness of autumn strangely curative. More often than not I recall Mother's words; out of demise comes renewal.

I cling onto this philosophy; it is, I trust, part of my recovery.

The leaves continue to tumble down, at the same time as mushrooms – robust ceps, leggy girolles – push upwards through the earth. At first, every time I spotted a mushroom I would excitedly scoop it up, pop it in my pocket for safety and then proudly show it to Pascal when I arrived home.

'What iz zat?' Pascal would ask, when I plonked it on the table and dragged him out of his chair.

'I'm not sure, I'm hoping you can tell me,' I'd reply with a little swagger in my step, as we both walked towards the farmhouse table in order to examine it more closely.

'Sam, Sam.' Pascal shook his head slowly. '*C'est rien ma chérie.*'

I had naively assumed all mushrooms could be eaten. After all, I now live in the land of *les champignons* so it stands to reason, went my naïve logic.

'Sam, never pick zee mushroom, don't even touch it eef you don't know eet.'

Pascal sat me down for one of his many nature lectures. In this one he went on to enlighten me with the fact that while yes, some rather lush 'rooms can be eaten, many are also life-threateningly poisonous specimens. Even a trace of one such fungus on my hand can result in a nasty tummy bug – or worse.

Lesson learnt; while Pascal indicated that I might be overreacting I still insisted on scrubbing the table down and removed the potentially Ebola-esque mushroom wearing a pair of sturdy rubber gloves.

Unless I'm with Pascal, I leave the rootling to others.

Nonetheless, it is a hive of hunter-gatherer activity in the Lotois countryside. Cars parked at the edge of forests indicate, more often than not, clandestine foraging for fungal delicacies. No one, it would appear, is in the least bit bothered by *Défense D'Entrer* signs. It isn't the only food sourced freely, however; I regularly spy bottoms of all shapes and sizes pointing skywards as women (and, curiously, it's usually women) confidently stake their place on the roadside gathering this year's crop of walnuts.

When I was first summoned to the building site, I was plagued with dread and insecurities; what if I hadn't located the right tool? But now just as often I'll pootle along to see how work is progressing. I relish the drive to see Pascal. It is a chance to take in the blazing glory of autumn. I pass the famed vineyards of Cahors, empty of their fruit maybe, but the leaves in turn rich crimson and golden blonde, shimmering in the valley bed surrounding the river Lot. On late October mornings the landscape is enchanting; wisps of mist thread through the vines – it is akin to watching a fairy tale come to life.

Pascal and Alberto are also a sight to behold. They work effortlessly with 100-kilo beams, shimmy up and down scaffolding and casually transport back-breakingly heavy wheelbarrows oozing with thick cement back and forth. They have an easy shorthand with each other; Alberto, who speaks in the thick accent of the south-west, bats questions at Pascal and he returns with commands quickly and efficiently.

I observe Pascal the carpenter in action. He's competent in ways I've never witnessed in a man before; turning raw materials into a home that will last for generations.

After a month the wooden structure of the roof, with complicated beams and joists, is already in place. I have learnt to arrive on site – in my sensible sturdy boots and dull dark-coloured fleeces – with bottles of beer in order to quench their thirst on the rare occasions they take a break. Pascal's preferred methodology is to work quickly and apply himself wholeheartedly to the task at hand – dawdling and idle chitchat are strictly forbidden.

When they're not on site, they're talking about what they need to do next, and perhaps inevitably such strategic discussions occurs around our lunchtime table. Plans for the roof, interior structure and terrace are coming alive at Pascal's drawing board, set up next to where we eat.

As Luisa works full-time, it has fallen to me to cook for both men. There are, as is to be expected, regular mishaps; I have misjudged when meat and potatoes might be ready, for example. Alberto, mercifully, says nothing when I urge him to get started on his mashed potatoes, promising that the meat will be ready '*dans un instant*', when I know full well it's still thawing in the microwave. Typically I am rewarded with a few spiky words of discontent muttered by a mortified Pascal. Alberto will not only eat anything I put in front of him, he is also easy company – even if we don't understand a word of what the other one is saying.

Yet as October gives way to November, I become accustomed to cooking for both men. *Steak haché*, pork chops and lots of Emmental-flavoured pasta continue to dominate the menu. It is simple fare – I haven't quite given up the title of Madame Congélateur just yet.

On one occasion, I hear two vehicles arriving. That's strange, I think. They normally arrive together in Pascal's little van. I peek out of the kitchen window and spy not only the Citroën, but also Alberto's red and green truck easing itself through the posts of our drive.

Pascal bounds up the stairs, I fling open the door and kiss him.

'*Ça va chérie?*' he asks, pulling off his muddy boots.

'*Oui, mon amour.*' I smile as he rushes through the door smelling of Gitanes and a deliciously musky odour. I indicate that the table is set for the three of us.

'*Ça sent bon*, Sam.' He gestures towards the kitchen where chicken breasts are slowly bubbling in a creamy garlic-laden sauce. He likes the smell of it! Always a good sign.

'*Chérie* make a place for one more,' Pascal says. 'Françoise is joining us.'

My ears prick up at this news. *Françoise? Who the devil is Françoise?*

'*Désolée,* I don't know she arrive,' Pascal whispers into my hair.

'*C'est pas grave,*' (it doesn't matter) I say.

I shoot into the kitchen and pull out more china and cutlery and hastily set up a place for 'Françoise'.

Merde! Never mind who Françoise is, do I have enough to go around?

I don't have time to clarify who she is either, because Alberto walks through the door, swiftly followed by Françoise herself. Elsea, who has been eyeing up the arrivals, has already greeted Pascal, jumping onto his lap and giving him a playful bite on his nose. As soon as she clocks Alberto, she grants him a flirty little lick on his outstretched hand. However, Elsea

221

sniffs cautiously around Françoise and, inexplicably, points her black snout in the air, giving her the cold, hairy shoulder, before trotting out of the door.

Formal introductions are made; naturally, we're both *enchantée* to meet each other. Françoise is – apparently – a colleague who works with Alberto in his forestry business. I shrug off an offer of help from her – only because I don't want her to witness the almighty mess that my first attempt at this latest dish has created in the kitchen.

Within minutes all three are sat down at the table. Rosé is sloshed into their glasses and, through a fug of their cigarette smoke, I discreetly check out Françoise; plump, easily in her forties, with large high breasts contained in a tight T-shirt. She has shoulder-length chestnut-brown hair, a wide smile, and her eyes crinkle when she laughs – which she does often. As she confidently rolls yet another cigarette, from what I can gather as their easy banter unfolds, she gives as good as she gets. I am, it slowly dawns on me, witnessing the archetypal French woman in action. I now understand precisely why she is feared the world over, for it is with good reason. This woman, who clearly hasn't succumbed to Botox, a high-maintenance hair regime or all-consuming yoga practice, has 'it' – charisma, magnetism, allure – in spades.

As we sit down to enjoy the first course, Pascal whispers endearments in my direction, thanking me for being so accommodating. I discreetly, impatiently, wave him away – far too busy playing spectator to the drama unfolding opposite me.

I scrutinise Alberto and Françoise, as intimate physical gestures pass between them. Alberto touches her arm, Françoise lights a cigarette for him, they talk easily in hushed tones. It's as though we're intruding; the atmosphere is electric!

'Anyone would think they're lovers,' I cluck to Pascal, unfortunately just at the moment that there is a lull in the conversation.

The silence that descends over the table merely serves to underline my faux pas.

'*Un ange passe.*' Pascal jokes that an angel passes – it's a French expression that I've learnt is used to gloss over an awkward silence.

Alberto looks at me sheepishly, while Françoise rewards me with a gaze that suggests I'm something unpleasant on her shoe.

A-ha.

Alberto has not one but two women in his life. I find this idea hard to fathom, but only because he bears an uncanny resemblance to a hobbit. Clearly in his own mind, and that, I'd wager, of Françoise, he is a fully-fledged sex god.

For the rest of the day I count down the minutes until I can 'casually' quiz Pascal.

Pascal is barely through the door when I start.

'Does Luisa know about Françoise?'

'*Peut-être,*' Pascal replies, as he picks up the remote control and begins his predictable search for Seasons, the hunting channel that is on constant rotation whenever Pascal is at home.

Perhaps? This isn't the response I was hoping for.

So I try again.

'Well, does she or doesn't she?' I insist.

'*Je sais pas*, Sam,' (I don't know) Pascal half-heartedly replies, as a programme on female hunters flickers into life. An extremely competent woman loads her shotgun. 'It 'appen 'ere all zee time.'

Oooooh, I want to throttle him!

Has he no idea that this is perhaps my biggest fear in marrying a Frenchman?

'Well, I want you to know, Pascal,' I say, trying to keep my pitch in check. I note, with my temper rising, that he continues to watch the woman on TV harp on about the type of gun she has. I am indignant! He can't even be bothered to give me his full attention. 'I want you to be perfectly well aware,' I repeat, 'that I wouldn't bloody put up with it!' My voice rises into an unfortunate squawk as I finish.

Pascal turns his attention away from the woman who now has her loaded shotgun poised and ready to shoot.

'*Je sais*, Sam.' Pascal lazily smiles at me.

I can see he is tired, but this 'talk' is important to me. It's laying down the foundation of our relationship, for goodness' sake. Fidelity is everything!

Pascal must know this, for he continues, 'I never do zat. You ees too precious to me. *Tu es la femme de ma vie.*'

'You cheat on me,' I reply, just for good measure, 'it's *over.*' My melodramatic finish comes just as the woman on the screen pulls her trigger, her bullet seconds later terminating the life of a male stag.

A smile breaks across Pascal's face when he swivels back to see what she has shot. 'Bravo!' he calls out in congratulations towards the television.

She stalks across to the animal and yanks a leg – presumably to check it's dead – revealing a pair of testicles.

'And I'll cut your bloody balls off too,' I mutter – just for good measure.

It is fair to say that, after mere months of living in France, most of the households I have come across are thoroughly matriarchal. What the women say goes. For that reason, then, we are summoned to meet with Pascal's grandmother.

Hélène lives in a swanky retirement home in nearby Prayssac. If the Lot were London, then Prayssac would be Notting Hill; full of dinky little boutiques, a plethora of trendy eateries and a market – much like that on Portobello Road – which pulls in tourists in their thousands throughout the summer.

Hélène, approaching her tenth decade, is as sharp as a tack and, so I've been told, adores her first grandson. When we pull into the car park, she is already on her terrace, beautifully turned out and waving at us.

A French retirement home is something else. As we walk along the sparklingly clean corridors, we pass the dining room, which is being prepared for lunch, with carafes of rosé and red wine being placed on each table. I'm agog! We mount the stairs and reach the first floor where Hélène lives. In front of us there are exercise bikes amongst other work out equipment, which – according to Pascal – the residents, some of whom are well over a hundred years old, are all encouraged to use daily.

We walk through the door of her apartment and she pulls Pascal into her arms – no mean feat, when she's not even 5 foot. She looks me up and down and says to Pascal, *'Bien, elle est belle.'*

I think I get the seal of approval. Unfortunately, it is only the first hurdle.

Her apartment is beautifully kept. Everywhere there are photographs of her grandchildren – pictures of Pascal and his siblings cover every surface. They both talk to each other in rapid-fire French. Hélène's lilt is a beautiful sing-song Parisian accent, testimony to the fact that she lived much of her life in the most chic city in the world.

It isn't long before I can make out the question that I dread the most.

'*Elle ne parle pas français?*' She doesn't speak French, Hélène asks incredulously.

'*Non mammie, un petit peu,*' Pascal replies, no, just a little.

I smile nervously and fidget in my seat.

'*Elle doit apprendre!*' she announces. '*Je veux parler avec ta femme, Pascal.*' I must learn, apparently! She wants to be able to talk to me...

Oh God – leave it to the old 'uns to cut to the chase. She is right, though; I must learn French.

So far I have muddled through each day, dictionary at my side, stock phrases next to the phone for whenever – horrors! – it should ring. Ridiculous, I know, but the sound of the telephone terrifies me. The irony isn't lost on me; before I had more phones than any human being should rationally possess. Now I'm terrified of handling the blimmin' thing.

We leave the retirement home and drive home along La Masse valley and turn into Les Arques, the village where Jan and Nick live.

And it's then I remember: Wendy! The language teacher I met at Jan and Nick's dinner soiree (I refuse to remember it as the night we had 'the row').

A call to Nick, who assures me she is very good, results in her telephone number being issued. Wendy, on learning I don't speak any of the language – no qualifications, let alone that other basic: 'schoolgirl French' – is nothing if not direct.

'We'd better get started as soon as you can – there's a lot of motivation for you to learn the language, isn't there?'

As November draws to a close, it is a race against time for Pascal and Alberto to finish their work before winter sets in. From sunrise until sunset I'm on my own running the house single-handedly. I can just about cope with this until, almost overnight, the temperature drops below freezing. One morning I wake up to see the countryside sprinkled in icing-sugar frost. It is stunning. Unfortunately, the downside is that the house is bone-achingly cold.

So cold that when I breathe, I can see the vapours of my breath escaping.

I can do this, I tell myself, trying not to panic.

For the house is kept warm by wood alone.

Pascal cuts it up with a chainsaw into wood burner-sized chunks – before setting off to work. I don't blame him for not being able to chip in with organising our winter wood. Even so, it is me who has to stack it, store it, load it into baskets and lug it into the house several times a day.

Needless to say, my nails are shot to pieces. I bite my lip to hold back the tears the first time I notice calluses on my hands.

This isn't me, I want to wail. I love a manicure! My lily-white soft hands are *always* commented on!

I don't, obviously, wail. Who'd listen to me harp on anyway? Instead, I just give myself a bloody good talking to and get on with it.

I have no choice; it's never-flipping-ending. Then there are the daily log-fire-related chores; dusting, sweeping, washing, mopping to combat the debris of the burning wood. Pascal is nothing if not a fusspot and is more than a little vocal about the pleasures of arriving home to a pristinely-kept abode.

The romance of a crackling fire has dimmed somewhat.

On each and every dog walk my eyes are trained for pinecones to use as firelighters. I scoop the precious items up and pop them into the basket that now accompanies me, swinging on my arm, on every canine outing. The only other alternative is to ferret about in Pascal's atelier for wood offcuts that are invariably covered in mouse droppings.

A whimpering phone call to Mother largely consists of my lamentations; I moan about my nails, the constant cleaning and the cold – oh, the cold! There is pitifully little about the joys of *la vie française*, rather I bore her to tears (I assume) about how much I miss the whoosh of the central heating boiler and how I'm convinced I'm developing chilblains (later inspection reveals that I'm not, but I could – in theory – develop them, at any time). However, my gripes are cut short at with the arrival of a package several days later.

The contents of which delight me no end.

Imagine my joy at pulling out thermal socks, long johns and a matching thermal vest.

Normally I only ever dream of slipping into a slinky Agent Provocateur matching bra and knickers set or beautifully cut Myla underwear.

Please don't ask me to choose between them; I fear that the knitted undies would win out.

Chapter Fourteen

Christmas

The ice queen December declares her arrival by showing us a flash of her ethereal wintry beauty, and another tumble in the temperatures. The first morning of December – or Saint Florence as it's known in France – is, just like a French woman, sensationally seductive. It's all about the show and putting on appearances. It's so easy to fall under her hauntingly beautiful spell; yet the allure of her Narnian wonderland is not without bitterly cold consequences.

Tiptoeing into the chilly living room, I pull my dressing gown tightly around me before gingerly opening the first of three windows, the one that offers the picture-postcard view of the valley facing our little stone house. Shivering, I quickly release the latch securing the shutters, push back the wooden doors and sharply breathe in the bitingly cold air. I catch my breath when I take in the rural wintry scene that greets me, for it is as though a Christmas card has come to life. The pine trees in the forest are all coated with frost, as if each and every branch has been individually sprinkled with a hefty dose of sugary frosting. Even the ineffective tumbledown wooden fence that haphazardly borders our land has been transformed into a proud-looking icy white creation. The fields behind the forest are also draped in wintry white veils of delicate icy lace. I can almost hear the tinkle of sleigh bells.

I open the shutters to the window that faces south-east and am treated to a spectacular sunrise; pinky tones of cherry blossom, flamingo and candy floss all streak across the sky, playing tag with each other. Stunning doesn't even begin to describe it.

The frost and below-freezing temperatures are unrelenting during the first week of December. I get used to stomping my feet, to maintain the feeling in my toes, on the tiled floor of what is now my domain – the kitchen. Fortunately, more discreet underwear packages arrive from Mother. Never have I been so relieved to slip into the reassuring, yet woefully unsexy, grasp of thermal leggings.

It is during the weekends that Pascal insists I join him in the kitchen and upgrade my culinary repertoire. I am to learn how to cook some of the Midi-Pyrénées' more traditional dishes and am given a crash course in the creation of typically French winter meals – *pot-au-feu*, *bœuf carottes*, lamb tagine. I am normally a diligent student, a desk-at-the-front-of-class sort of girl. However, Pascal is *not* a patient man. Rather, he is the schoolteacher all students fear; the grumpy one who shouts a lot and rarely, if ever, gives out praise. So when things get burnt, overcooked and don't go as planned, well, let's just say that the atmosphere in our house prickles with barely contained tension. Pascal, who is sublime in the kitchen, does try to hold his tongue. Strangely, then, it is the little things that cause his temper to ignite.

'Sam, Sam, SAM, *NON*!' he will shout, genuinely vexed with me. *'Pas comme ça!'* He will then whip the knife, spoon or any other utensil out of my hand and make what to my mind appears to be a miniscule adjustment in my chopping, stirring or blending. '*Voilà, comme ça!*'

In my defence, I do try. It is desperately frustrating that I'm not a natural cook.

It's around this time that I learn that rule number one in this French kitchen is *mijoter* – that's simmer. Or, as Pascal pleads each time I boldly fire up the gas cooker, 'Just leetle, leetle gas, pleeze, Sam', doubtless dreading the prospect of yet another overcooked, tough 'n' chewy dish.

Pot-au-feu is arguably the most popular winter dish in my part of France, the French equivalent of the Sunday roast. It typically consists of leeks, carrots, turnips, onions, potatoes and select cuts of beef; all cooked together in a *cocotte minute* (which I'm tickled to discover is that seventies throwback – the pressure cooker) with each of the ingredients added at specific intervals. Sounds easy? Wrong, if you're me. I have scorched the meat, I have mistimed when to cook the potatoes and I have forgotten to close the vent on the pressure cooker.

The fact that I can't even pronounce the dish doesn't exactly bode well for me cooking it. Antonio collapses into fits of giggles when he hears me proclaim, '*Pot au fou* for dinner tonight, chaps!' Pascal lets out a deep sigh, slowly shaking his head. This is because '*pot au fou*' literally translates as a 'pot of madness', whereas '*pot-au-feu*' is the rather more tempting 'pot on the fire'.

Repeatedly overcooking the meat isn't the only culinary cock-up I make during the wintry December weekends, when there is precious little else to do. It's not that I spend every weekend cooking, mind – only those forty-eight hours when

Antonio is with us. When he's not, I can think of plenty of other activities that keep us warm and amply distract Pascal's attention from my woeful attempts in the kitchen.

My first shot at *bœuf carotte* isn't much cop either. I forget to put the ingredients into the pressure cooker first – to thoroughly cook through the meat and the vegetables. Instead, I put them straight into the Le Creuset casserole pot, and am puzzled as to why – two hours later – the meat has yet to transform into the tender soft morsels that are normally in evidence when Pascal cooks this seemingly easy dish.

I am still vegetarian – just. My current philosophy, which I know would horrify most vegetarians, is to eat everything barring the meat. I know I'm failing miserably – my veggies simmering in animal fats! But it takes my inept self so long to cook for Pascal and Antonio that unless I want to keel over with exhaustion, it is my only available option.

It is one December Friday night that Antonio and I transform Fridays into *fun*-days. The irony isn't lost on me; a year ago I was putting on a brave face and holding court at Soho House in London or the Sky Bar in LA. Now my plus-one is a ten-year-old boy. The VIP lounge is our *salon* – at least there is a trendy log fire, I suppose. Squint your eyes a little and we could easily be in the drawing room in any private members' club in London.

And so, that Friday night, I finally discover the way to Antonio's heart – hamburgers. Don't necessarily believe all you read in those tomes about French children positively embracing the prospect of life as a Gallic gourmand. *Les enfants* I've met over these last few months are foodies on a par with children all over the world – they'd gladly swim across the river Seine in December for American fast food.

My skills as a short-order cook advance quite nicely on these evenings. Antonio takes his hamburger – that's two, if you please – in a lightly toasted bun. Ketchup is slathered on each half and gruyere cheese is melted over the burger under the grill. *Et voilà!* I hold the contents together with cocktail sticks and a sticky label on top with 'Master Rubinat' emblazoned with stars and stripes on it. His little face breaks into an adorable smile.

'*C'est vraiment régal*, Sam,' (this is really delicious) he announces between ginormous bites. While eating his American creation he quizzes me about the times I've travelled in the US. He loves to hear about the ritzy Vegas hotels, the skyscrapers in New York and the boulevards of endless palm trees in Los Angeles. When he has finished he thanks me with a sticky kiss on each cheek. It might be bitingly chilly in our house, but I am flooded with a deliciously warm feeling inside. I catch Pascal's eye and his face lights up in response to the scene unfolding before him. I wouldn't want to be anywhere else in the world.

It is on one such evening, in the middle of December, that we decide to sit Antonio down and tell him we have news.

It is a conversation I would happily shrink away from. Having swotted up on how we're expected to approach this tricky subject according to various sanctimonious step-parenting books, Pascal and I are in agreement. We need to do it together and face-to-face with Antonio.

I peek out of the window and spot Antonio's arrival with Papa. They fall into step easily with one another. Pascal takes his son's school rucksack and his bag for the following week, slinging both effortlessly over his shoulder. His other arm he drapes casually around Antonio. I adore observing Pascal the carpenter at work, but it is something else to watch Pascal the father interacting with his son. It takes my breath away.

The instant they both walk through the door, I skittishly ask Antonio if he would like *un coca* or *un chocolat chaud* – he opts for the latter. He can sense something's 'up' and so boldly requests a sprinkle of marshmallows too. I clock Pascal's expression, easily readable; it tells me that I should get a blinking move on, as he wants to get 'it' over with. Hands trembling, I pour a glass of rosé for Pascal and me, while the milk seems to take forever to boil in a little pistachio-green pan on the stove.

When everything is eventually ready, and I enter the *salon* with the steaming bowl of *chocolat chaud*, Pascal calls Antonio, currently lost in a television show, to the table.

'Antonio,' Pascal begins, the emphasis, as always, on the first two parts of his name only.

'*Oui Papa?*' His freckly little face turns towards Pascal and he gives him his full attention.

'*Alors*, we 'ave set a date for *le mariage.*'

Crikey, I know Pascal isn't one to beat about the bush, but really! Even I'm agog at how direct he is.

'*C'est vrai, Papa?*' Antonio stares boggle-eyed at both of us. They're virtually out on stalks at the announcement.

'*Oui*, Antonio,' Pascal replies. '*Tu es content?*'

For a moment Antonio fixes us both with an expression I can't quite fathom.

Oh God, I think, please don't kick off... the atmosphere in the *salon* as we wait for his response prickles with anticipation. '*C'est génial, Papa!*' Antonio leaps to his feet after announcing that it's great news, and gives Pascal a hug and a kiss before throwing himself onto me and treating me with the same shower of cuddles.

I catch Pascal's eye while this commotion is unfolding and he winks at me. *Result!*

When Antonio has finished with the hugs and kisses he sits back down at the table, and a contemplative expression descends over his face. After a couple of minutes he looks up at me.

'Sam?' he asks, his demeanour particularly pensive.

'*Oui*, Antonio?' I smile. Inside I'm thinking oh no, what now?

'Pleeze, for *le mariage*,' he starts and then stops before continuing on in English, 'can I 'ave a suit, shoes wiz zee laces and a trilby?'

My mouth involuntarily drops open. But nothing puts Antonio off his stride.

'I want a shirt and tie too, pleeze?'

This time it's Pascal's turn to look alarmed. There is no way Jose Pascal will say the French equivalent of 'I do' wearing a tie.

I look at Antonio, in his trainers, baggy jeans, little cap and camouflage fleece top. Then I imagine him transformed, little Lord Fauntleroy in a suit. Maybe my high-maintenance ways are rubbing off on Antonio after all. I suppress the urge to giggle.

'*Bien sûr*, Antonio!' Of course, I reply. Naughty, I know, not having even discussed it with Pascal. Yet the expression on my fiancé's face says it all. He is beyond thrilled. Surprised, I'd suspect, but nonetheless tickled pink that his son is happy with our news – and already dictating the terms of the outfit he wants to wear.

There's another surprise waiting for Antonio – a chocolate-filled advent calendar.

Rural France takes the arrival of *Noël* extremely seriously, and across the Lot, preparations to welcome in Christmas are well underway. I mosey about Cazals village daily, ostensibly to buy Pascal's *flûte blanche* from the *boulangerie*. In reality, it means that I get to absorb the Christmas spirit that descends over Cazals as it is enchantingly transformed into a winter wonderland

Each store – *épicerie*, *pharmacie*, even L'Auberge de la Place – has a Christmas tree proudly standing outside of it. Each window is charmingly decorated with the chosen colour scheme for the village. This year it is crimson and gold. An enormous tree goes up in the village square, overseen by the gimlet eye of Madame Blanco who runs the local television repair store. She prudently ensures it is proudly erected just so, before conducting its embellishment with bows, faux presents and fairy lights.

The little streets and lanes of Cazals don't escape the Christmas cheer either. Twinkling lights are strung above and carols are played from speakers discreetly dotted throughout the village.

I am, I confess, nervous about spending Christmas in France. It's not that I mind being away from my family. For the previous decade I've spent pretty much every festive season abroad, chasing the sun on one exotic beach after another. Yet it is the first time I have been asked to assist in the selection and purchase of a Christmas tree; I've never gone to the effort of decorating my home before. There never seemed any point without a family to appreciate it.

Pascal is in high spirits at the prospect of celebrating *Noël* together. He insists we buy not just one tree, but two – one for our terrace and one for the living room. Climbing into the little white van, we venture into the village one Sunday morning to La Mine D'Or, the local *quincaillerie* (hardware store), where an enticing selection of Lotois spruce and fir trees are on sale. Pascal is insistent; not only must we buy locally, we must also purchase the largest tree we can find. We have been startlingly well organised, having already prepared a place for our new resident in the *salon*. Pascal approaches each tree and sizes her up, with the level of deliberation a Miss World judge might use. Too fat, too skinny, what about her bottom, does she have enough personality? All these assets are discussed with Pierre, the proprietor of the La Mine D'Or. I am tasked with selecting one for the terrace. I unashamedly follow my nose and opt for the tree with the most enticing scent. To my mind, she also has a rather charming full skirt and will be the perfect mannequin for our terrace.

Although what Barney and Ambrose will make of the tree, I dread to think. I have already plonked Father Christmas hats on both of their furry (and dirty, to my eternal shame) heads for a Christmas photo to send back home. Elsea, of course, was having none of it and slinked off the moment I pulled out a smaller hat and waved it in her direction.

Pascal easily straps both trees onto the little van. As it is Sunday, it is also market day. We visit other stallholders, who coax us into buying bunches of holly and sprigs of mistletoe. It doesn't take either of us much persuasion to stop for a glass of spiced wine either.

Within hours our little home is transformed. Pascal chose well; our new resident looks splendid. Her potent pine scent perfumes our house. I catch my breath each time I walk into the living room – the fragrance is delicious.

Rural life is usually on lockdown from November through to March, while everyone cocoons and focuses on staying warm. Except, that is, during December, when the markets and fairs entice almost everyone out of their homes. Christmas markets spring up everywhere.

Cazals' Christmas fair is no different. Traditionally it is held on the first Friday of December. Christmas presents – of the craft variety – are on sale in the village hall and there are refreshment stands tempting passers-by with oysters, hot cider and sticky fresh crepes. Father Christmas, or *Papa Noël*, to give him his correct name around these parts, also finds time in his busy schedule to put in an appearance.

But best of all, L'Auberge de la Place also opens its doors, proffering a crustacean winter menu. I am in heaven! Pascal, knowing only too well that I would happily run through the village square naked for a platter of *fruits de la mer*, has already reserved us a table.

Throughout the evening, as we pass around the village square, Pascal proudly announces our news.

'We're getting married!' mingles with cries of *'Félicitations!'* as we pass from one well-wisher to the next.

Pascal's *artisan* colleagues shout and roar their approval. There is much back-slapping and gentle ribbing involved. Everyone we tell is automatically given an invitation to our wedding. I try not to twitch when totting up the number of locals Pascal has casually invited to our nuptials. There's just no stopping him! He adores his rightful place in the centre of attention and has, I note, a permanent smile etched across his face. I too am positively giddy from the congratulatory kisses and hugs.

Huddled against each other, with a December wind whipping around us, it is an extraordinary season to be in love.

Christmas Eve starts off so well.

Plainly, I was lulled into a false sense of security.

'Joyeaux Noël!' Pascal whispers to me as I slowly waken in his arms. I peek over the duvet. Brrrr, it's cold. But for once the plunging temperature that has, yet again, seen the inside of the windows ice over doesn't trouble my mind.

Instead, my thoughts turn to the preparation of Pascal's beloved foie gras, oysters for me, champagne for both of us and the yummy dessert only eaten at Christmas – *une bûche de Noël*. I have excitedly spent the last few days carefully selecting all of the essential ingredients for a traditional French Christmas. I desperately want our first *Noël* together to be perfect.

I don't even let the fact that I've never cooked an English Christmas meal put me off.

It took me by surprise to learn that we celebrate, exchange presents and eat *the* meal on the evening of Christmas Eve. Not that I was worried; I had it all under control, or so I thought.

Pascal had decided he wanted to eat chicken, as opposed to the traditional goose that is eaten in these parts. We painstakingly selected our bird over a week ago and stored it safely in a fridge in the *cave*. After a lazy breakfast together – *pain au chocolat*, *croissants* and bowls of steaming, sugary *café* – we finally begin to prepare the vegetables together.

'You want take zee *poulet* from zee *cave, mon amour*?' Pascal asks, as he carefully peels potatoes.

'*Pas de problème, chéri*,' I reply as I pull on my huge black parka and bolt down the stairs outside.

I tiptoe into the *cave*, not entirely trusting I'm not going to come across an unidentifiable creepy-crawly or worse.

That's strange, I think as I notice that a sliver of light beams through the partially opened fridge door. I warily approach the fridge, my brain slowly calculating what could possibly have happened.

Oh no.

I vaguely recall Pascal warning me that the fridge door can be temperamental at the best of times…

Surely not?

I hastily estimate when I popped the bird into the fridge. I vaguely remember that the afternoon I unloaded the shopping, I could hear the phone trilling in the *salon*. Did I check that the door was properly closed? Or did I focus on my pre-arranged and much longed-for girly catch-up instead?

I can't put the moment off any longer and open the door.

The stench is one of those odours that triggers projectile vomiting in those with the strongest of stomachs.

The bird is well and truly off.

What a disaster!

Even by my counts, it isn't my finest hour in France.

I panic, yet know I must instantly confess all to Pascal.

On inspection of the bird he is, for once, speechless.

At the speed at which it has gone off? At my ineptitude – which seems to take a turn for the worse each day? Who knows?

Yet it is my turn to be stunned, because he takes it surprisingly well – all things considered.

Pascal, ever resourceful, instantly calls his parents. I try not to dwell on the fact that I've ruined our first Christmas together.

'*Bonne nouvelle!*' Pascal says with a smile when he's finished talking to his father. 'We can eat wiz my mummy and daddy.'

Thank you, God, I mutter softly, looking skywards. Later on, I pack up the foie gras, the oysters, the cake and the champagne, placing everything into an unwieldy basket.

It's early evening when we arrive and are ushered into the toasty warm living room, where a fire is roaring in a large open grate.

I stop and stare.

In front of the fire is *sanglier* (wild boar) slowly turning on a mechanical spit. Christmas carols are playing softly and fairy lights twinkle across the fireplace. Hélène, Pascal's grandmother, is also seated in 'her' chair. Antoine, Pascal's father, places a flute of champagne into my hand and settles me down in front of the fire. Danielle, Pascal's mum, waves away all offers of help in the kitchen. Instead she smiles, watching Pascal snuggle up next to me.

Christmas Eve dinner, then, turns out to be thoroughly unexpected, but nonetheless passes exactly as it should – surrounded by the love of Pascal and his family.

After we've eaten more than I dare admit, any thoughts of my struggles with the French language are put to one side when Hélène challenges me to a game of dominoes. The woman fights dirty and more than once *'salope'* is muttered in my direction when I have the gumption to win a point. She is ruthless and, to the amusement of the family, shamelessly beats me.

As we drive home, I weave my fingers through Pascal's hair. Even by night the journey is still magical; we shoot through vineyards, drive slowly and respectfully past churches – their congregation leaving midnight mass. Watching over us all the while is the grand chateau at Grézels, positioned high above serving as guardian and protector over the Lotois valley and vines.

It is during the drive home that I feel the vibration of my mobile in my pocket. I open the phone and read a text from Philippe wishing us a happy Christmas. It would seem he is happy for us too.

It is New Year's Eve and, this time, Pascal and I are determined to mark the end of the year together – just the two of us. It is inky black outside. The only light is from the twinkling stars and a crescent of moon, waning in its cycle. An owl hoots in the distance, there is the usual nocturnal rustle of animals rowdily passing through the rural neighbourhood.

What an astonishing end to my annus horribilis, I think to myself as Pascal hands me a glass of champagne and slips an arm around my waist. We boldly make the move out onto the terrace, where the temperature is just above freezing and the Christmas lights are twinkling towards their allies in the midnight-blue sky.

I sip from the flute and reflect back over the last twelve months – and how I have unexpectedly ended up in love and attempting to carve out a new life in France with my fiancé.

I won't deny it; it's been a demanding few months. I still barely speak the language, my L-plates are firmly in place when it comes to keeping house, and as for taking on the role of stepmother, I know I truly have to up my game before I'm deserving of such a title. Perhaps most poignantly of all, it's only in living together that Pascal and I have truly begun to get to know each other.

'I know you change for me,' Pascal begins, whispering into my hair, 'your life, your home, your work – everyzink. I know your life before was exciting and 'ere eet isn't.'

I shake my head, thinking, if only you knew.

'But you are a real compliment to Pascal Rubinat,' he continues, 'you change my life. If I know you exist before, zen I would 'ave 'unted you down, seduced you and taken you 'ome many years before, Sam. You are *la femme de ma vie*.'

'And you are my world,' I whisper. 'You've not only saved me but given me a new life. One that's worth living.'

He places his fingers over mine, easing the flute out of my hand, puts both of our glasses down onto the terrace and, taking my face in his hands, kisses me as the little Norman church, two fields across, rings in the New Year.

Chapter Fifteen

Los Angeles, and Closing the Door on My Old Life

I'm grateful for the diminutive slithers of sunshine which are just about all that qualifies for daylight during those harshest of months, January and February. The notion 'daytime' takes on an entirely different meaning in the heart of a French winter.

The eerie silence of these brutal months in the Midi-Pyrenees is simply something I hadn't anticipated; the birds have long ceased their chorus song and instead peer nosily into our house in their never-ending search for food. As quickly as we put out grains and seeds, they're voraciously eaten. The dozens of farm animals – dairy cows and Quercy sheep – which normally populate the fields around our little house are nowhere to be seen. Not a bleat or a moo can be detected, carried on the wind. The only sound that pierces my winter mornings is that of a dog half-heartedly barking in the distance. Elsea barely lifts her head; even she doesn't want to expend precious energy on a reply.

I'm astonished to discover that a blanket of fog descends over the Lot for winter's bleakest period. Locals and expats alike have neglected to mention the ghostly miasma of mist that rolls into the valleys, nestling down for seemingly weeks at a time. It is a thick freezing fog, *'comme la soupe'*, as the locals are prone to say, clucking and despairing over its firm hold. Even the dogs don't like to scurry too far into it, fearful, I imagine, that they will become lost in the supernatural-like haze.

Driving along *le causse* towards Cazals allows me to take in the full bleakness of the wintry landscape. The immediate fields left and right are no longer a hive of countryside activity. Rather, it is as though they are suspended in animation, having taken a heady sleeping draft from the winter queen herself. Subsequently they are frozen, draped in powdery dustsheets, captured and immobilised for all time. None of the surrounding valleys are visible, hibernating in their duvets of fog; only the tallest of treetops peak through. Closer to the road, the thick mist clings to chimney pots and log piles – nothing escapes its grasp. Driving past the lake in Cazals, I slow down because I don't quite believe my eyes. For it is an ethereal vision that unfolds in front of me; will-o'-the-wisp, ghost-like maidens dance across the surface of the water. It is a Victoriana ghost story writ large.

And the silence – oh, the silence. On days like this – when the headlights are on full-beam at midday, and I can barely see in front of me – I turn on radio Nostalgie and uncertainly sing along to Charles Aznavour or Brigitte Bardot.

I have taken to using candles to light our home throughout the day. It isn't a wholly romantic gesture. Our isolated position means that we are at the end of the electricity line. We suffer frequent power cuts; too many people demanding too much electricity at the same time. I soon become acquainted with the regularity with which we are plunged into darkness. I can virtually set my watch by the twice-daily milking at the farm at the top of *le causse* – when the dairy shed's electrical system kicks in to signal the arrival of the cows. The dim in our lighting sends me scuttling around the house turning off all non-essential electrical items. Consequently, I time my laundry and cooking around the needs of Mesdames Les Vaches.

The wintry solitude of the days is frequently and, to my sheer pleasure, adorably broken by the latest development in the love story that doesn't just belong to Pascal and me.

That of Elsea and Barney.

Elsea has finally opened her heart and surrendered to the unwavering romantic overtures from Barney. His unrequited love of the last six months has paid off. Such dogged devotion has clearly softened her flinty heart (which is normally reserved for Pascal only).

She has now made room in her life for Barney; they sleep in the same basket together, Elsea curled into Barney's snugly warm chest. Each morning, whoever has finished eating first patiently waits for the other one (behind the oak tree in front of *la grange* – their furry little heads intermittently poking out, to ensure Pascal hasn't clocked they're off on their daily jaunt). When the other has finished they then trot off together, making their rounds of the neighbouring countryside.

For they have a routine; even Coco, our neighbour, knows when to expect them. He is used to listening out for Elsea's paw frapping on his door to remind him yes, she would quite like some of last night's leftovers – *maintenant s'il vous plaît Monsieur*. Other locals tell us delightedly of their sightings of *Madame Petite* and *Monsieur Grand* roaming the countryside together. At first it pained me to think of Barney unleashed – what if he gets hit by a car? These days, admittedly, I just shrug, knowing he's better protected with the wily little terrier he has fallen in love with, who knows the comings and goings of every *paysan*, than he could ever be with me.

Elsea, who Pascal frequently claims is quite simply his best hunting dog ever, is of course no stranger to *la chasse*. Pascal has trained her well – so well, in fact, that she frequently takes herself off to hunt. On one particular day she returns with a present for Barney.

It is Ambrose's howling that first alerts me to the gift, loudly performing an 'it's not fair' dance and growl around Barney – who is doing his very best to ignore him.

When I spy Barney, nestled quietly under the oak tree, enjoying his gift, my shrieks echo around the valley.

Within seconds Pascal flings open our front door.

'What eez zee problem, *chérie*?'

'Look! Just look at Barney!' I squall. 'What's he doing to that poor thing? Get it off him!'

Pascal, puzzled, calls Barney, who turns, with the lower half of a rabbit lodged between his jaws.

I shriek again. Pascal roars with laughter.

'*Dis donc* my leetle *femme de la ville*,' he begins, 'Barney eez country dog now, Sam.'

Pascal regards Barney with a newfound admiration.

Barney looks from me to Pascal, thinking 'what's the big deal?', if I know my blimming food-obsessed hound. All the while the carcass continues to hang from his mouth.

'Get it off him!' I yell.

'Sam.' Pascal grabs me by the shoulders. 'Elsea give it to 'im to eat. He live 'ere now, *mon amour*.'

I shudder, yell out for Ambrose to follow me (which he does, though with great reluctance, I note) before stalking back into the house.

Quite what Ambrose makes of the love affair from which he is explicitly excluded is anyone's guess. It's fair to say Ambrose detests the countryside; he has been subjected to more electric shocks than he can shake a paw at from the wire fencing which the farmers insist on using (''E learn, Sam,' is the only response Pascal will deign to give me when I pester him to 'have a bloody word' with the farmer). Oh, Ambrose does try, though; on the rare occasion he has been brave enough to bark at the sheep, he is usually repaid with angry bleats from the severely peeved ewes, which send him cowardly scurrying back in my direction.

If truth be told, he's not too keen on Pascal either. He cocks a deaf ear when Pascal calls him, and certainly takes not a blind bit of notice when Pascal insists he does his 'business' in the field opposite our house. At every opportunity he joins me in the bedroom, even though the sight of Ambrose snoring in 'his' place is always guaranteed to send Pascal into a potty-mouthed rant.

But his epilepsy remains under control – and for this I am eternally grateful. His thick wintry coat has grown out to protect his osteoarthritis-riddled bones from the plunging temperatures and while Elsea isn't in love with him, I certainly am.

It is rare we pass wintry evenings alone. While the two bars in Cazals remain almost deserted for much of winter, the same cannot be said of our home.

Pascal's work colleagues drop in when the fancy takes them; between 8 a.m. and 8 p.m. I must always be ready to make coffee or prepare an *apéro*. This means that, as it's winter, there is a constant fug of smoke in our house. I learn how to make pastis, getting the doses of water versus alcohol right for each of Pascal's very particular friends, how to pour the correct slugs of the locally produced ratafia (it's delicious, but goodness is the liqueur – made from unfermented grape juice – strong) and how to serve the perfect *demi* of beer.

None of our visitors is more regular than Alberto. It's not even been discussed, no formal invitations are ever issued, yet he arrives every lunchtime and evening in his little red and green truck. I'm usually alerted to his imminent appearance by the put-put of his engine as he descends the lane to our house. The dogs are so used to his appearance they don't even bother to bark anymore. I lay an extra setting for him each evening and button my lips when I discover that our food bill has doubled, that our wine supply drains far quicker than I have ever budgeted for.

Each day before we eat, both Alberto and Pascal walk in the forest behind the house, where they'll scatter grains and maize for the passing deer and birds. Observing their robust male silhouettes, it's plain to see that Alberto's physique is markedly different; shoulders down, body hunched over, his aura flat and lifeless.

But there's a tragic reason for this; Françoise, his mistress, has died.

I am flabbergasted to hear the news. Françoise was so full of life. But a routine procedure in a local hospital had turned into septicaemia. There was nothing anyone could do – her own body poisoned itself to death.

Alberto refused to go and see her – from what I can glean – and is now tormenting himself with grief and regret.

I have urged Pascal to talk to him about it, yet each time I raise the subject, he looks at me in horror – explaining that it just isn't the done thing. But anguish and despair drips from Alberto. It's plain to see that he needs to talk to someone – he is a broken man.

I berate myself for not knowing enough French to tackle death and loss.

Instead, Alberto has found solace in alcohol – and drinks himself into oblivion most evenings. When he eventually passes out, Pascal and I haul him onto our sofa bed and make him as comfortable as possible. Each morning when I tiptoe into the living room, I'm invariably greeted by an empty sofa; the eiderdown is always neatly folded, with the pillows plumped up and left on top of it.

Quite what his wife Luisa has to say about all this, I dread to think.

One evening when we three are filling up the wood supply beneath the stairs, I look at Alberto, his body with us, yet his heart and soul plainly elsewhere. I touch his arm and haltingly attempt, '*Je suis vraiment désolée*, Alberto.'

His eyes meet mine; I recognise the emptiness in them.

He simply nods and continues to stack the wood.

While I no longer suffer as Alberto does, I can empathise with such intense pain of grief and loss.

February is a month I have been dreading. I have been just about coping with the adjustments to my new life; I stopped taking the antidepressants within weeks of arriving in France and only allow myself a sob in the bath once a week. While emails no longer ping into my inbox with the same reassuring frequency as they used to, the scarce few that do arrive are a pleasure to receive, for they are from genuine friends.

I am slowly putting myself back together; no longer a television executive, those skills are useless in rural France. Instead, I have to unpick those thorny professional traits from my personality. During a stand-off with Antonio about tidying his room, with me demanding to know exactly *when* the task would be completed, he shouted, '*Insiste pas*, Sam! I just don't want make when you insist *tout le temps*!' Well! It was a light-bulb moment for me.

All those years I'd spent micro-managing my colleagues, hovering over them, constantly 'checking in' to see if they'd finished. If I had just backed off, they'd have got on with things anyway – and probably much quicker. It has taken a ten-year-old boy to expose one of the many ugly sides of my character.

On the flip side, I'm slowly discovering other talents I didn't know I had. In the kitchen my culinary skills are slowly but surely getting better. Around the home, I – she who relied on a cleaner for over a decade – now do everything myself. I'm even book-keeping and client-liaising for Pascal.

While I'm no linguist, I am enjoying the challenges involved in learning a new language. As Wendy my teacher has lightly commented on more than one occasion as I squawk through my conjugation, 'There'll be no danger of anyone mistaking you for a French person, will there?'

But none of that protects me from the realities of formally closing the door on my previous life. There is little left to face now – yet the final formidable obstacle is something I have been dreading.

I am scheduled to appear in court in LA; to bankrupt my US television company.

Shame doesn't begin to describe the end of my American dream. I have scrimped together air miles to pay for most of the flight; the remaining pounds I have secured by selling my Cartier watch.

The journey is a difficult one. I sit in the cabin during the long-haul flight, unable to watch any of the films on offer, my mind awash with painful memories of my former life. The months I lived in Los Angeles, the dreams I had of creating a life there.

As I pass through immigration, I'm amazed not to be stopped, to be informed that the likes of me aren't wanted and to hop it on the returning flight. At the baggage carousel, I keep my head down, fearful of recognising anyone. Television executives use transatlantic flights with the frequency of taxicabs.

It doesn't help that I find myself next to the svelte form of the actress Sienna Miller at the baggage claim. I unwittingly follow her out through customs and into a burst of paparazzi flashbulbs. She elegantly folds her tiny figure into a waiting limo and I, shuffling further along the pavement, go to wait for a bus.

It is the ultimate humiliation and a reminder that without money, you're nothing in LA.

If I'm honest, it is a chapter in my life I have mixed feelings about closing. I lived in LA for six months near the ocean. I walked my dogs, practised yoga and cycled along Venice Beach daily. I fitted right in with the LA work ethic – up at 5 a.m., gym at 6 a.m., office by 7.30. I loved it. A few calls with a large dose of humble pie are all it would take to return to such a lifestyle. After all, everyone loves a comeback kid, right?

And yet, and yet... I can hand on heart say that I know such a life isn't what will make me happy anymore. It's taken losing everything, a cliché, I know, to appreciate being loved. Waking up each day, secure in the love of a man who I respect and who challenges me every single day, in the knowledge that we are shaping our future together.

So in the twenty-four short hours I am in Los Angeles I have deliberately checked into a cheap hotel downtown, near the courthouse, and I consciously refrain from telling any of my former work colleagues and friends that I am 'in town'.

After a fitful sleep, broken constantly by nightmares, the following morning I nervously pull on one of the few suits I have left over from my executive life. I walk into the entrance of the courthouse, where a security guard points me in the direction of the courts, urging me to have a nice day. I smile anxiously at his greeting and try to suppress the waves of nausea rippling through my body.

I have been assured by the company I have hired to handle the Chapter 7 bankruptcy procedure that someone will be here to meet me. I hover by the court noticeboard and am approached by a lawyer straight out of central casting; grey skinny shiny suit, cowboy boots and hair slicked back into a ponytail. He enthusiastically pumps my hand and rattles through what I need to say to the judge.

I wait for sixty long minutes for my case to be called. I listen to tales of the lives of other women – and it's mainly women seeking bankruptcy in front of the judge today – who ashamedly tell of credit card debt, the sudden death of their partner, giving their children funds they don't have.

My lawyer is next to me, leaning back in his chair, noisily chewing on a piece of gum, feet crossed on the chair back in front of him. The old Sam would have told him to 'bloody belt up', and most likely 'show a bit of bloody respect'. But the last twelve months have stripped away all of my former confidence in such social situations.

Instead, I watch one woman after another shuffle forward and tell her story. My stone-hearted lawyer has doubtless heard it all before. Eventually, he indicates it's my turn. My stomach flip-flops when I hear my name called. I wobble forward in a pair of ill-fitting heels – more Birmingham Rag Market than Beverly Hills boutique.

After confirming my name, age, date and place of birth, I too confirm my story.

The judge, on hearing the details, softens. 'Are you sure you want to do this?'

'Yes,' I reply, haltingly, aware that I most likely will never be allowed to launch a business in the United States of America again. 'Yes, I am.'

It is all over in minutes.

Four hours later I am at LAX airport, where I buy a snowstorm model of Los Angeles for Antonio.

It doesn't surprise me to discover it has broken when the plane finally touches down on European soil.

When the Kia pulls into the drive, some seventy-two hours since I left, Pascal and Antonio are excitedly waving to me from the terrace.

They both rush down the stairs, Barney, Elsea and Ambrose enthusiastically leading the way. All five are jumping up and down, alternately pawing at me, kissing me and hugging me.

'*Ça va?*' Pascal mouths to me over the commotion.

'*Oui, chéri,*' I reply, with more certainty than I feel.

'Sam, Sam!' Antonio shouts, pulling me towards the stairs, 'you must come quickly, I 'ave surprise for you.'

Pascal grabs my suitcase and we head indoors together. I haven't had a chance to take my bag off my shoulder before Antonio shouts, '*Voila!*'

He hands me a large envelope. I turn it over in my hand, and mouth '*merci*' towards him.

I deliberately, slowly put down my handbag and root out my reading glasses, making an extravagant show of putting them on, all the better to receive my 'surprise'. Pascal laughs, while Antonio, impatient, cries, '*Vas y!*' Go on!

I carefully peel back the envelope and pull out the hand-made card that is nestled inside.

Both Antonio and Pascal watch me open it.

I study the front of the card, tears pricking at my eyes. It is a picture of our home with the three of us outside it. Pascal in camouflage, Antonio – smaller, but also in camouflage – and then next to Antonio is me. He's captured me perfectly; blonde hair flying in a ponytail, wearing jeans, and he has painted a red-lipsticked smile on my face.

'I make at school,' Antonio explains, 'my teacher say to make eet for our family.'

We *are* a family?

I'm not Antonio's mummy and I'm not yet Pascal's wife, but we're just about making a fair fist of life together. It dawns on me that while Antonio and I might not have wanted that much to do with each other at first, we are slowly accepting one other.

The following morning while out walking the canine crew, after much huffing and puffing, I get to the top of what I now think of as my track. *Finally* the fog is beginning to clear! I take in the azure sky that greets me and I can't honestly remember when I last saw it such a delicious shade of blue. Even the dogs making a greedy beeline for the cowpats in the field in front of us can't distract me from this moment. I cover my eyes while they adjust to the intense luminosity of our surroundings. It is then that it occurs to me. I spin three hundred and sixty degrees and, laughing and hugging myself, I gaze at the familiar network of planes streaking across the sky, their silhouettes leaving their usual evocative trail – because it finally hits me.

I no longer dream about where they are going.

I have zero desire to be a passenger on one of them.

I've finally realised, I'm one of the lucky ones; I've already found my paradise destination.

As the bitterness of February comes to a close, *apéros chez nous* become a firm fixture on the social calendar. One couple, Leticia and Bernard, are regulars around our table. They are similar in age to Pascal and me; except they are one of those couples who have been together for so long they have worryingly begun to look like each other.

Leticia and Bernard are typical of many couples that live, work and love together. They run a convenience store in a neighbouring village. Yet she is the undisputed boss; these French women who run rural businesses are scarily competent, equally at home barking out orders from the seat of a tractor or seductively directing her husband's clumsy hands *comme ça* from between her exquisitely ironed sheets.

Leticia is nothing if not up front. Her biggest headache, she announces, is her non-existent sex life.

I have listened agog to her trials of the last few months; their disastrous attempts with amyl nitrate (I dread to think where they purchased that banned substance from in rural France, until Pascal witheringly points out that there is such a thing as the Internet. Hark at him, who didn't even have such a connection a year ago). Then there is the Viagra they both took – which left Bernard eternally frustrated and extremely hot to trot, while Leticia steadfastly refused all advances, owing to hot flushes and firmly closed thighs. They have even tried a Rampant Rabbit that I purchased for them. I discreetly urged one on Leticia, having 'heard' good things about them.

Ahem.

I was convinced that a vibrator would allow Leticia to discover that certain parts of her body worked perfectly well with or without a man. She could quite easily become, I teased her, a wanton sex goddess. I was mightily miffed (not to mention running out of options) when she gave it the thumbs down. I have to confess I don't think I was able to hide my dismay when Leticia could only grumble about the uncomfortable rubber and the alleged rash it left her with instead.

One morning just after 11 a.m., I swing by her store. I have timed my visit deliberately; just after *les grandes dames* have done their daily shopping (and gossiping) and just before *les ouvriers* dart in before lunchtime. Leticia whistles to her assistant (that'll be her husband) and orders him to man the till while we have a coffee together.

We disappear through the door at the back of the store. Leticia prepares two silky smooth cups of coffee and we each perch on a bar stool around a tall barrel-shaped table.

I've barely dropped a sugar lump in my coffee before Leticia begins.

'Can you look at somezing for me?'

'Of course!' I reply.

She jumps up, yanking up her blouse and pulling down her trousers at the same time.

I very nearly spray the room with the coffee that happened to be in my mouth at the exact moment.

'*Mon dieu*, Leticia! *Qu'est-ce que tu as?*'

What on earth does she want to show me, I ask, as she fiddles with the top of her knickers.

'I zink zis is my problem,' she replies, deadly seriously.

I nervously peer over into her trousers and see a miniscule pouch of skin sitting above her knicker line.

'Pah!' I say. *'C'est rien!'* It's true. For a woman who has had two children – it's nothing.

'Non, c'est pas vrai, Sam,' Leticia responds grimly. 'I 'ate it, it disgust me!'

Leticia goes on to tell me that for the last few months she has been doing sit-ups every night, in a bid to get rid of her muffin top and allow herself to feel more desirable at the same time.

'What I make?' she asks.

'I have no idea. Surgery?' I say jokingly.

'Non, Sam, I 'ave a better idea.' Leticia leans in. 'I zink I take a lover.'

This time my coffee does spray the table top.

Ever alert for scandal, I automatically cry, *'Non,* Leticia, *non*! Think of Bernard!'

'Bah! Bernard, he ees zee only man I make love wiz.' She twirls her empty coffee cup in front of her.

I try not to get my knickers in a twist. But I do try to impress on her that this is a bad idea. Instead, she promises me to do 'nozink' without talking it through with me first.

An unconventional one, maybe, but I feel like I might finally have found myself a friend.

Chapter Sixteen

Wedding Preparations and Marriage Hiccups

'*Tu vois*, Sam?' an excited Coco calls out from his terrace, as I stride purposefully towards my neighbour's little cottage, the three dogs excitedly zigzagging around my legs. '*Elles sont belles, non?*'

'*Oui*,' I reply, slowing down, one eye on the hounds, all of whom are already bouncing on ahead without me. 'I've seen them, Coco, *elles sont magnifiques*!'

Coco is proudly pointing out his daffodils – *les jonquilles* – that have pushed up and out in their hundreds during the recent days. Impatient spring can wait no longer and has bid winter a firm *au revoir*, insisting that she packs her bags and goes. We have been rewarded for spring's insistent efforts, for the temperatures on waking the last few mornings are astonishingly mild. During the last few days I have – oh joy! – pottered about outside in just jeans and a light jumper, and have not had to engage in the rigmarole of hat, scarf and gloves. The sun reassuringly affirms her presence, warming my cheeks when I peg out the laundry. It gets better; even Ambrose has taken to sunning his osteoarthritis-riddled bones on the terrace.

Coco, a large, round man with an equally large, round face, whose default setting is cheery, is cautiously reversing his too-tiny moped out of his *cave* in order to make his daily jaunt into Cazals. He continues to chatter and frequently pauses to beam in the direction of the pretty little trumpet heads.

Coco, like most of the French here, is known to everyone by his diminutive nickname (it's all Didi this, Bron-Bron that, in these parts), and he lives alone during the winter months. His partner, the extremely elegant Mélanie, refuses to reside in the Lot during winter's brutal sojourn. It is almost as if Coco swaps one mistress for another, Mélanie returns to her cosy chic Parisian apartment, while Coco surrenders to winter's icy grip along with the rest of us hoi polloi.

For Coco, the daffodils don't just indicate that spring is on its way, they also signify Mélanie's return. Her arrival, I'd wager, must be imminent. Mélanie is now retired, yet when she worked she specialised in fitting and selling lingerie to the Parisian bourgeois. My reaction on hearing this news was to clutch at my woeful little bosom and think, 'Heavens! What must she make of the dodgy push-up bras I rely on to hoick the girls up?'

Coco's observations are spot on – the flowers *are* pretty. His lawn slopes down towards the pine forest, and the bank is dotted with hundreds of their sunny yellow bonnets gently bobbing in the breeze, as though admiring the view around them.

The thought had crossed my mind, naughty I know, of waiting until he had left one morning to go and take his daily *café* in the village – and then sneaking in to swipe a bunch. He wouldn't miss a dozen or so, I reasoned to myself. I've resisted, of course. I'm slowly coming to appreciate that those flowers don't actually belong to any of us – least of all me. Rather, Mother Nature has provided her floral presentations for all to enjoy.

Spring continues to march inexorably on, buds shooting forth from each fruit tree. It's almost as if they take it in turn to put on their individual blossomy spectacles; first the buds on the plum tree burst into flower, providing dainty, sweet-smelling, waxy white blooms. Next up, the cherry tree is adorned with the most darling garlands of flowers, their fragrant bloom releasing a scent that perfumers the world over have greedily attempted to replicate. Finally, the enormous quince bush releases the prettiest of floral displays. I gasp when, on opening the bedroom shutters one morning, I am greeted by her vanilla-coloured, deliciously scented floral glory. It's also, to my admittedly untrained olfactory senses, the most pleasing of all.

It is to the Lotois flowers that Pascal and I turn for inspiration for our wedding invitations.

For our wedding date – 31 May – is drawing ever closer.

Heavens! The whole sum of our wedding preparations – and it's March already! – amounts to pitifully little. So far our total efforts have resulted in the sending out of lackadaisical emails urging friends and family to save the date (and, on my side, a not-so-subtle nudge to everyone to jump online and book those precious low-cost flights). Frustratingly, Pascal has also issued similar announcements to colleagues, acquaintances and just about anyone else he happens to remember having once shared a glass of wine with, ooooh, at any point within the last two decades.

I'd love to proclaim we plumped for a spring wedding for romantic reasons. A year to the day after we finally consummated our relationship would technically be correct. Unfortunately, such a scandalous reminiscence would give my dad a coronary were it ever to be announced in front of *tout le monde* at the wedding. Lucky for Dad's blushes (and my honour), then, it isn't the guiding motivation.

The logic is much more simple; having so many teachers in the family makes it difficult for them to take time off work. Our wedding has to be during the school holidays – and one of the less heart-stoppingly expensive ones of the winter or spring.

So Whitsun holiday week it is, then.

Pascal has turned to his *papa*, an artist of some international repute, to design our wedding invitations. It is his generous gift to us. The only downside of this is that what he and Pascal decide goes. Consequently, they spend hours on the telephone discussing motifs, sketches and fonts.

It is crystal clear I'm not going to get a look in.

They decide on using a local flower as the motif. The dog rose grows abundantly in the Lot. Its charming little bowl-shaped, pinky-white blossoms dominate the hedgerows of this region. Antoine has decided on a rose, he announces, because I am the flower and the thorns represent Pascal. I daren't break it to Pascal's staunchly Marxist family that the dog rose was once the symbol of the European monarchy.

I'm not proud of myself when I admit this, but the wording of the wedding invite results in a major quarrel between Pascal and me.

For some reason – inelegantly trying to assert myself and dig my heels in, I shouldn't wonder – I announce to Pascal that I'd prefer just our names on the wedding invitations, rather than including his three children. Well! Talk about up in arms. The wedding is very nearly called off on several occasions during our week-long stand-off.

I'm perfectly aware I probably seem like a self-obsessed narcissist, but, in my defence, I wanted just one teensy-weensy aspect of the wedding to be about us as a couple.

Yet it is one of my best friends, Sally Ann, who very tactfully delivers some sound advice. She diplomatically points me in the direction of various websites which show how successfully 'blended' families celebrate weddings. Stepchildren are seamlessly woven into the celebrations. My friend, in a beautifully composed email, wisely reminds me that Pascal's children are my family now and that they too are inextricably woven into my future. They are most definitely not an add-on, decoration, or – whisper it – an afterthought. I very humbly log off and finally grasp that I am displaying all the traits of a self-deluded ninny.

After giving myself a bloody good talking to and, having consumed a large amount of humble pie, I say to Pascal that of course the children – all three of his offspring – must be named on the invitations. His elder children, both of whom are in their early twenties and who I have met briefly, are adorable.

He looks at me with such tenderness and love when I say this, that I wonder how on earth I ever could have been such a selfish little madam in the first place.

'You know, Sam,' Pascal says, smiling, 'I wait and I 'ope you change your mind. I tell myself "Pascal, *attends*. She arrive at zee right idea." I know zat you ees a good woman.'

So our wedding invitations are printed with our names and then those of the children – for it's together that we invite our guests to attend our family celebration.

Our wedding is being plotted and planned on a micro-budget. Any half-baked aspirations of champagne cascades and firework displays are reluctantly pushed to the back of my mind.

We have pulled together a back-of-an-envelope budget that takes into account the cost of food, wine, aperitifs and the wedding cake. Looking at the projected digits in front of us, my heart sinks when Pascal frowns and then announces there is absolutely no way we can stretch to flowers.

I harrumph to myself as yet another wish of mine is steamrollered before we've even discussed it. We'll see about that, the devil on my shoulder whispers into my ear.

As usual, though, I have to hang my head in shame – because funds are being secretly squirreled away for my benefit.

I am enticed into the village of Prayssac with Pascal and Antonio – both men assure me my presence is required. Pascal expertly glides around the hairpin bends that carry us along the valley of the river Lot. Their ruse is a cunning one; to take Antonio for a haircut. Those lovely long locks that distinguish so many French boys at *école maternelle* are going to be lopped off for the wedding.

So it comes as a surprise when, after we've finally parked the Kia, we dawdle along the main shopping boulevard, within window-shopping proximity of a quaint little jewellery store. 'Eyes forward, Sam,' I mutter to myself. Those days of eyeing up to-die-for little numbers are long gone. The remainder of my jewellery collection has been sold off to pay my contribution towards the wedding and to ensure I have the necessary funds to pay for the flights and accommodation for Dad and his family to attend. Any 'jewellery' I eye up in the future will most likely be purchased at Claire's Accessories.

'We 'ave a leetle look in 'ere *chérie*?' Pascal asks me. Antonio is a bundle of excitement, rocking back and forth on his feet.

'Errrr, OK,' I reply. I hadn't given much thought to our weddings bands. Well, except for the fact that the only ones we can afford to buy have to be going for a song.

I am touched that Pascal wants the three of us to choose them; so this is what they were planning!

I insist that we opt for the inexpensive models. We select traditional gold rings, slim and plain – rather elegant, if truth be told. Antonio is in firm agreement, elongating his approval: that they are truly *'mag-nif-ique'*.

It is just as Pascal is paying for our purchases that Antonio steers me in front of a selection of engagement rings.

'Antonio!' I cry, knowing perfectly well that Pascal will blow the French version of a gasket if he sees what we're up to. Surely he will blame me.

'Look, Sam, look.' Antonio indicates a little princess-cut diamond, simply set.

'Yes, it's lovely,' I concede, but really, what's the point in looking?

'You like eet?' Antonio presses – boy is he being persistent!

'Well, yes, but...'

'Aha!' Pascal cries.

Oh no! Now I'm for it, I think.

'What you look at?'

'It's Sam,' Antonio starts, before turning to point the finger, in more ways than one, 'she like zat one!'

The little telltale!

'*C'est vrai?*' Pascal asks me, a huge smile breaking across his face.

And then I cotton on.

They've planned today's surprise excursion. *For me!*

The jeweller, grinning behind the counter, is clearly 'in' on the ruse, because – quick as a flash – he already has the ring out on the counter in my size.

Pascal takes it and gently slips it onto my finger, all the while looking intensely at me with those chocolate-brown eyes.

'Ees for you, *ma chérie*,' he whispers, 'if you want.'

I do want!

My *bague de fiançailles* – chosen for me by my 'boys'.

The first engagement ring I had was, at my insistence, all about having the right bling. Yet this one is first and foremost an expression of love. I know it's a fraction of the price of my previous platinum job; and yet I adore it so much more.

As March comes to a close and with – frighteningly – just eight weeks to go until we're due to be hitched, Pascal and I decide that, moving forward, planning the celebration of our nuptials will be a lot easier if we each take different tasks.

Pascal reasons that he should be on food and alcohol duty. Oh, and that he should draw up the invitation list. Then there is the village hall. Isn't it better, he reasons, if he books it with our mayor? Talking of which, he announces, he can confirm the marriage booking at the same time. And, he reminds me, let's not forget the outfits. He insists, owing to his self-proclaimed 'good taste' in clothes, that he will be signing off on any white dresses that take my fancy.

I gape at him in horror.

I am staring at Groomzilla.

I eventually wrestle the invitations off him – only after he has provided me with a catalogued list of virtually all of the residents in our hamlet, dozens of family relations and countless friends. I'm mortified to admit it, but the number of people on his list that I genuinely know (excluding Pascal's family), I can count on one hand.

Still, at least I get to write and then mail the invitations. It's something, I convince myself.

Meanwhile, Pascal is having a whale of a time.

He orders two sheep from the local farmer and has a discussion with Alberto, which goes on deep into the night, about the precise type of scaffolding erection they will need to build in order to roast said sheep on a spit (if you please!) outside our village hall. What do they think our wedding is, I ask myself crossly, the Last Supper?

The following day we are driving to the village butcher's to discuss the charcuterie table 'arrangements' (who knew slices of chorizo and Bayonne ham merited such intensely debated presentations?). I struggle to keep a straight face when our journey is significantly delayed by the appearance of over fifty sheep idly trotting back and forth along *le causse*. Is it a surprise they are from the very same farm Pascal has ordered two to be 'prepared' for our wedding celebrations? I am convinced they're trying to escape their fate.

Another week passes and I find myself one morning at Leticia's table mulling over the wedding preparations.

'*Tout se passe bien?*' she asks. Is everything going well?

'*Je pense…*' I half-heartedly reply.

'*Mais?*' she replies excitedly, goading me on, ears pricking up at the possibility of scandal.

'*Pas de fleurs,*' I respond with a shrug, before grumbling, 'No money.'

'*Oh la la*, Sam,' Leticia shrieks. '*C'est pas vrai!*'

It is true.

I have needled and nagged Pascal. I have grilled him while massaging his back, I have also propositioned him with my floral desires while massaging somewhere else, just that *little* bit more pleasurable – after which I can normally have anything I like… alas, to no avail. The answer is always *non*.

I haltingly explain this to Leticia, who shakes her head in dismay.

Suddenly she can't bear to listen to any more of my mithering.

'Stop!' she cries. 'I make for you, OK?'

I wouldn't go as far as to describe Leticia as a florist, but it is true that she stocks seasonal plants and flowers; chrysanthemums for All Souls' Day, Christmas trees during the festive season. *Of course!* It stands to reason she'd know how to put together floral arrangements for a wedding.

'Are you sure?'

'*Bien sûr!*' she exclaims. 'You pay me when you can, OK?'

I leap up and hug her.

'*Merci, merci beaucoup,*' I say into Leticia's hair.

The rest of the morning passes by pleasurably. This is how every girl should spend at least some part of her wedding preparations, I think dreamily to myself. Leticia settles me at a pistachio-green wrought-iron table on her terrace, where I sink into a cushioned chair. She pours me a glass of champagne and leaves me to flick through endless books showcasing utterly enchanting floral arrangements. I am torn over the multitude of species of rose – who knew there were so many? I imagine Antonio, Dad, Norman and Pascal sporting scarlet roses in their buttonholes and just *know* Pascal won't mind this expense. I save the best until last, though, when I finally allow myself to coo over the pièce de résistance – the bouquets. I weep girlishly at the thought of my little nieces – Madeleine and Lola – clutching the petite version of the bouquets I am hankering after.

It is when I'm reminded about the bridesmaids that I involuntarily shudder. Most women would baulk at the idea of their other half sticking his oar into such traditionally female-led decisions.

Nonetheless, I *had* already discussed my bridesmaids quota with Pascal. I'd made myself perfectly clear! It went without saying I would ask my sisters – Joanne and Fiona. Likewise, I also wanted their daughters – Madeleine and Lola. I also asked Debra. Did she think, I asked, Sophie and Victoria would like to be bridesmaids too? Debra, wisely, told me not to be ridiculous. She appreciated me formally asking my two half-sisters, but she was more than happy to forgo their role.

Four in total, then – not bad, by noooo means excessive.

Logical, in fact.

I'd thought we were agreed: four bridesmaids, in pink.

Pascal, however, for reasons best known to himself, also decided to ask the daughters of other acquaintances in the village.

Apparently, he informed them that as he would be wearing a red shirt, if they'd like to wear a red dress too, then that would be just fine.

When he casually happened to mention this to me… well, that was when I finally lost it.

'Are they your bridesmaids or mine?' I yelled. 'Because I already have quite enough, thanks very much!'

'Zey just *enfants, chérie,*' Pascal reasoned.

'But do they know the colour scheme?' I shrieked. 'Because it's pink! Pink, Pascal! Not bloody red!'

Pascal looked at me, hands on hips, ready to reply, but thought better of it.

'Do you understand me, Pascal? My bridesmaids are wearing pink!'

'And,' I continued, 'if you're thinking of inviting every child in France you come across over the next few weeks to be my bridesmaid, can you just bloody make sure they're wearing pink? P-I-N-K!' I spelled it out – just for good measure.

Naturally, we weren't on speakers for another, let me see, day, or perhaps it was two, after that particular meltdown on my part.

Why should it matter?

In the grand scheme of things, I know, I know... it shouldn't matter one jot.

Yet it was the one little facet of our wedding that I was organising myself. If we'd discussed it first and I'd been able to ask the girls themselves (who are utterly lovely), I'm sure I wouldn't have had a problem.

Which is why I know that my fiancé will – if he's wise – keep schtum when it comes to my flowers.

Even if they are, as Mother disdainfully notes, bought on 'tick'.

The only other fly in the ointment is our first dance.

It is no exaggeration to say that my husband-to-be is of the Latino snake-hips persuasion. Expats such as Jan talk in rather excited, breathy tones when they describe Pascal's expertise on the dance floor. 'He really can move,' I've heard her whisper rather enthusiastically within a group of girlfriends.

Unfortunately, I cannot.

There was a brief period when I was, oooh, eight years old, when Mother insisted my sister Jo and I attempt to trip the light fantastic in one-to-one private classes. It was all Jo's fault, she was borderline fanatical about the original BBC ballroom series *Come Dancing*. I seem to recall I'd have made Ann Widdecombe look like Darcey Bussell; it's fair to say I wasn't a natural. I have neither waltzed nor rumba-ed ever since.

In my defence, during my student years I used to dance in intimate, sweaty clubs (naturally at the time I thought they were the height of glamour) where the likes of Boy George used to DJ; but as that just involved sitting on a swing one week and energetically gyrating on a podium the next, skill hardly came into it.

It stands to reason, then, that I weakly suggest dance rehearsals; and so it is one spring evening when Pascal disappointingly discovers I am the proud owner of two left feet.

Unperturbed, Pascal persists in teaching me some basic moves.

After an hour, during which time Pascal realises I have zero coordination, all that can be heard echoing around the French countryside is Pascal roaring, '*Arrête! Arrête! Saute pas,* Sam.' He repeatedly urges me to stop my enthusiastic bouncing.

Our rehearsals are far from a perfect ten.

'You 'ave no rhythm, Sam!' is Pascal's conclusion after my bid to master the jive. His caustic commentary doesn't put me off. I love swirling underneath his arms, before returning into his embrace.

I fare little better with the more traditional ballroom dances such as the waltz. I'm sure his hand isn't supposed to go on my bottom and that neither are our lower bodies supposed to touch in quite such an intimate manner. We'd give Len Goodman an attack of the vapours with our risqué manoeuvres.

I really do try, but there is little I can do about my ineptitude as a dance partner. Pascal's cursory conclusion is that I have about as much grace as the dancing hippopotamus in the Disney film *Fantasia*.

At the same time as our plans are falling into place, Antonio's love life is also moving up a notch. He has met and fallen head over heels in love with a heartbreakingly beautiful Parisian girl.

While spending weekends with friends in a neighbouring village, their eyes – as I understand it – literally met across the village square. That was it – for Antonio, anyway.

Over recent months, our trips in the car – to school, to see his friends, to the shops – are no longer dominated by the tick of the clock in the little Citroën van. Oh, how relations have improved! No longer do I attempt to fill the awkward silences with spelling tests or the repetitive questions about what Antonio gets up to at school, which have resulted more than once with Antonio retorting in frustration, 'Why you ask me zee same question *tout le temps*, Sam?'

These days he happily chatters away, for the little van is Antonio's confessional box, and his preferred topics don't stray much from the things important in Antonio's world: namely, his blossoming love life, for French girls are nothing if not forward. As Leticia has pointedly informed me more than once, 'Zey grow up much quicker in zee countryside, Sam.'

Listening to him rabbit on, it would appear that Antonio, now eleven years old, just has to sit back and let the girls come to him. Rarely a week goes by when he isn't in receipt of this love letter or that poem, or embroiled in some flirtation or other. Even I get used to girls phoning the house demanding to talk to Antonio. Honestly!

For that reason, then, I am intrigued when I discover that he is head over heels in 'love'. What's more, it is me Antonio has chosen to confide in.

''Ow can you know when a girl like you, Sam?' Antonio asks. We are in the little C15 returning from his friend's house.

'Well,' I say, shifting around, sitting upright, aware that this deserves a proper answer, 'do you ever look her way and catching her staring at you?'

'*Oui...*'

'Does she spend more time with you than anyone else when you're all together?'

'*Mais oui...*'

'Well, then I think she likes you!'

And with that a huge smile breaks across Antonio's face.

It is on the first day of the Easter holidays that I first hear her voice when I answer the phone (it's taken me eight months to control the terror that consumes me when I do this).

'*Oui, allô?*' It also took me a while to clock that very few French actually say '*Bonjour*' when they pick up the phone.

I'm quite taken aback by the gravelly little voice that replies. I am charmed to be spoken to by a confident young girl with an impeccable command of English.

'Ees zat Sam? Pleaze may I speak wiz Antonio?'

I trot off down the hall to hunt out Romeo himself, who I discover is on a serious tour of duty, in command of a Lego-created war zone in his bedroom. Cool, Sam, play it cool, I remind myself.

'Antonio!' I shriek, failing miserably. 'There's a call for you – it's you-know-who-oo.' My voice rises annoyingly at the end. I sound like someone out of an eighties sitcom! Yet I can't help myself; what's more, I even wink and continue to make a grand show of the fact that the object of his affections is on the phone.

Ye gods – I'm turning into Mother.

Eavesdropping on their call, I note that Nicole has, cutting to the chase, invited herself over for the afternoon.

She *does* like him, then, I conclude – with sneaking admiration.

For the next hour Antonio and I race around his bedroom, scooping up his toys and throwing them under his bed. I whip off his favourite Pokémon duvet cover and slip on his recently purchased WWE matching bed set. The wrestler Batista – replete with naked chest and six-pack – smoulders back at me as I wrestle his form over Antonio's duvet and onto the bed. Antonio swipes some of my incense sticks from the bathroom and sets about creating a chilled out tween pad. It is something of a transformation.

'What are you going to do with Nicole?' I ask, when we're done tidying.

'I want try to kiss her, eef she let me.'

'*What?*' Calm down, Sam, I warn myself, before recovering, and making a feeble attempt to brush off my reaction. 'You're eleven years old, Antonio. You've got plenty of time for that later on.'

'I want learn, Sam,' he implores. 'I must try!'

Help!

I recall Leticia's warnings about children in the countryside 'developing' much younger. Sex is all over the television here; the British 9 p.m. watershed just doesn't exist. We can be sitting at the table eating dinner at 7.30 p.m., and a couple can suddenly be humping away on one of the mainstream channels. It really is sex, sex, sex over here. Mary Whitehouse was born in the wrong country.

Well, Antonio's attempts at pre-teen fumblings are certainly not going to occur on my watch.

Nicole is delivered by her mother. I am stunned when they pull up, for they look like they have walked out of a Dolce & Gabbana advertisement. Both have jet-black long hair, strong sultry features and beautifully maintained figures. Nicole (think a mini Monica Bellucci) proves herself to be a scarily confident ten year old – and is more than a match for an amorous prepubescent boy.

It is clear from the start that Nicole is in the driving seat, ordering him to play on this game, cycle over there, listen to that CD. No wonder Antonio turned to me for advice on wooing her. She is *une fille de la ville*!

It's unsurprising, but nonetheless heartbreaking, when Nicole breaks it off with Antonio some weeks later.

She sends him a text message telling him she loves him – but only as a brother.

Ouch!

Chapter Seventeen

Our House: DIY SOS

With less than a month to go before the wedding, Pascal and I decide to embark upon an extremely logical mission.

To gut and then redecorate the entire house.

I know.

Ever since Pascal gave me the key to both his home and his heart, he has repeatedly given me his word that we will spruce up our little pad. The depressive brown wooden ceilings, the heavily flocked (not to mention suspiciously hairy in places) wallpaper that looms large in each and every room – rendering them gloomy on the sunniest of days – *must* go. It is also time to bid *au revoir* to some of Pascal's rickety French furniture and say a hearty *salut* to a selection of mine; Laura Ashley coffee tables, IKEA sofas and Heal's lamps. The majority of Pascal's fixtures will remain – my 'French-style' pine kitchen table is a ridiculous imitation of his authentic farmhouse one. Yet I desperately crave the finishing touches that will hide some of our home's less attractive details.

I *know* our wedding guests – well-meaning friends and family – will cast their critical eyes around the place, on the hunt for something, anything to support their worst fears about my new life.

That the French really are *different*.

That I've made an almighty cock-up in moving here.

It isn't just in our rented abode that the decor by and large leaves a lot to be desired. Homes in the French countryside are all functionality first; the pompous add-ons are, at best, an afterthought. Admittedly, it is mainly people like myself who excel at the slightly ridiculous notion of 'Does this chair/cushion/champagne glass reflect who I consider myself to be in the world?' Consequently, interior design in most of the French homes I have been into – how can I put this delicately – tends to be resoundingly conservative. So, at the risk of coming over all Hyacinth Bucket; I do *not* want my twenty-odd friends and family, all house-proud Cath Kidston, ELLE Decoration or IKEA aficionados, to see the current state of the place.

Rather, I'd prefer that they swoon and fall in love with my version of *la vie française*.

Our admittedly beautiful-from-the-outside home is, on entering, currently akin to waking up in an unfashionable French movie circa the 1960s, liberally festooned with old-fashioned country-scene wallpaper – some of which makes woodchip look alarmingly chic. It would crush me if this was their lasting memory of the Lot.

However, it isn't just a *Changing Rooms*-style cosmetic makeover we're planning.

Nope.

Pascal, for reasons I can't quite fathom (well, I can, but not mere weeks before a wedding), has *big* plans.

Pascal will focus on removing numerous interior walls (yes, you read that correctly). Such structural changes are being single-handedly carried out by my fiancé. With the permission of our landlord, who is clearly over the moon that his house is getting hauled – gratis – into the twenty-first century, we are creating an open-plan living room and kitchen. This means that the hall wall will be removed, an oak supporting lintel will be hoisted into place to support what remains of the wall, a 'bar' opening in the kitchen wall will be knocked through and a new hallway will be fabricated by moving a doorway to the opening of the bedroom area. Oh, and the new open-plan kitchen and living room will need to be rewired throughout too.

Pascal's plans, rather horrifyingly, also include me. He has patiently talked me through my DIY contribution – which is by no means small. For he is intent on overhauling the studio next to the *cave*, painting it throughout, so that Mother and Norman have somewhere to sleep. Worryingly, my expertise with a bristled brush doesn't much go beyond trying to define my cheekbones or varnishing my nails.

For the next few weeks our lives will be *Grand Designs* on fast-forward.

It was, perhaps, predictable that Antonio and I would get roped into the demolition of the walls.

One Wednesday, the day off that French children usually view with undisguised glee (they get to lie in until mid-morning), Antonio is unceremoniously yanked out of bed at the crack of dawn and urged to don his 'work' clothes. These are really a mini version of Pascal's. I am in a checked shirt that has seen better days and a pair of dusty 7 For All Mankind jeans; any hope of salvaging these beauties for future nights out is long gone. Both Antonio and I are wearing sturdy gloves – Pascal, of course, wouldn't dream of sporting such unmanly garb.

As the wall consists of building blocks, Pascal, rather logically, decides to use an extremely large saw, with the longest blade I've ever encountered, in order to carve out cube-sized portions of it.

'Errr, I think it's going to be too heavy, Pascal,' I mumble between mouthfuls of chalky white dust, which christens all three of us and the room, as I eye the portion of the wall he is currently carving up. '*Mon chéri*, I really don't think I can...'

''Ere, take eet!' Pascal roars as he eases the section out.

'Who me?' I squawk in a panic. 'Now?'

'*Mais oui*, Sam, *allez*!' my dust-covered fiancé hollers at me. Honestly! It's as though I'm just any ole lackey, rather than the alleged love of his life.

I genuinely stagger under the weight of the blocks and end up lurching down the staircase, shouting at Barney and Elsea, entwined together on the landing, to 'shift it', while trying to keep the bulky blocks in my arms. I shouldn't be doing this, I whimper silently to myself, this isn't *me*.

But then the light bulb pings on and the advantages of such physical work instantly occurs to me; and I silently, even gleefully, contemplate the toning of my upper arms that such manual labour will result in. I unceremoniously dump the blocks at the rear of the house, then bolt up the stairs and demand heavier ones.

Antonio is, *bien sûr*, far more proficient than I am. A dusty papa and son duo work neatly and efficiently together with an easy shorthand. There are none of the lumbering pauses as I, grumbling and moaning, shift a section of wall from my lap and into my arms, before staggering crab-like out of the front door. The work is back-breakingly hard. Yet I constantly remind myself that the tightening of my thighs and the resulting pertness of my derriere will be my reward as I clamber up and down, up and down the stairs.

Unsurprisingly, it takes us the best part of the day to remove the wall and create the bar space in the kitchen wall.

But goodness is it worth it!

At the end of the day we sit together in our new living space; Pascal and I sip a glass of rosé and Antonio knocks back a bottle of Coca-Cola in record time. I discreetly roll up the sleeves of my checked shirt and squeeze the tired flabby skin under my upper arms to shrieks of disbelief from Pascal – '*J'y crois pas*' – and laughter from Antonio. They can mock all they like – my bingo wings have *definitely* reduced as a result of today's efforts.

But the real gain is the additional light. The fourth window that previously belonged to the hallway, along with the window in the kitchen, are now part of the newly created open-plan area – and as a result the magical, ethereal white light that typifies southern France at sundown streams into the living room. The effect is stunning.

Later, I gaze out of our new window as the sun finally sets. Entranced, I watch her slip out of view as she tosses her silky strands of reds and golds behind her, streaking across the sky and fanning out in my direction. It's another evocative, beautiful scene in this corner of France which I consider myself blessed to call home.

Pascal turns to Bernard for advice as to where to buy paint. Bernard comes over alone to share this information. Before we know it we have passed another evening consuming countless glasses of rosé and have been privy to yet another eye-popping instalment in the saga of his non-existent sex life with Leticia. I'm running out of suggestions – and it sounds as if they are running out of patience with each other. Nonetheless, thanks to Bernard, we buy great vats of white gloopy paint at a markedly reduced price. This is after I have managed to talk Pascal out of the intense palette of Mediterranean colours he had set his heart on for our too tiny rooms. Talk about impractical! I involuntarily shudder at the very idea of life in a tangerine and lime-green living room.

It is a miracle we finally get around to daubing any paint on our walls at all. The battle to remove the stubborn wallpaper is nothing short of unarmed combat. When the paper finally surrenders, waving its metaphorical white flag as sheaths of the hideous, thick, sticky 'matter' tumble down around me and it is finally bagged and disposed of, even Pascal gives a sigh of relief. We look around each room – *salon, cuisine, salle de bain, chambres* – and want to cry with happiness. There was nothing nasty lurking beneath the paper! But then there wouldn't be, it was so thick it was bound to protect whatever was underneath it – even in the event of a nuclear spillage, what lay beneath would remain untouched.

The bare walls, to our undisguised delight, are already white and – thank you guardian angels – completely smooth. We literally whistle while we work! Well, most of the time we do. That is, when Pascal isn't roaring with frustration in my direction. I'll confess, I am more than a little slapdash.

It appears I consistently, yet inexplicably, apply paint to the windows, to the floor – even to myself.

But we finish in speedy time. For the large part of the painting job we get away with two coats of white. All demonstrations of my talents with French cuisine have staggered to a halt, not, I hasten to add, because of my former (I like to think) incompetence in the kitchen, but because I don't have time to cook. So every lunchtime we decamp to L'Auberge de la Place. Goodness, how times have changed! Far from '*la bombe*' I might once have considered myself to be, strutting into the restaurant, nowadays I don't look at all out of place with the rest of the male *artisans* in my shapeless work clothes, coated in cement, paint and dust.

We eventually rebuild the doorway and attempt to paint the ceilings. Our work is punctuated by continual bickering. I keep reminding myself this is only a temporary status, that I must keep at the forefront of my mind the Pascal I fell in love with. The brooding, beefy hunter, so macho he leaves a trail of testosterone in his wake. That *homme*, I tell myself, isn't the picky, at times effeminate and demanding wannabe interior 'designer' who has temporarily moved in and is constantly finding fault with my work.

This isn't how I had envisaged the countdown to our wedding. At one stage I had permitted myself to daydream about indulging in a spa day and a sprinkling of luxury beauty treatments in preparation for the Big Day. I'd even heard talk of being able to swing free visits to certain spas for water therapies, known here as a '*cure*' – complain loudly enough to your GP about a bad back, so the rumours go, and *le cure* is paid for by the French health system. I should be so lucky! The only hydro-treatments I might possibly have time to expose my tired body to before the wedding is a blast under our lukewarm, finicky shower. The reality, after this bout of do-it-yourself madness, is that my nails are shot to pieces, my hair is paint-splattered and the ends are split. My own personal hygiene standards are plummeting daily – I don't remember the last time I pulled a wet wipe across my face, let alone pampered myself with a face pack.

It's official – I'm going to rack and ruin. I can't help thinking that this is supposed to be my fairy tale. Aren't I meant to transform into the Disney Princess, not the haggard old crone...?

As Pascal insists that only he is capable of pristine paintwork, he elects to take over painting the studio. I am relegated to the lowest geographical part of the house: the *cave*. Ugh! I can't begin to describe what lurks in its gloomy corners. I normally run in and out quick smart when loading up the washing machine – and that's it. On closer inspection, it is no exaggeration to say that this basement hasn't been cleaned in over a decade. It is *filthy*.

Undeterred, I prepare what can only be described as an outfit first for me. Securing one of Pascal's dust masks over my nose and mouth, donning a pair of plastic goggles and then stuffing my hair into a shower cap is only the start of it. The pièce de résistance is stepping into and then zipping up an all-in-one workman's jumpsuit – I look like a reject from *Ghostbusters*. You'll never see this trend adorning the pages of *Grazia*.

I snigger when I find a walkie-talkie (or *talkie-walkie*, as the French call them) rigged up in the *cave*. Pascal told me it belonged to the former tenants, who kept in communication with each other at all times. I frantically hunt for the connecting wire around the base of the contraption; if I know Pascal, he will be badgering me in here, wanting to know if I'm using this cleaning product or have found that piece of hunting accessory he left down here at some point during the winter of 2004.

With a sharp tug on the cord, I extinguish all possibility of *le talkie-walkie* squawking between us.

For the rest of the afternoon I gingerly clean out decades-old spiders' webs, banish mouldy old rubbish, and try not to squeal when I come across dozens of dead mice and dead goodness knows what else. I then set about dumping everything that doesn't belong in this century, leaving to one side any items which look remotely like an antique. I've no doubt David Dickinson would be sobbing at the things I deem fit for the *poubelle*. I also jettison jar after jar of what appears to contain animal fats. I only open one, but the vegetarian in me wants to hurl everywhere on inhaling the putrid (to my mind) contents. I chuck out somewhere in the region of fifty of the icky pots.

It is Pascal's turn to feel queasy. When he ventures into the *cave*, he is speechless to discover that the place is spotless – and glaringly empty of numerous items he'd been planning on keeping. He quietly informs me, temper held remarkably in check, that the duck fat inside the fifty or so containers is mouth-wateringly delicious, and furthermore it is an essential in every French kitchen. In fact, he goes on, the jars alone are worth an eye-watering amount of money.

Whoops.

Nonetheless, utterly fed up of playing Cinderella, the unpaid skivvy, I ungraciously announce that if he wants them, then he is perfectly within his rights to hoick them out of the bin. To his credit, Pascal says nothing more of them. Instead, he sets about breaking up the suspect items of furniture we have both agreed can go to the great *brocante* in the sky.

It is with some satisfaction that I watch a mixture of Pascal's personal history – alongside some of my own mementoes – burst into flames on the bonfire we have created and smoulder into the night. I didn't bring much with me, most of my personal effects were ruined in the flood in the UK, but I don't need to hold onto certain photographs and letters which have no place in my new life.

Desperately childish, I know, but it is with a gratifying sigh of relief that, the following morning, I discover all that is left of certain parts of our past is a smouldering pile of ashes.

After close to three weeks of hard labour, Pascal and I are as proud as punch to announce that the house finally shines on the inside. It's an as-near-as-perfect Franco-British fusion as we can create in the silly amount of time we have given ourselves. Outside, the garden and forest have also been busy sprucing themselves up. The lilac bush that faithfully guards over the letterbox has already blessed us with fragrant blooms, bunches of which I have been unable to resist, guiltily snipping them off and then dotting their heady blossom in jam jars and jugs around the house. The pale purple colour is adorable against our fresh white walls. The scent of the tiny flowers is gentle, yet exquisite. It's a busy time amongst the other trees, bushes and hedgerows too, for the lime blossom is about to burst forth any day now and the honeysuckle is biding her time to put on her alluring spectacle.

I walk with the dogs along one of my new Pascal-designated off-road routes, further along the lane towards the neighbouring village of Thédirac. The verges froth with blossom and dinky buttercup-yellow cowslips are pushing through everywhere. I have already christened the path 'butterfly lane'. Dozens of species of nature's prettiest insects flutter to and fro – they are a joy to watch.

My heart positively sings when Ambrose takes himself off into a field, skipping through the vibrant meadows, stopping to smell this flower or pass his pink tongue over that silky sheaf of moist grass. He'll still jump out of his skin when he hears a neighbouring sheep bleat across a field in his direction, and reciprocate with a 'who goes there' yelp – yet he appears to be more accepting of the countryside. At home, Elsea has taken to snoozing on my knees when I sit at the table; even Barney and Ambrose aren't allowed to approach me when her majesty is in residence on my lap. She'd reduce an Alsatian to a trembling wreck.

In these weeks before the wedding I secretly adore popping into Cazals; for I am treated like a princess. Everyone appears to know all about the impending *mariage* (in more intimate detail than I do myself!) and, to my utter astonishment, I'm greeted with genuine warmth and bonhomie. People know which herbs Pascal is using to cook the meat in, what wine he has chosen – even where he is buying the foie gras. This being rural France, where gossip is traded faster than a tweet, everyone has something to say to me.

Madame who runs the *boulangerie* excitedly asks about my dress. The proprietor of the *pharmacie* tells me she has been surveying the weather forecast and warns it's not looking good. But I'm not to worry if it rains, she says. Clocking my puzzled expression, she explains, '*Mariage pluvieux, mariage heureux*' which means that if it rains when you say 'I do', you'll be rewarded with a happy ever after. Meanwhile, Francette, over a glass of wine in her bar one evening, confidently assures me '*Mariage plus vieux, mariage heureux*'. That is: marry older, and your marriage will be a happy one. Whichever saying applies, I can't deny the fact that we are indeed a couple of oldies getting hitched. While there is precious little we can do about our age or the rain, Pascal and I have put into place plans for the unpredictable weather.

Leticia has been working tremendously hard for us too and mocked up an achingly pretty bouquet. Pascal took the news of the flowers surprisingly well – all things considered. He only shouted at me for approximately ten minutes when this bombshell was dropped and '*Merde*, Sam!' was roared just half a dozen times. I have had to pledge that I will resist splurging even a centime without his say-so between now and the wedding day.

Over *un café* one morning Leticia tells me that Maggie, one of our mutual expat friends, was strong-armed into a conversation with Miriam about 'the wedding'. My stomach automatically flips over. I have purposefully kept out of Miriam's way since moving in with Pascal. Settling into the foreign rhythms of life in France has been difficult enough, without anyone else trying to sabotage my attempts at each step of the way.

'She ees *vraiment* jealous,' Leticia begins.

'Oh really?' Raw fear runs through my veins.

'Maggie tell me,' Leticia continues, 'that she sit wiz 'er in Francette's and she ees angry because you ees getting married. She never zink it 'appen. She 'ope you 'ate eet 'ere.'

I do *not* want to hear this.

'Oh *merde*,' is all I can manage, as guilt rockets up into my temples. I predict a tension headache any moment now.

'Ees not your fault, Sam.' Leticia takes a sip of her coffee. 'She don't want you live 'ere, *mais bon, tu es là, elle se débrouille.*' She shrugs and grins when she states the obvious: you are here and she'll have to cope with it.

'*Merci*, Leticia.' The band tightens round my head.

'*Mais tu sais*, Sam,' Leticia continues, clearly not quite finished with 'news', 'Maggie tell 'er stop to complain. Maggie say to 'er everybody 'ere like you. She tell 'er zee problem ees wiz 'er, *pas toi.*'

What?

Did I just hear that correctly?

People here actually like me and accept me? I assumed because I'd made that many cock-ups – at the school gates, in company with expats, not to mention around Pascal's friends – that I was persona non grata in many parts of the village.

I wordlessly squeeze Leticia's hand and she responds with a big smile, which breaks across her beautiful olive-skinned face. On cue, the tears spill over and Maybelline's finest streaks down my cheeks.

Change is everywhere.

I have already spotted that other gauge that marks spring is officially here; geraniums. It is *obligatoire* in these parts to have pots of the little star-shaped flowers on balconies, in tubs on tables – even large containers on stone doorsteps spill over with them. Cazals Sunday market expands in size each week to accommodate them: stallholders introduce more and more colours and variations for sale; the range is beyond tempting. The dozens of little pots of herbs and shrubs that jostle for space alongside them barely get a look in.

Pascal has a 'plan' for the floral decoration of the exterior of our home. He is as faithful as an old Labrador when it comes to purchase power. He has headed off all of my whiny requests to buy our flowers when we see them. No, we must go to the nursery he has bought them from ever since he arrived in the area. We spend hundreds of pounds on flowers for the outside of the house, baskets, boxes, specially filled *sacs* which trail flowers down the front of the building – flowers spill over everywhere. It's not quite the Hanging Gardens of Babylon, but we can hold our heads up high with our green-fingered neighbours.

It goes without saying that Alberto is rewarded with best-man status at the wedding.

Luisa and Alberto had already popped by to talk about shirt styles and sizes. I meticulously noted down all of Alberto's chest, underarm and back measurements in a bid to buy the correct shirt.

'Find zee shirt wiz a "L" in eet,' Alberto had said, practising his English with me, while flexing his *forestier* biceps and puffing out his chest, pigeon-style. 'I am zee large man, you see?'

Before they had left, Luisa had pulled me to one side and whispered, 'Zat "L" ees "L" for leetle.'

I'd nodded my head and, biting my bottom lip, tried not to laugh.

Luisa, undeterred, and with a glint of mischief in her eyes, insisted, ''E ees not large, my 'usband, you understand?'

Is it my imagination or has Luisa got the *exact* measure of her husband?

After much palaver we eventually manage to locate two red silk shirts – this search took up far more time than tracking down my eBay-purchased wedding dress. I'd like to say it was a painless process – it wasn't. It involved Pascal and me having a stand-up row in one store, which resulted in him stomping out and me, red-faced, apologising to the rather bemused shop assistant. Two perfect red shirts finally revealed themselves in the least likely of places – a store close to my sister Fiona's house in Birmingham. We breathed a sigh of relief when Pascal's fitted him perfectly. The only question that remains is whether the one we bought for Alberto will fit.

We have arranged for Alberto and Luisa to have lunch with us, in order to try on the shirt.

Luisa joins me in the kitchen. I am making chicken breasts wrapped in prosciutto for lunch. She pours both of us a large glass of the locally produced ratafia aperitif. It is delicious and extremely strong. I practically sway with the first sip.

'I want try my English wiz you, OK?' asks Luisa.

'No problem.' I smile. I rub flour into four chicken breasts and gently place them into a large frying pan, which splutters and pops as their skin kisses the hot buttery base.

'I want zank you and Pascal for 'elping finish zee roof.' She pauses before continuing, 'Alberto... 'e ees difficult zis winter. You know... 'e don't want go on wiz it, wiz anyzink.'

Help!

What on earth do I say if the woman whose name begins with 'F' is mentioned? Those 'well-meaning' books that smug French women churn out about their rose-spectacled life have yet to tackle this tricky social snafu.

'I know 'e stay wiz you,' she goes on, looking down into her glass, which she is involuntarily swirling in her hand. 'Ees difficult for 'im to go on wizout Pascal to 'elp 'im.'

The silence in the kitchen is only broken by the soft bubbling in the large frying pan and the hiss of the gas which tickles its base. At a loss as to what to say, I peer into my glass of ratafia and stare at the intense rich red liquid, before finally lifting my eyes to meet her gaze.

'But zee 'ouse ees nearly finish.' Her eyes lock with mine. 'So I zink 'e ees OK now.'

I think, but don't dare confirm, that Luisa is assuring me that Alberto is over Françoise, there will be no more overnight stays on our sofa. I don't think I could have handled such a conversation with the grace Luisa has just displayed.

Chapter Eighteen
The Wedding

The days leading up to the wedding pass by in a blur.

I'd love to say we are totally prepared... Pascal is still frantically rewiring the electrical sockets in the hallway when I have to leave him in order to collect Mother and Norman from Bergerac airport. I tiptoe out of the front door to the sound of him effing and blinding at the inexplicably complicated cabling.

I spy Mother, impatiently waiting for her luggage, before she sees me. The expression on her face is one of obvious anticipation and excitement, a marked difference from the fear and worry that was etched across her features when we last parted ways at this wee airport.

Now, eight months later, I stride confidently towards her as she and Norman pass through the arrivals door and I instantly envelop her in my arms. She hugs her first-born daughter tightly, before holding me at arm's length and giving me a thorough inspection.

Her eyes search mine and I sense she finally grasps that I have undergone a dramatic transformation. I *think* she likes what she sees, for even I know I am a markedly different woman. I would need to use all of my fingers and toes to tot up all of my recently acquired 'talents'.

I have changed – for the better.

For I am someone who no longer believes a crisis is being unable to locate her favourite MAC lipstick or that an extravagant amount of retail therapy is the only antidote for down days. Instead, my mother is looking into the face of a woman who, over the last year and a half, has had to cope with losing her home and being booted off the career ladder, who has adjusted to life without a penny to her name, has found that most – but not all – of her friends deserted her, and was plunged into (at times suicidal) depression.

Today that same woman is slowly carving out a new life amidst the idiosyncrasies of a foreign country, sometimes flourishing, admittedly more often struggling, for she is still to master even the basics of the language. Yet none of this matters because, most poignantly of all, she is head over heels in love with a man who just so happens to be her polar opposite.

In spite of it all, I am a better woman for it.

We drive through the Bergerac vineyards, their shiny green leaves pushing through signifying the beginnings of their rebirth. My hands firmly on the steering wheel, I am yakking away to Norman, who is eager for news of the latest exploits in the canine world of Barney and Ambrose. Out of the corner of my eye I catch Mother glancing at my profile. She reaches forward and pushes a strand of hair behind my ear. I briefly turn to meet her gaze and for the first time in what seems like an age I bestow her with a genuine smile – it is one that reaches the corners of my eyes and the depths of my soul.

The following day Dad and my sisters arrive. Blimey! It's as though Birmingham has descended onto Cazals. And I, for one, couldn't be happier. Dad, nervous and unsure about his stay in France, only relaxes when a cold *demi* is thrust into his hands at Francette's – where he is instantly welcomed like a long-lost friend. For once the patois isn't that of the Lot; it is of decades-old in-jokes, jibes amongst my family. Such pleasantries are all underpinned with love and an unmistakeable fondness for each other.

The next day is the eve of the wedding, and Madame le Maire grants us access to the *salle des fêtes*, the village hall, to organise it for the wedding meal. Fiona commandeers the children in preparing each of the table settings. My brother-in-law Sam and I place the tables in the familiar long rows that define so many French village events. My sister Jo unleashes her Type A personality and orders all of the men, including a bemused Alberto, to decorate the hall beams with the branches of honeysuckle she has picked that morning.

The tubular flowers hang down from the wooden frames, their intense fragrance scenting the hall, the twining branches inadvertently creating a Disney-esque grotto; maybe I'm going to get my fairy-tale wedding after all.

Of course, not everything goes to plan.

When Pascal sees that I have blithely waved away his instructions of not placing a table near the entrance, he equally blithely boots said table in the air.

'Sam!' he roars. 'What I say?'

Before I can count to ten, I ungraciously tell him to eff off.

Here we go, the wedding is once more cancelled.

The pressure and tension of the last few days is released as we hurl insults at each other like a pair of drunken old navvies. We each give as good as we get, launching one profanity after another at each other, striking our target with the exact amount of damage intended with each brutal missive fired. Of course, our war of words is in full flow when the door flies open and Jo walks in, arms full with branches of honeysuckle.

Poor Jo – what a ridiculous spectacle to witness.

My sister, to her credit, says nothing, simply raises her eyebrows at me and reverses out of the door.

The rest of the day Pascal and I swap sulky glances. It is he who eventually declares a ceasefire and extends to me a peace offering: a lusty kiss.

That evening, in return for their efforts, I cook for twenty-five members of our family and friends. Two enormous roast beef joints infused with garlic, *haricots verts* tossed in butter and sautéed potatoes. Sophie and Victoria, who normally turn their pert little noses up at anything that hasn't been prepared bespoke for them by Dad, wolf it down, their plates thrust forward for seconds. I constantly monitor the table; is everyone's glass full, do they have enough bread, is everyone engaged with someone in idle banter?

I discreetly notice that various members of my family regard me at different times throughout the meal. Their look each time is identical – it is one of utter amazement; they are witnessing me in a new light. I see it in their eyes – the recognition that I've *changed*. Before, the extent of thought and effort that would have gone into this would have been a thirty-second phone call to secure a reservation and a credit card slapped down on the table afterwards. Now, though, I appreciate that food is love and a thought-through, home-cooked meal is the biggest gift I can give my family and my husband-to-be.

I also know, as he slips his arm around my shoulders, that no one in the room is prouder of me than my fiancé Pascal.

I wouldn't say Madame Congélateur has gone forever, but she is getting less and less evident.

I wake at 6 a.m. and Pascal is beaming back at me.

The day has finally arrived.

I smile coquettishly at him, allowing myself to reminisce that it was a year ago to the day that I first woke in the arms of this man, known locally as *'L'Ours'* – the bear – and I blush.

I am rewarded with a, *'Bonjour*, Madame Rubinat.'

I reply, almost shyly, *'Pas encore!'* Not yet... we're not married just yet.

Pascal insisted I spend the eve of our wedding with him. He waved away all talk of bad luck and superstition. His reasoning wasn't lost on me – this is the first time in days we are alone together. We spend the early morning on the terrace, waiting for the sun to rise and, wrapped in chunky white dressing gowns, we sip on hot steaming bowls of *café au lait*. Ambrose is softly snoring in his bed, four furry legs in the air. Elsea and Barney are in their basket together, all eight paws touching; it is difficult to see where Barney's hairy coat ends and Elsea's scruffy one begins. They are inseparable, their passionate canine love affair something neither Pascal nor I had anticipated. I lazily pass my hand over Barney's fur and turn my face towards the rising sun. I am greeted by a haze of iridescent pink light shooting through the thick branches of the oak tree and descending all around me on the terrace.

I turn to Pascal and I smile: it is as though our day has been blessed by the gods.

At last, I treat myself with the luxury of a soak in the bath. It is with some amusement I note that I *have* lost weight, albeit in a thoroughly unconventional manner. There is no reliance on the Dukan *régime* or the Atkins diet; instead, the pounds have dropped off owing to sheer physical labour. Pascal has also commented on my shrinking tummy and my smaller bottom. I didn't believe him – but the results are in. As I slip into a pair of jeans and a baggy top, in preparation for the beauty rituals ahead, I hear shuffling outside indicating Mother and Norman are on the terrace. I leave the steamy air of the bathroom behind me and find Pascal in the kitchen brewing more coffee. I kiss him softly on his bristly cheek. For it is the last time we will be alone today.

Mother and I are the only ones who venture into the village hairdresser's. When I eventually emerge from the salon, half choking on lacquer and other unguents, I'd say the others got it right. For my dodgy up-do is far from the Grace Kelly elegant chignon I'd dreamed of. I wait until I am in the car with Mother before I howl with frustration. It isn't the hairdresser's fault. But when oh when will I learn? If someone is speaking rapid-fire at you in a foreign language about what they intend to do with your hair, don't just blankly nod your head – dig out a sodding dictionary, woman!

Mother calms me down, orders me to point the car in the direction of the *pharmacie* and moments later is back in the passenger seat armed with hairgrips, a large tin of old-fashioned lacquer and a can of dry hairspray.

When I have recovered from my first (and undoubtedly not my last) bout of hysteria of the day, we drive to the *gîte* where my sisters are staying. Dad and his family are already there. It is mid morning when we pull up and already some sort of party appears to be in full flow. My family have turned into party animals – *fêtards*! Champagne is poured, beer is consumed, music is playing. In amongst the revelry, clothes are ironed, hair is straightened and make-up is studiously applied.

Leticia arrives, arms laden with boxes of buttonhole roses, posies of flowers and pretty bouquets. Everyone gasps on seeing them. For her talents go beyond the definition 'florist' – the creations she has fashioned are exquisite. Someone thrusts a glass of champagne in her hand and she responds with a *merci*.

'*Tu es belle!*' she cries on seeing my expertly applied make-up, courtesy of a television presenter friend who is also in attendance and has taken over my woeful attempt at bridal beauty.

'*C'est pas moi,*' I say, pointing to my girlfriend, who is patiently waiting to finish off my powder and paint.

My wonderful, faithful girlfriends undeniably bring a touch of glamour to the rustic event, decked out in Manolo heels, designer tea dresses and achingly trendy (not to mention expensive) frocks – I am as pleased as punch that they have been able to come. I know they are here to support me in my peculiar new life, yet I am perfectly aware they can't resist seeing if Pascal really is the man in a million I've made him out to be.

Their appearance is heartily appreciated by the local male population who have, slack-jawed, watched them and my sisters strut through the village over the last forty-eight hours. It is much to my amusement that I have noted the numerous men who have called on us at home. Honestly! I feel like charging them each time they gawp as they 'stop by' with some obscure request.

It is still sunny – just – when I slip into my dress. The forecast is worryingly mixed and I pray that the sun which has been in abundance over the last four hours continues to shine. At the time I considered my Internet purchase a steal at twenty-five pounds. As Jo spends half an hour sewing me into it (it is too 'roomy' around the chest area), I repeat to myself it's only for a few hours. I'll never wear it again – and then won't I be pleased I didn't drop thousands on a wedding dress?

As I look at my reflection in the mirror, I think that if I remind myself of this enough times, maybe I'll eventually believe it.

Before everyone leaves to go to the *mairie*, we raise a toast together – the British contingency of the wedding party. At that moment, a bolt of lightning spears the sky and a crash of thunder bellows its approval in the distance.

Everyone optimistically agrees that the storm is far enough across the valley not to disrupt the nuptials, and I hope they're right.

Eventually it is just me and my bridesmaids; my sisters and my nieces, Madeleine and Lola. Madeleine has blossomed into a beautiful young tween in the months since I last saw her. She is wearing a baby-pink dress and her long slim legs are shown off to their best advantage by a pretty pair of sandals. She looks beautiful. Lola is wearing a miniature version of the same dress. She has already informed me of her intention to be an actress and, judging by her look of studied concentration, I'd say she'll be taking her old Aunty Sam to the Academy Awards – for she is taking her role extremely seriously. I take picture after picture of them with their posies in their hands. My beautiful nieces – oh, how I miss them.

Without allowing any further time to linger, Fiona shepherds us all into her hire car and, with Duran Duran accompanying us, we giggly girls set off for the village.

As is the British tradition we arrive late – twenty minutes late, to be precise.

I instruct Fiona to cruise around the village square – we excitedly wave at everyone – and finally park near the *salle des fêtes*. We then make the walk to the *mairie* together, the bride and her four bridesmaids linked arm-in-arm.

Everyone claps us in on our arrival; a silly, bashful smile spreads across my face. Jo and Fiona confidently yet discreetly support me – just as they have always done in life. Lola and Madeleine beam with delight at the attention their arrival attracts.

However, not everyone is cheering.

Pascal marches up, his bridesmaids fluttering behind him, and shouts, 'Why you so late? Everyone tell me you go! My 'eart, Sam...' He pats his chest, his expression still fretful. I clock my brothers-in-law, Sam and David, beautifully turned out, yet smirking in the background. 'Scallywags' is the polite version of the 'B' word I'm tempted to shout at them – which repeatedly streaks across my mind. They clearly 'forgot' to explain to Pascal that of course I'd turn up late.

To my left, under the large tree that provides shade in the hot arid months, I see my future in-laws sitting on the bench. The same tight-knit family group who welcomed me so warmly into their clan on the camping trip last summer. I wave at Jane, Carlos's English wife, who hastens over and greets me with a warm embrace. There is Hélène, who I rush to greet, the matriarch of the family in an elegant dress. Her hair, I note, is magnificently coiffed. Next to her are Pascal's elder children, Joëlle and Hélios, who hug me hello. Joëlle is stunning in an utterly fabulous cocktail dress and Hélios is breathtakingly handsome in a sharp suit. With them is Antonio, looking movie-star attractive in his three-piece suit. He proudly saunters over – his buttonhole red rose in place – and when I tell him how striking he looks, he thanks me with a cheeky smile.

Madame le Maire clucks in our direction; she is wearing a pretty black linen suit and the obligatory sash across her body informs us of her prestigious role. We are late and she wants us to get a move on.

The tiny room where the ceremony is held is no bigger than the living room in a semi-detached. Close to fifty people manage to squeeze inside, with many more crowding around and listening in at the open windows. The sun pours in through the windows, and I put to one side all thoughts of the earlier burst of thunder.

Pressed against Pascal, and with my two witnesses, Fiona and Sally Ann, one of my best friends, behind me, the ceremony begins. It is a thoughtful gesture for Madame Le Maire to provide an interpreter. The official vows are first read out in French and swiftly followed by an English translation. It is sobering to hear what the vows actually are, for I hadn't thought to check what I would actually be consenting to before the wedding. Marriage vows are the same the world over, right? Wrong.

I gulp involuntarily when I agree to allow my stepchildren a say in every aspect of my life from this day forward.

From that moment on, before I say *oui* to anything that Madame le Maire fires at me, I warily hear out the translation first.

Pascal is outraged!

When I am asked the French equivalent of 'Do you take this man?' and there is an unseemly pause while I listen to it word-for-word in English, Pascal can contain himself no more.

'What you wait for?' he shouts at me. 'Just say yes!' Everyone roars with laughter.

As we exit the town hall, cheers and confetti rain down on us. I look around and notice that it's not just family and friends who are shouting out their approval, but also those local faces I have come to adore too – our neighbours Coco and Mélanie, our French friends Bernard and Leticia, Alberto and Luisa and even my expat buddies Jan and Nick. I finally understand that these people had already accepted me, they had already taken me into their hearts.

That I am now Madame Rubinat, French wife and stepmother, is something that matters to Pascal and me only. I pull my stepchildren to me and give them a shower of kisses and sentimental hugs before giving Pascal his first well-earned *bise* as my husband.

Pascal is shadowed by his bridesmaids, prettily dressed in their red frocks, who happily trail after him; where the male lead goes, the crowd follows. He makes a fuss of them, as I do too. Together with my English bridesmaids, we stand in the middle of our village square and pose for photo after photo. Even though the bridesmaids' dresses are a sea of pink and red, I've already come to the conclusion – seeing the beaming smiles on their faces – that colour coordination really doesn't matter a jot.

The sun is beaming down on us and both Pascal and I are in agreement – those weather forecasters were clearly wrong.

There is to be no rain on our wedding day.

Phew!

One of the countless differences between French and British weddings is that the drinks – to which everyone is invited – are held before the more intimate celebration dinner. It is called the *vin d'honneur* and we have prepared the garden accordingly to receive our guests. Benches have been hired from another village hall, the tables have been decked with flowers and wine and punch has been chilling all morning.

Everyone piles into cars and heads back to our *maison en pierre*. Hélios and Joëlle have already spent the morning tying balloons to trees and road signs to mark out the route to our home. A caravan of cars pulls off amidst much horn tooting, waving and flashing of lights.

Pascal and I lead the way, our car decked with ribbons. There is no mistaking the proud groom and his radiant bride.

As we drive along *le causse*, we take in what until now we have studiously avoided acknowledging – ominous rain clouds gathering over our valley.

'Merde!' Pascal calls out despondently.

Within seconds of arriving home, the heavens open and treat us to a downpour of torrential rain. *Merde* indeed. Everyone gathers sardine-fashion in our living room, on the terrace and under the shelter by the studio.

A unanimous decision is taken: to hold the *vin d'honneur* in the *salle des fêtes* where we are due to eat. It is a risk; I have heard many rumours of guests unwilling to leave and inviting themselves to stay on for the meal, only for the bride and groom to run out of food. If your guests leave hungry then you have committed the ultimate faux pas at a French wedding.

However, if stragglers do decide to settle in for the evening, I know there is no danger of us running out of food. We have enough to feed the five thousand.

Less than an hour later, the downpour having receded and the sun making a cheeky, are-you-waiting-for-me appearance, we are nonetheless settled in the village hall. I tour the room nervously, haltingly introducing myself to friends of Pascal, while at the same time bashfully accepting the congratulations poured over me.

It isn't long before the meal is underway. I barely see Pascal throughout the rest of day – he is lost in the final touches of the feast he has spent months preparing. This part of our celebration is undoubtedly his baby and the control freak that I know is one aspect of my French husband wants to see it through. He has several friends overseeing the barbecue and kitchen. Guiltily, I have no part to play in the feast that Pascal has created.

And it is a feast – moans of appreciation, demands for seconds echo around the hall. My normally picky father declares it the best lamb he has ever tasted and goes on to help himself to what surely must be a fourth portion.

It is during a lull between courses that Leticia pulls me to one side.

'You know,' she begins, 'I don't know what 'appen next wiz me and Bernard.'

'Oh no,' I cry. Don't say they're splitting up?

'*Non, non,*' she reassures me, when she realises my mind is leaping to a conclusion even she hasn't reached yet, 'but I want you know zis. Life wiz a Frenchman eez not easy. I am always 'ere if you need me.'

'Really?'

'*Oui,* I am your friend, Sam,' she says, holding my shoulders and looking into my eyes earnestly. 'Know zat you can call me whenever you need me.'

As I rejoin my guests, I turn to see Leticia ruffling Bernard's hair – she shrugs her shoulders and gives me a wink.

I consider myself blessed to have found a genuine girlfriend.

Dad has been akin to a cat on a hot tin roof for hours. Refusing all whisky chasers and sipping on one *demi* since the meal started, I'm fearful he is ill.

Sick with nerves more like – he's been plotting a surprise.

Earlier on in the day my father, totally coincidentally, got talking to my French teacher, Wendy. Between them they have been scheming over when and how he can deliver his speech.

I had already told him that the French don't *do* speeches. Obviously, he hasn't listened to a blinking word!

I shouldn't be surprised, though. In my family, when someone has set their mind on something, it's like convincing Tiger Woods to stay faithful – nigh on impossible – to get them to change their mind. And so after the main course Wendy, who has commandeered the DJ's microphone, hauls my dad on to the stage.

Oh God – it's 'the talk' all over again. How Pascal must look after me – or else.

I needn't worry, though; my father could give the comedian Dara O'Briain a run for his money when he's on form. His speech is funny, yet adorable.

He starts off with an apology, that as an Irishman he can barely speak English, let alone French. It is the perfect ice breaker. I beam at him – for I know how nervous he will be in front of just under a hundred and fifty people.

His speech continues, 'When Pascal asked me for Samantha's hand in marriage I was pleasantly surprised as these days the father is always the last to know! Straightaway, I knew that here was a man who I could trust with my daughter. He has always been nothing but respectful to me. I expect only the best for Samantha.'

Pascal and I grin at one another. Dad continues to read out each sentence in English, and Wendy (with the enthusiastic gusto of an am-dram performer, it must be said) repeats it in French. After each phrase there are roars and roars of approval.

'Samantha,' Dad says, 'it is lovely to see you so happy here in France with Pascal. I am so proud of you. You are beginning a new chapter in your life and I wish you every happiness.'

When Dad has finished I kick off my shoes and run to meet him descending the stage where I hug him in a huge embrace.

However, he has clearly started a fashion, for not only do my stepchildren quick smart make for the stage to welcome me endearingly into the family; they are sharply followed by my sister Jo, who has darted onto the platform after them, where with undisguised relish she reads out her pre-prepared missive to Pascal.

I laugh out loud when she begins with, 'Some advice to Pascal from a Brick girl who knows what she's talking about.'

She continues along the lines of, 'Whenever you're wrong, admit it; whenever you're right, shut up,' before concluding, 'Listen to my sister, she is always right.'

Pascal's eyes are out on stalks.

It doesn't end there; yet another friend also surprises me with a speech she has prepared in French – it is adorably sentimental, not to mention wickedly funny. Not to be outdone in the oratory stakes, several of Pascal's friends line up on the stage to tell us in painfully long detail just what they think of Pascal, me, our wedding, oh – and life in general.

After what seems like hours of heartfelt homilies, the DJ – yet another friend of Pascal's – discreetly turns up the music, drowning out the final words of the last well-wisher.

I'd like to say that our first dance goes off without a hitch.

Yet it doesn't happen at all. Pascal is caught up in assisting a friend who has been at the French equivalent of the sherry in the kitchen all day. It is painfully clear that he needs to be taken home. So Antoine and Veronique – my new in-laws – start the dancing off instead. Within seconds the French part of the room (and there *is* a divide) are lured onto their feet by the siren call of the music. The British contingency take their own sweet time in shrugging off their stiff upper lips.

Instead, as I had feared, of Pascal bossing me about as I lurched around the dance floor trying to keep up with him, I boogie with all of my bridesmaids. While it's an unconventional first dance – the spotlight is on them – their efforts are applauded and that's what counts. When we sit down I pull Madeleine on my knee and ask, 'Happy?'

'Yes, Sam.'

'You know you're always welcome to come and see me here.'

With that she hugs me tightly and I pretend not to see the tears in her eyes.

Pascal and I eventually dance together, performing a safe and conventional sway discreetly in the middle of the other revellers who continue to perform their enthusiastic moves around us. When Pascal leans forward and whispers into my ear, '*Je te protège tout le temps*, Madame Rubinat,' I know that this is a moment I'll treasure forever.

The evening is deemed a huge success. There are no rows, there are no hissy fits, and there are no embarrassing moments.

When we arrive home I am instantly reminded that there are two extremely important males who have, as yet, to share in the day's celebrations. I clamber out of the car, wincing at the stones beneath my bare feet (my shoes were discarded long ago) and tiptoe to the boot where I lug out several plastic bags full of bones. I shamelessly went round the wedding reception urging our guests to tip the remnants of their meat (admittedly not much) for those who would without question appreciate them the most – our dogs.

Pascal grabs a couple of the sacks from me and opens the *cave* where he stores them in the coolness of the space, out of the reach of inquisitive paws.

As we head towards the terrace, Barney and Ambrose leap up and down, excitedly barking, while Elsea skips a dance along the wall. I sit down on a chair and don't care that my beloved hounds leap excitedly over my already rather grubby wedding dress.

We open one of the bags we have saved and each dog's bottom immediately hits the floor. I might not have liked Pascal's strict attitude towards my pooches at first, but his approach has paid off. I hand out a lamb chop bone to each of them, which they gently take and, one by one, retreat to 'their' basket. As they begin to gnaw at their bones, I reflect on how much they have aided my recovery and helped me transform into the woman I am today.

Pascal scrambles inside and pours us each a glass of champagne. I look up at the crescent moon and realise how lucky I am. Although at times in the past I had feared that we were just too different, what I overlooked was our similarities. We are both strong characters, who tackle life – by and large – head on. It is this outlook on life, I believe, that will carry us through the inevitable trickier moments.

When we eventually fall into bed, I immediately launch myself into Pascal's arms. I am happy to note the fact that my current status is tired yet overwhelmingly content.

Although, it is with admittedly the tiniest bit of apprehension that I realise I am about to embark on the next chapter of my life. I glance down at the rings on my left hand and I can't help but wonder what I'm letting myself in for.

Life as a French housewife?

Whatever happens, I know it's going to be an adventure.

About the Author

Samantha Brick worked full-time in television for sixteen years, producing TV shows in the UK and America. An award-winning producer, she has worked with everyone from Russell Brand and Tess Daly to David Beckham, and has sold and produced documentaries and reality shows for every major channel, including ITV, BBC and Channel 4 in the UK, and MTV and Fox in the US. She is co-creator of the *Bridezillas* franchise on the Women's Entertainment network.

Samantha moved to France in 2007, where she continues to work part-time consulting for television companies and broadcasters. She is a regular contributor to the *Daily Mail*, *The Sun*, *You* magazine and *Grazia*. She frequently appears on television and radio.

Tout Sweet

Hanging up my High Heels for a
New Life in France

KAREN WHEELER

NEW LIFE

LOVE?

TOUT SWEET

Hanging up my High Heels for a New Life in France

Karen Wheeler

£7.99

Paperback

ISBN: 978-1-84024-761-9

In her mid-thirties, fashion editor Karen has it all: a handsome boyfriend, a fab flat in west London and an array of gorgeous shoes. But when Eric leaves, she hangs up her Manolos and waves goodbye to her glamorous city lifestyle to go it alone in a run-down house in rural Poitou-Charentes, central western France.

Acquiring a host of new friends and unsuitable suitors, she learns that true happiness can be found in the simplest of things – a bike ride through the countryside on a summer evening, or a kir or three in a neighbour's courtyard.

'Hilarious account of a fashion guru who swaps Prada for paintbrushes and Pineau in rural France.'   Mail On Sunday Travel

'Perfect summer reading for anyone who dreams of chucking away their Blackberry and downshifting to France.'   French Property News

a delicious love story, with recipes

LUNCH
in
PARIS

ELIZABETH BARD

LUNCH IN PARIS

A Delicious Love Story with Recipes

Elizabeth Bard

£8.99

Paperback

ISBN: 978-1-84953-154-2

Has a meal ever changed your life?

Part love story, part wine-splattered cookbook, *Lunch in Paris* is a deliciously tart, forthright and funny story of falling in love with a Frenchman and moving to the world's most romantic city – not the Hollywood version, but the real Paris, a heady mix of blood sausage, pains aux chocolats and irregular verbs.

From gutting her first fish (with a little help from Jane Austen) to discovering the French version of Death by Chocolate, Elizabeth Bard finds that learning to cook and building a new life have a lot in common. Peppered with recipes, this mouth-watering love story is the perfect treat for anyone who has ever suspected that lunch in Paris could change their life.

'A truly delicious love story... this delectable delight is the perfect way to enjoy lunch in Paris if you can't be there yourself.'   Living France

'Escapism doesn't come much more delicious than this... ambrosial and uplifting, this international bestseller will have you stifling a giggle as you read it on the bus and endeavouring to control your food cravings until you get home. If you enjoy French cuisine and are a sucker for a well-written romance, Lunch in Paris *will go down a treat.'*   France magazine

Have you enjoyed this book?
If so, why not write a review on your favourite website?

If you're interested in finding out more about our books,
find us on Facebook at **Summersdale Publishers** and
follow us on Twitter at **@Summersdale**.

Thanks very much for buying this Summersdale book.

www.summersdale.com

MAD, Bad
and Just Plain
Dangerous
ROMANS

John
Townsend

illustrated by
Matt Lilly

LONDON·SYDNEY

First publi   2013 by Franklin Watts

Created and dev   d by Taglines Creative Limited
Tex   y John Townsend
Illustratio   and layout by Matt Lilly
Cover de gn by Cathryn Gilbert

Franklin Watts
338 Euston Road London NW1 3BH

Franklin Watts Australia
Level 17/207 Kent Street, Sydney, NSW 2000

The author has asserted his rights in accordance
with the Copyright, Designs and Patents Act, 1988.

A CIP catalogue record for this book
is available from the British Library.

(ebook) ISBN: 978 1 4451 21956
(PB) ISBN 978 1 4451 2191 8
(Library ebook) ISBN 978 1 4451 22397

1 3 5 7 9 10 8 6 4 2

Picture credits:
The author, packager and publisher would like to thank the following
for the use of their copyright material in this book:

p.6 Maisna/Shutterstock; p.8 SimonHS/Shutterstock;
p.9 grafalex/Shutterstock; p.14 ARENA Creative/Shutterstock;
p.16 irisphoto 1/Shutterstock; p.19 IgorGobvniov/Shutterstock;
pp.22 Andrei Nekrassov/Shutterstock; p.23 The Art Archive/Alamy;
p.26 Danilo Ascione/Shutterstock; p.31 Danilo Ascione/Shutterstock;
p.33 Bocman 1973/Shutterstock; p.34 Vladimir Korostyshevskly/Shutterstock;
p.40 Lakov Kalinin/Shutterstock; p.42 Ivy Close Images/Alamy;
pp.44–45 Stewart Smith Photography/Shutterstock;
p.53 Henrik Larsson/Shutterstock; p.54 Eric Isselee/Shutterstock;
p.55 (top) Sergey Goruppa/Shutterstock;
p.55 (bottom) Stephane Bidouze/Shutterstock; p.56 Paul Bevitt/Alamy;
p.58 kiep/Shutterstock; p.68 Hong Vo/Shutterstock; p.69 Matthew Lilly
p.73 Filip Fuxa/Shutterstock; p.75 James Steidt/Shutterstock;
p.78 Joseph Calev/Shutterstock; pp.84–85 SueC/Shutterstock:

Every attempt has been made to clear copyright on the photographs
reproduced in this book. Any omissions, please apply to the
Publisher for rectification.

Printed in Great Britain

Franklin Watts is
a division of Hachette Children's Books,
an Hachette UK company.

www.hachette.co.uk

WARNING

THIS BOOK IS FUN!

It could seriously change the way you think about history!

What do you think teachers will make of this book?

It's so mad and dangerous they'll cry!

CONTENTS

Keep turning for a right good Roman read!

Chapter 1

ROMANS on the Rampage

Over 2,000 years ago the Roman Empire stretched across North Africa and Europe, including Britain. The Romans brought great changes, as well as mad, bad and dangerous ones! Rulers were assassinated, soldiers were killed, ordinary people were executed and slaves were murdered. These could be scary times for everyone.

Where are we?

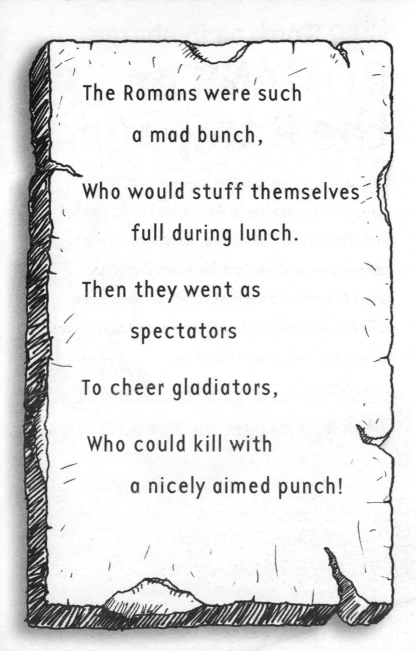

The Romans were such
a mad bunch,

Who would stuff themselves
full during lunch.

Then they went as
spectators

To cheer gladiators,

Who could kill with
a nicely aimed punch!

Romans in charge

For the first 200 years or so, the Romans were ruled by kings who would pick a fight with anyone. Then the kings were kicked out. For the next 500 years, Rome was a 'republic' led by a series of over 140 different leaders. Many were totally mad, bad and dangerous.

I'm a mighty dictator but you can call me GOD.

Mad and dangerous Roman times

753 — 509 BCE Roman Monarchy
War leaders in charge, known as 'kings'

509 — 27 BCE Roman Republic
Kings replaced — but still lots of wars

27 — 476 CE Roman Empire
Emperors in charge — and still lots of wars

Early emperors

The first Roman emperors all came from the same family line. This is called a dynasty.

- -

Julio-Claudian Dynasty 27 BCE — 68 CE

Augustus Caesar	*First Roman emperor*
Tiberius	*Killer emperor who lived in Capri*
Caligula	*Evil emperor who proclaimed himself a god*
Claudius	*Emperor who conquered Britain*
Nero	*Mad tyrant*

- -

Flavian Dynasty 69 — 96 CE

Vespasian	*Fond of money but did some good*
Titus	*Destroyed the great Jewish Temple in Jerusalem*
Domitian	*Murdered thousands of Christians*

- -

Nervan-Antonine Dynasty 96 — 192 CE

Nerva	*Good ruler*
Trajan	*Another good guy*
Hadrian	*Built the big wall in Britain*
Antoninus Pius	*'The Excellent Emperor'*
Marcus Aurelius	*Last of the five good emperors*
Commodus	*Nastier than Domitian and madder than Nero*

> I'm Trajan and I can see all the Roman Empire from here!

The best of the best...

Trajan, 98 — 117 CE

Many experts think Trajan was the greatest Roman emperor of them all. Under his rule Rome reached the peak of its power, around the year 117 CE.

Marcus Aurelius 161 — 180 CE

He was called the 'Philosopher-King' and the last of the 'Good emperors'.

The Roman Empire at its peak

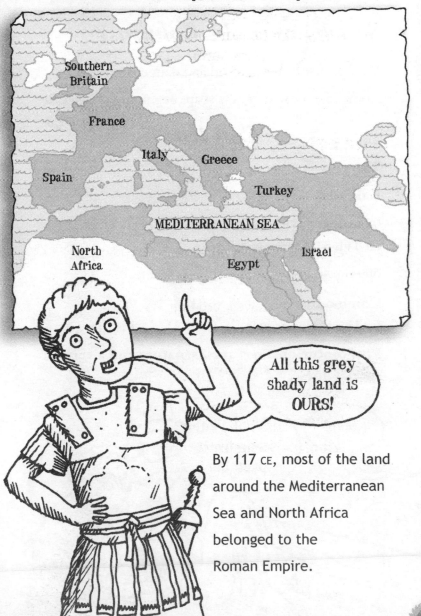

Southern Britain

France

Italy

Greece

Spain

Turkey

MEDITERRANEAN SEA

North Africa

Egypt

Israel

All this grey shady land is OURS!

By 117 CE, most of the land around the Mediterranean Sea and North Africa belonged to the Roman Empire.

Romans  the Soap

So who were the Romans?

Meet some of the mad, bad and dangerous rulers of Rome in our exciting new soap, beginning on page 28.

Cast list:

Tiberius   14–37 CE

Caligula   37–41 CE

Claudius   41–54 CE
(and his wife Agrippina)

Nero   54–68 CE

Commodus   180–192 CE
(and his sister Lucilla)

Plus centurions, servants, senators and a very special horse.

How mad could it be in Roman times?

 Roman girls got married at the age of 14. A girl's father would choose her husband. She wouldn't have much say in the matter!

 Some Romans used powdered mouse brains as toothpaste. Not nice for mice.

 The closest thing Romans had to underwear was a subligaculum – a rather long word to describe rather short pants!

Oops... I forgot to put my subligaculums on this morning!

Chapter 2

MAD Myths

Ancient Romans believed in a lot of different gods. People thought that if they upset the gods, bad things would happen. There were lots of stories or myths about the gods and how mad, bad and dangerous they could be.

Neptune

It's no fun being god of the sea. It's 'turtley' boring – or am I just being a bit 'shellfish'?

A Roman god, so says

 a myth,

Fell in love with a certain

 Miss Smith.

He flew in through her door,

Smashed his teeth on

 the floor

And in tears he lisped,

 "Give uth a kith."

(NB This is made-up twaddle – just like
many myths!)

Terrible twins

Rome was the centre of the Roman Empire. As you might have guessed, it has a mad story behind it...

Once upon a time, Princess Rhea and Mars (god of war) had baby twin boys called Romulus and Remus. To save her babies from attack by other gods, Rhea set them adrift on the River Tiber. Guess who found them? A mother wolf — yikes! But instead of eating them, she fed them — phew! They were later said to have been adopted by a shepherd and his wife.

Bad boys!

When the boys grew up they wanted to be kings (as you do). So they built a city by the River Tiber and had a bit of a fight. Romulus picked up a rock, killed his brother and made himself king. How bad is that! And that's how Rome got its name (well, the Rom bit).

Supergods

The Romans stole a lot of their gods from Greek myths. They just changed their names. The most powerful Greek god, Zeus, became the Roman god, Jupiter. He was afraid of nothing (apart from Juno, his wife). He would often hurl a thunderbolt just for fun. But his best superpower was to change himself into anything he wanted, especially animals.

Today, I'm playing cards with Juno so I've turned into a cheetah!

Good gods

☆ Janus was the god of doors. He had one face to look forwards and another to look back — so he could watch both ways from the doorway. The month of January is named after him because we look forward to a new year, while still looking back at the last.

Feels like I've got eyes...

... in the back of my head!

☆ In Ancient Rome, each home had its own god that kept things safe. Some homes had a whole room as a shrine to their god.

☆ Jupiter's sister was called Vesta, the goddess of homes. Romans would throw a small cake into the fire in their dining room to keep her happy. Lucky Vesta!

Silly superstitions

Of all the things to be scared of in Ancient Rome, people chose owls! If anyone saw an owl, they believed bad weather,

illness or death was coming. They also believed they had to kill the offending owl and nail it to their door. Then their house would be safe — but they would have a yucky door knocker!

Watch out, watch out, there's an owl about. Twit twoo!

Left behind

It wasn't good to be left-handed in Roman times! They believed the left side of anything was evil. It was important to get up from the right side of the bed, and to enter a house with the right foot first.

Pass the salt

In Ancient Rome, salt was very important for preserving food. Without salt to keep food safe to eat, people would die of starvation. Salt was so important, soldiers were paid with it. This is where the saying 'Are you worth your salt?' comes from.

Potty plot

Julius Caesar (100—44 BCE) was a powerful leader in Ancient Rome. He was so powerful that his senators became worried. They feared he would take over the government by force and ignore everything they said. So they came up with a grisly plan to get rid of him. According to legend, a fortune teller warned Caesar of the plot by saying: "Beware the Ides of March".

I just heard an owl... but I don't give a hoot.

Warned by an owl and a fortune teller!

I'M JULIUS CAESAR... BOW NOW.

> The Ides of March was the Roman way of saying March 15th. Each month had an Ides (usually the 15th).

What's the point?

So, who would kill Caesar? They all would! On 15th March, 44 BCE, a group of about 60 senators led by Gaius Cassius and Marcus Brutus surrounded Caesar. They all stabbed him at the same time. He fell with 23 wounds and died.

Ouch, that's my hand!

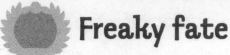

Freaky fate

Ancient Romans believed in an underworld
where they went after they died. To reach the
underworld, you had to cross the River Styx. How?
On a ferry boat, of course. Charon, the ferryman,
would decide whether or not to take you across.
People buried a dead person with a coin in their
mouth to pay the ferryman.

SURVIVAL QUIZ 1

Team up with friends or try the quiz yourself to see how you would survive in Roman times. Add up your scores for each answer. When you've done all the quizzes, check out the final verdict on page 88.

1. Are you scared of owls?

A Definitely

B Certainly not

C Just a bit

2. Are you left-handed?

A Yes

B No

C Now and again

3. Do you like money?

A Yes, please

B Just give me gold

C I don't mind how you pay me

Scores for answers:

1. A = 9 B = 1 C = 5 (You'd fit in well to Roman life if you feared owls)

2. A = 1 B = 10 C = 5 (Left-handers were thought of as evil by the Romans)

3. A = 2 B = 0 C = 9 (You'd have to like being paid with salt as a Roman soldier)

25

Chapter 3

BAD and Brutal Beings

Emperors aren't mad, just misunderstood!

Ancient Rome had its share of vile villains and rotten rogues. Some of the Roman rulers were far worse than the worst mega-scary mad, bad or dangerous villains. Many emperors were bonkers killers who got away with murder — again and again and again.

How horrid was

vile Agrippina?

Few Romans were fouler

or meaner.

To Claudius she sighed,

"On my nice floor

you've died...

Yuck! Nero, go get me

the cleaner."

Romans  the Soap

Episode 1: Twisted Tiberius

Scene 1: A public square in Rome. Date: 14 BCE.

Action

Centurion: Citizens of Rome, I bring grave news. Our first emperor, the mighty Augustus has just died at the grand age of CXXVI years (76). Please welcome our second emperor – Tiberius.

Fanfare of trumpet and loud cheers

Tiberius: Shut that row! Take that man away and torture him. Oh yes, and while you're about it, strangle a couple of children.

Mind where you put that spear!

Scene 2: Many years later, on the island of Capri.

Tiberius: I love these high cliffs. Time for some fun. Guards, grab that slave and hurl him off the cliff into the sea. Just look at him splat on the rocks! Ooh, he's not quite dead. Quick, send over my boat and finish him off with a harpoon. Perfect!!

Oh no! I'm ending on a real cliff hanger...

The trouble was, the next emperor was far, far worse...

29

Romans  the Soap

Episode 2: Cruel Caligula

Scene 1: The third Roman Emperor was Gaius – nicknamed Caligula (12–41 CE), which meant 'little boots'. He started well, but after a fever he went stark raving bonkers.

Action

Caligula: *(Shouting)* Why does everyone think I'm mad?

Senator: Well, you've just married your sister and had breakfast with your horse and given her a collar of jewels.

Caligula: So? You're fired, and my lovely horse, Incitatus, is going to be a senator.

How's your sore throat this morning?

Still a little hoarse!

Senator: What will I do, Emperor?

Caligula: Feed the cats.

Senator: With sardines?

Caligula: No – with you. I'll throw you to the lions. But first, go and chop the heads off all the statues of the gods and replace them with my head.

That's better!

After dressing as a god, executing anyone he didn't like and chopping off people's hands for fun, Caligula was assassinated by Roman guards. Who will be the next Roman Emperor? Turn the page to see...

Romans  the Soap

Episode 3: Fearsome Family

Scene 1: Caligula's Uncle Claudius is shaking behind the palace curtains after Caligula's assassination. Date: 41 CE.

Action

Soldier: Hail, Claudius. You are our next emperor.

Claudius: R..r..really? But I dribble, stutter and I'm always ill.

Soldier: You'll do!

Scene 2: Claudius marries Agrippina, who is Caligula's dodgy sister. Bad move!

Agrippina: Nero, my son, now you are 12 years old I shall murder Claudius and make you emperor. I've made a pizza topped with deadly mushrooms for dinner.

I've made him a pizza with extra mushrooms...

Claudius: Mmm, tasty pizza, my dear. It's... ergh ugh glglglglg *(Dies)*

Nero: Yay! I'm the new emperor!

Nasty Nero

Nutcase Nero hated his mother and tried to poison her three times. He failed. Time for another plan.

Killing looks easier than it is.

He made the ceiling fall on her. He failed.

He sank the ship she was on. He failed.

Finally, his soldiers stabbed her to death. Job done.

At the age of 30, Nero tried to kill himself. He failed. His servant had to finish him off.

Will the Romans ever get a decent emperor?

Romans the Soap

Episode 4: Crazy Crackpot

Scene 1: Over 100 years after Nero, mad Emperor Commodus (161–192 CE) strutted about Rome like a mega-cool gladiator. But he was really a super-wimp bully. He wanted to prove how manly he was by killing thousands of people and animals in the gladiator's arena.

Everyone wants curls like mine.

Action

Lucilla: Commodus, I must talk to you.

Commodus: Ah, Lucilla, my sister, what is it?

Lucilla: You are a complete and utter nincompoop.

Commodus: How dare you!

Lucilla: All Romans laugh at you as you strut around like a gladiator in the arena. You're a total joke.

Commodus: They love me. I chop bits off the other gladiators and they all cheer. I'm actually a superstar. They adore me.

Lucilla: They hate you! And I know that you killed our father. I'm going to have you killed...oh, what's going on...?

> Why are your guards carrying me away, Commodus?

> They're going to kill you, my dear sister. Bye bye!

Aaarrgh!

Scene 2: Ten years later, in Commodus's bathroom

Action

Narcissus: Shall I scrub your back, Emperor?
(servant)

Commodus: Very well, Narcissus, but be gentle.

Urgh... you're strangling me.

Well you've always been a pain in the neck.

Commodus: Ergh ugh ggrrrllll *(splash, gurgle – dies)*

The end!

As Commodus comes to a soapy end we come to the end of the Soap. There was still another 280 years of Ancient Roman history with the empire going down the plughole, but that's another story.

See what you and your friends score for each of these questions. Add up your scores for each answer and check out the total below. When you've done all the quizzes, check out the final verdict on page 88.

1. Do you always do as you are told?

A Of course — always

B It all depends

C Not much

2. Would you ever worship your country's leader?

A You must be joking!

B Only if I had to

C Yeah — no problem

3. Would you laugh at a crackpot with daft ideas?

A Maybe

B You bet!

C Not likely

Scores for answers:

1. A = 10 B = 4 C = 1 (Disobeying Roman rulers could be fatal)
2. A = 0 B = 8 C = 9 (Disobeying Roman rulers could be fatal)
3. A = 6 B = 0 C = 9 (Making fun of Roman rulers could be fatal)

Chapter 4

DANGEROUS Days

Romans liked to add extra danger to their lives. If they didn't take part in risky activities themselves, they were happy to watch others dabble with danger. Emperors liked to keep the bloodthirsty crowds happy with free gladiator games and other mad, bad and dangerous entertainment.

To the death!

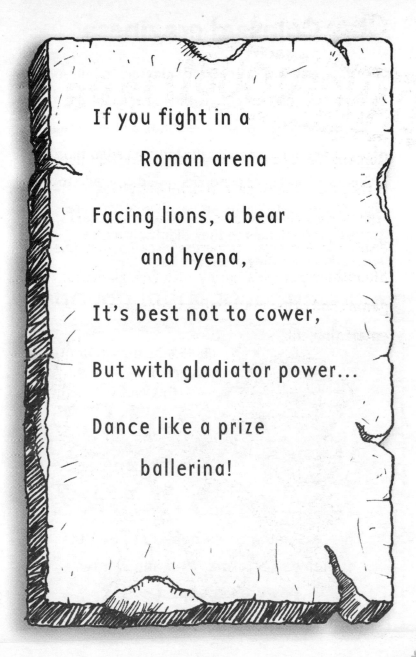

If you fight in a
Roman arena

Facing lions, a bear
and hyena,

It's best not to cower,

But with gladiator power...

Dance like a prize
ballerina!

Colossal craziness

A grand space was needed for emperors to put on shows that could be seen by the masses. So, the Emperor Vespasian began the building of an arena the size of a modern football stadium called the Colosseum. Slaves or prisoners would be made to fight to the death in the arena. Gladiators were trained professionals so they didn't always kill each other, but they often got badly hurt.

This Colosseum will look great when it's finished.

The Colosseum could hold up to 50,000 standing spectators. Men and women were kept apart.

Fierce fights

When a gladiator was beaten but not quite dead, the audience would wave scarves or put their thumbs out if they wanted him killed. If he'd fought well, and they wanted him to live, the people would close their thumbs into their fingers and the gladiator would be allowed to live to fight another day.

Bad luck chum, all I see is thumb!

Perilous pastime

Chariot racing was the Formula One of its day but much more dangerous. On average charioteers lived until they were 22 years old. Crowds flocked to the great race track called the Circus Maximus, which could seat over 150,000 people.

It's much safer doing it this way!

Many children trained as charioteers and became professional racers in their teens.

Lethal crashes

No lanes were marked on the track. Twelve chariots, each pulled by four horses, thundered round the track for seven laps. The charioteer tied the reins around his waist and kept a sharp knife in his belt to cut himself free if he was thrown from his chariot. Many charioteers were trampled to death.

I need to go to 'horse'pital.

Why the long face?

Bleak Britain

Roman soldiers also lived dangerously. They had to invade strange, unknown lands, fight mad tribes and then build roads. One really dangerous place they went to was ... Britain!

It took three attempts for the Romans to conquer Britain. First they had to cross the scary sea. Julius Caesar tried to invade twice, but his ships were wrecked in storms.

What a dump! They haven't even got any roads!

Bad Britons

It took almost another 100 years before the Romans dared to go back to Britain.

In 43 CE, the Emperor Claudius sent 40,000 troops across the Channel. They were so terrified of crossing the sea that they nearly didn't go! When they finally arrived, the troops refused to leave their boats to face the mad Britons. But then they did ... and the rest is history!

Is this the way to Colchester?

Go away, you nasty Romans.

See what you and your friends score for each of these questions. Add up your scores for each answer and check out the total below. When you've done all the quizzes, check out the final verdict on page 88.

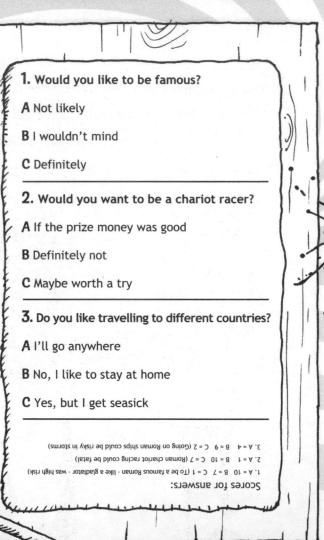

1. Would you like to be famous?

A Not likely

B I wouldn't mind

C Definitely

2. Would you want to be a chariot racer?

A If the prize money was good

B Definitely not

C Maybe worth a try

3. Do you like travelling to different countries?

A I'll go anywhere

B No, I like to stay at home

C Yes, but I get seasick

Scores for answers:

1. A = 10 B = 7 C = 1 (To be a famous Roman - like a gladiator - was high risk)

2. A = 1 B = 10 C = 7 (Roman chariot racing could be fatal)

3. A = 4 B = 9 C = 2 (Going on Roman ships could be risky in storms)

Chapter 5

MAD Medicine

The Romans tried all kinds of mad, bad and dangerous treatments for illness and injuries. Soldiers often needed medical help after battles, but it was likely to be grim. Treatments could be worse than the illness or injury.

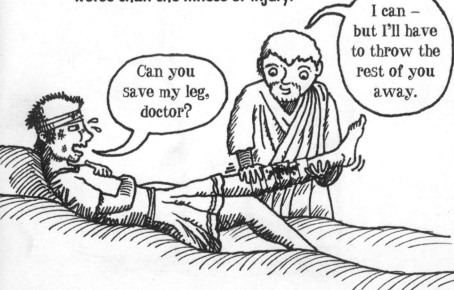

Can you save my leg, doctor?

I can – but I'll have to throw the rest of you away.

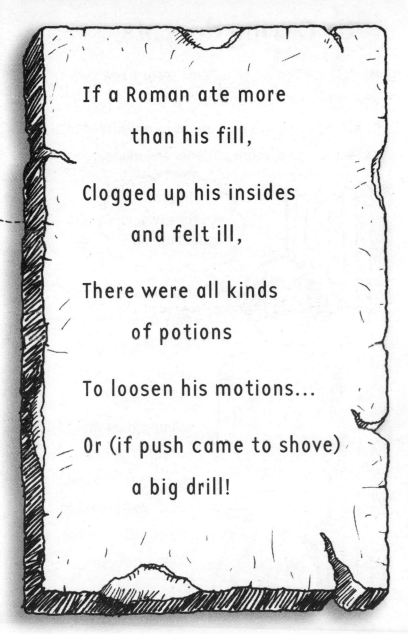

If a Roman ate more
than his fill,

Clogged up his insides
and felt ill,

There were all kinds
of potions

To loosen his motions...

Or (if push came to shove)
a big drill!

Daring doctors

Many doctors in Ancient Rome were freed slaves who didn't have much training. Doctors would sometimes do quick operations on the street to attract a crowd, more patients and money.

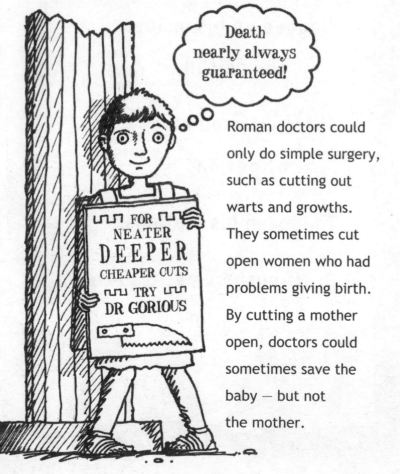

Death nearly always guaranteed!

FOR NEATER **DEEPER** CHEAPER CUTS TRY DR GORIOUS

Roman doctors could only do simple surgery, such as cutting out warts and growths. They sometimes cut open women who had problems giving birth. By cutting a mother open, doctors could sometimes save the baby — but not the mother.

Potty poison

Roman doctors didn't know why so many people became sick. But we know one reason — a metal called lead. Roman water pipes and pots were often made from lead. Many Romans boiled grape juice in lead pans to make wine. Bad move! Lead poisoning made people ill and could kill them — but it also affected their brains. Maybe all those mad emperors had simply drunk too much lead in their wine.

This is going straight to my head...

Rotting Romans

Roman troops looking for new places to conquer often had to march through swamps. Nasty insects and snakes would bite their feet, but there was worse — mould!

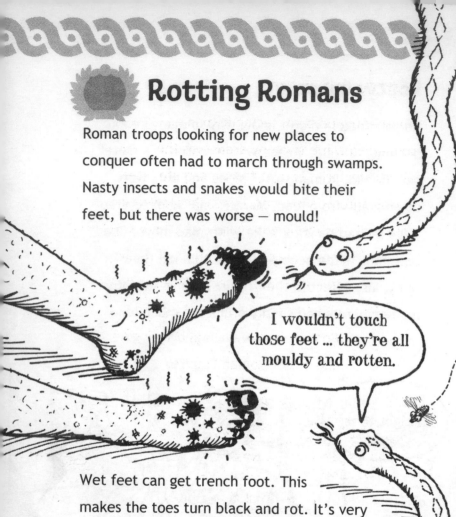

I wouldn't touch those feet ... they're all mouldy and rotten.

Wet feet can get trench foot. This makes the toes turn black and rot. It's very painful and if it gets bad enough, the foot has to be amputated. The Roman answer? Leather sandals that let water in, but also air, so the feet could dry out. When the Romans invaded chilly Britain, they simply put on woolly socks and kept marching.

Mozzy mayhem

Another big problem facing Roman soldiers in warm swampy areas was the disease malaria, caught from mosquito bites. The symptoms are fever, headaches, sweating, cold chills, vomiting and diarrhoea. There was no treatment and malaria killed many soldiers. Some experts think malaria played a big part in making the Roman army weak and bringing an end to the Roman Empire.

DANGEROUS

Just popping out for a quick bite.

Maggot attack

Doctors looking after wounded soldiers on the battlefield didn't know about germs and infection, they just knew wounds could become smelly and turn black.

Yuk!

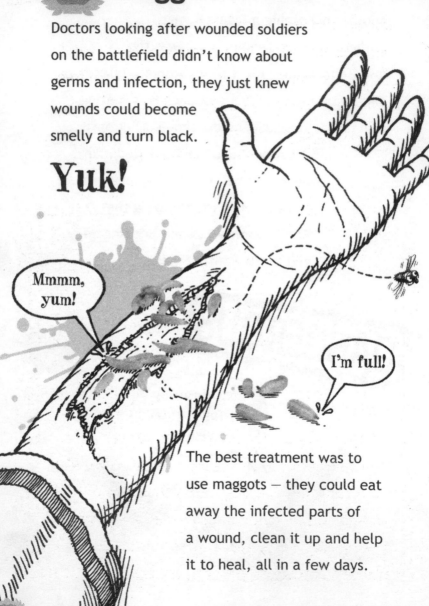

Mmmm, yum!

I'm full!

The best treatment was to use maggots — they could eat away the infected parts of a wound, clean it up and help it to heal, all in a few days.

Lively leeches

Doctors also used leeches to heal wounds. They put them on boils to help them shrink, and even inside sore mouths and throats. Leeches were free – they are found in wet, swampy places. Roman soldiers could collect them and stick them all over their bodies.

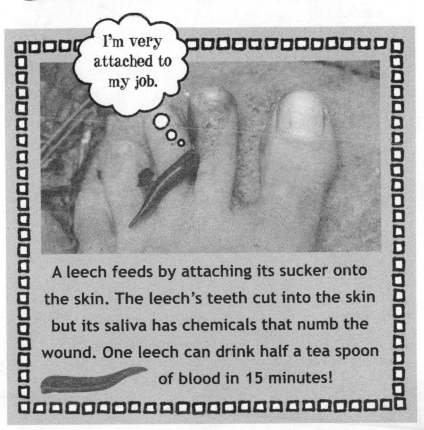

I'm very attached to my job.

A leech feeds by attaching its sucker onto the skin. The leech's teeth cut into the skin but its saliva has chemicals that numb the wound. One leech can drink half a tea spoon of blood in 15 minutes!

Crazy cures

The Romans thought head pains or fits were caused by spirits trapped inside a person's head. So the best way to let them out was to drill holes ... right through the skull. Yikes! Many Roman skulls have been found with holes drilled into them.

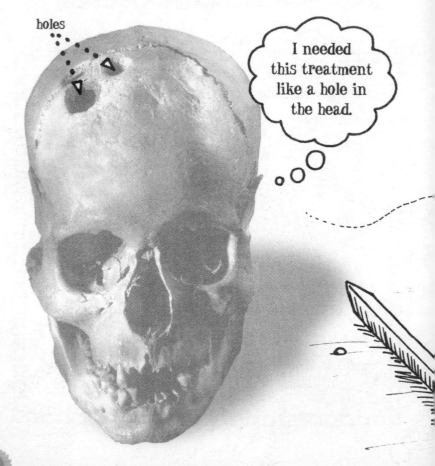

holes

I needed this treatment like a hole in the head.

Stand and de-liver

The human liver and blood were thought to be great treatments for epilepsy — especially if fresh and from someone healthy, strong and brave — like a gladiator.

For anyone feeling ill, it was worth a trip to the Colosseum in case one of the gladiators got the chop. If a gladiator was killed in the arena, there would be a rush of sick people to drink his blood — while it was still warm. Gross!

I'll have a pint.

Just a half for me.

Potty potions

Ancient Rome had a lot of dodgy medicines made
from plants or animal parts.

 To stop bleeding — slap on a cobweb.

To cure baldness — rub sulphur, tar and
animal urine on the head.

 For sore eyes — use boiled liver.

 For most other problems — chew wild garlic
or rub it on the body.

To stop hiccups and sneezing —
kiss the nostrils of a mule.

I'm only kissing
you because I've
got hiccups.

That's what
they all say!

58

SURVIVAL QUIZ 4

See what you and your friends score for each of these questions. Add up your scores for each answer and check out the total below. When you've done all the quizzes, check out the final verdict on page 88.

1. Have you ever been bitten by a mosquito?

A Never

B Not sure

C Ouch — yes

2. Could you touch a live leech?

A Easy — no problem

B No thanks

C AAGH don't go there!

3. Have you got a headache right now?

A Yes — another one

B No, but thanks for caring

C I never get headaches

Scores for answers:

1. A = 10 B = 5 C = 1 (Mosquito bites in Roman times could be deadly)
2. A = 10 B = 3 C = 0 (Romans sometimes put leeches over their bodies)
3. A = 3 B = 8 C = 10 (Roman headaches could lead to holes in the head)

Chapter 6

BAD Behaviour

Some people in Ancient Rome could be scarily cruel, nasty and just plain horrible. This was a time of slavery, public torture and painful punishments. Laws were strict and people breaking the law could be in for a terrifying time. Runaway slaves and prisoners were forced into the gladiator arena to fight each other or animals to the death.

My agent didn't say anything about working with animals!

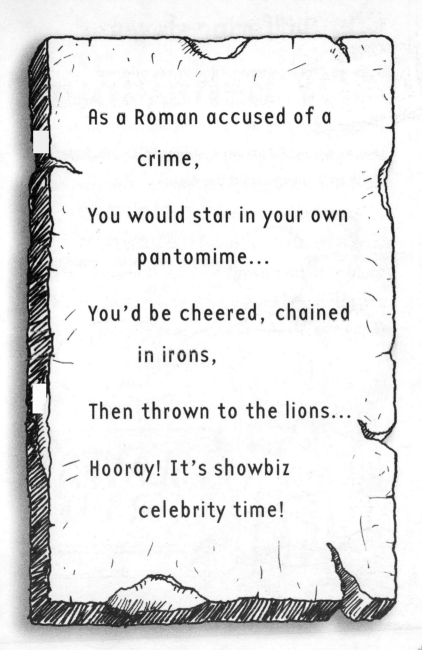

As a Roman accused of a

crime,

You would star in your own

pantomime...

You'd be cheered, chained

in irons,

Then thrown to the lions...

Hooray! It's showbiz

celebrity time!

Suffering slaves

Soldiers captured people for slaves on their travels and in battles, then brought them back to Rome. Children as well as grown-ups could be sold as slaves. Parents sometimes sold their older children if they needed the cash.

Slaves did all the chores in the house, but they also worked on farms, building sites and down mines.

I wish I'd tidied my room now...

SLAVES FOR SALE

Rotten rules

Owners of slaves had to look after them for life, but they often treated them badly. Slaves could only buy their freedom back if their owners allowed it, and it was almost impossible for a slave to save enough to pay back the money their owner paid for them.

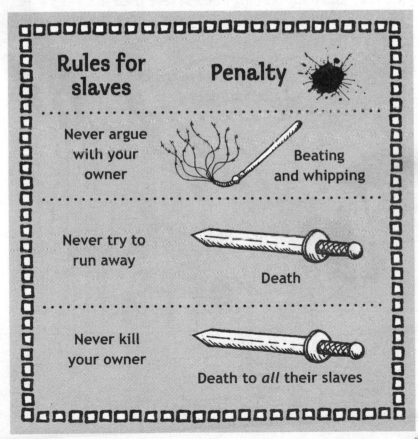

Rules for slaves — **Penalty**

Never argue with your owner — Beating and whipping

Never try to run away — Death

Never kill your owner — Death to *all* their slaves

Crushing Christians

From 60-40 CE the new religion of Christianity grew fast. Some Roman leaders were determined to crush Christian beliefs before they spread. Nero made sure many Christians were executed in public. His victims were tied to poles and set on fire, and their burning bodies were used as torches to light up his garden.

I do like a midnight barbecue.

Grim for Christians

Many Christians were nailed to crosses made of wood. Romans used this form of punishment (crucifixion) on Jesus Christ.

Roman crucifixion was seen as the most shameful way to die. Only slaves or the worst criminals were crucified. It could take hours or days to die in agony.

Saint Peter was crucified upside down because he did not think he was good enough to die like Jesus Christ.

Quick, turn the page... the blood is rushing to my head...

Blame the Christians!

In 64 CE, part of Rome burned down. Emperor
Nero blamed the Christians, so he arrested lots
of them and executed them in horrific ways.
One way was to cover them in wild
animal skins and leave them
to be eaten by dogs.

Excruciating executions

Many Roman leaders came up with more and more gruesome ways to execute people.

Mad Emperor Caligula was fond of sawing people in half. The victim would be hung upside-down and a large saw would cut their body down the middle all the way to the head.

Emperor Constantine (274–337 CE) boiled alive his own wife and strangled to death his relatives. One of his favourite ways to kill criminals was to pour red-hot liquid lead down their throats. Apart from that, he could be quite friendly!

Pain and punishment

Romans had many nasty ways to punish different crimes. This was the punishment for anyone who killed their father (this is called patricide).

1. Taken to a field. Stripped and whipped.

2. Still naked, tied in a sack with a snake, a chicken and a dog. (Why these three? Who knows!)

3. The sack thrown in the River Tiber. End of.

Hard times

These were some other common punishments for criminals:

- Beheading
- Strangling in prison
- Throwing a criminal off the prison roof
- Throwing a criminal from a high cliff
- Burying a person alive
- And there were always hungry animals ready to help!

Not too much garlic on mine!

SURVIVAL QUIZ 5

See what you and your friends score for each of these questions. Add up your scores for each answer and check out the total below. When you've done all the quizzes, check out the final verdict on page 88.

1. Are you always good and never get in trouble?

A I'm an angel

B Usually OK

C Oops, I get told off lots

2. Do you work hard at all times and never complain?

A Of course

B Not likely

C It all depends

3. Do you celebrate Christmas?

A No

B Yes

C I like Easter, too

Scores for answers:

1. A = 9   B = 5   C = 1 (It could be dead risky getting into trouble in Roman times)

2. A = 10 B = 0   C = 4 (As a Roman slave you would have to work hard — or else)

3. A = 0   B = 9   C = 10 (Romans sometimes got fed to the lions for enjoying Christian events)

70

Chapter 7

DANGEROUS Doings

For all their violent and cruel ways, the Romans came up with some really brilliant inventions that were bold and daring in Roman times. Some of their ideas were so amazingly clever that we still use them today. Some were just plain mad, bad and dangerous!

This aqueduct isn't dangerous.

It is if you fall off it!

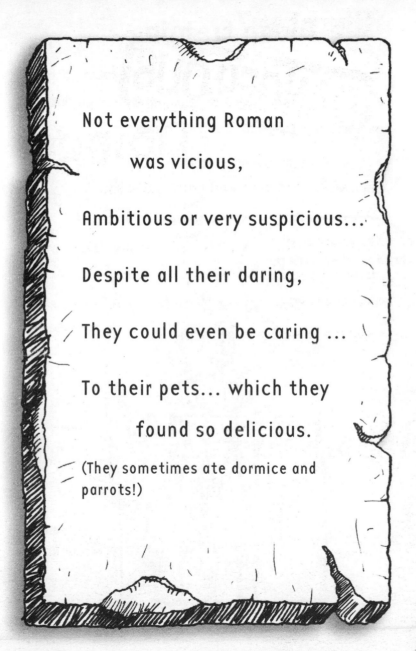

Not everything Roman

was vicious,

Ambitious or very suspicious...

Despite all their daring,

They could even be caring ...

To their pets... which they

found so delicious.

(They sometimes ate dormice and parrots!)

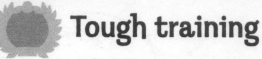

Tough training

Roman soldiers trained hard and were expected to win all their battles. If a soldier fell asleep on duty he could be stoned or clubbed to death.

As well as tough training, Roman soldiers had great kit:

Never mind all these wicked weapons and kit – I just want some warm tights.

Iron or bronze helmet

Spear

Dagger (pugio)

Large shield

Heavy body armour

Sword (gladius)

Mine's bigger than yours...

Roman armies had massive catapults that were used to hurl huge rocks that could knock down walls. They also used large crossbows called ballistas to fire long spears. All of this, plus giant battering rams and flying burning tar, meant their enemies didn't stand a chance.

Bubbling bathtime

Roman public baths were like naked leisure centres! You went there to relax and gossip — oh, and get clean. First you did a few exercises and had a swim in the pool — all naked. Next you'd go into a series of heated rooms, which got hotter and hotter, to make you sweat out the dirt. A slave would scrape dirt, sweat and oil from your skin with a metal scraper called a strigil. Then a final plunge into a cold pool. Phew!

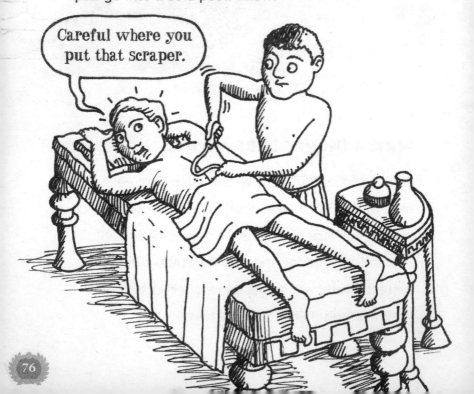

A great day out

The baths were often packed, with hundreds of people bathing at once. No children or slaves could use the baths.

Roman baths were an important part of Roman daily life. They were a great place to catch up on all the latest gossip (or do a bit of plotting) and had hair-cutting salons, reading rooms, libraries and shops. The Romans could be mad, bad and dangerous, but they were clean!

Waste worries

The big problem for any growing city is how to get rid of smelly human waste. Rome had the answer — toilets with running water. Romans went to the toilet together in rooms seating up to 30 people at once. Friendly or what! Seats were placed over channels of flowing water to flush away the waste. Instead of toilet paper, they shared a sponge on a stick to wipe their bottoms.

You know the saying, "To get hold of the wrong end of the stick?" Well, I think I just have...

Gross!

Wonder wee

Some Romans relieved themselves
in pots on street corners. When
the pots were full of urine, they
would be collected and (wait for it...) taken to the
laundry to use for washing clothes! The ammonia
in urine made bleach which whitened tunics. A
slave had to stand in the tub of urine, stomp on the
clothes, then rinse them. **Phewee!**

Get your clothes
**WIDDLE
WHITE**
at our new
Roman Laundry
(next to the piddleorium)

*

'You're in' for
a wee treat!

Fab food

Rich Romans enjoyed lavish banquets with many courses. They liked to show off with menus such as jellyfish, boiled ostrich, stuffed sow's udders or flamingo boiled with dates.

Anyone for fried flamingo with dormouse pasta?

It isn't true that Romans had a special room called a vomitorium for being sick in after a banquet. A vomitorium was the passage leading out of the Colosseum — named to describe crowds 'spewing' from a show. However, sometimes a slave would bring round a bowl during a feast for anyone wanting to bring up the first course and make room for some pud!

Grave event — come die with me?

One daring dinner party was given by the totally mad Emperor Domitian. His guests were sent to a room decorated in black — black marble, black paint and black curtains — it was lit only by funeral lamps. Each guest's place was marked with a gravestone with his or her name. The terrified guests feared they were about to be murdered by the emperor. All the food was dyed black and served on black plates. Each guest took their own gravestone home.

I can't see what I'm eating.

That's probably a good thing!

See what you and your friends score for each of these questions. Add up your scores for each answer and check out the total below. When you've done all the quizzes, check out the final verdict on page 88.

1. Would you ever take a bath with other people?

A Certainly not

B No big deal

C Only if I kept covered up

2. Would you ever share a toilet with other people at the same time?

A Not too bothered

B Never in a million years

C I'd have to be desperate

3. Would you ever eat ostrich, flamingo or a dollop of jellyfish?

A Yum — delicious

B Only in a curry

C I'm a vegetarian

Scores for answers:

1. A = 0 B = 10 C = 2 (To be a clean Roman, you'd have to share bath time!)

2. A = 9 B = 0 C = 3 (Romans couldn't be fussy)

3. A = 9 B = 1 C = 0 (You'd be a hungry Roman if you were a fussy eater)

Chapter 8
And Finally ...

Rome ruled land around the Mediterranean
for over 1,000 years. By 400 CE the empire was
crumbling and the city of Rome finally fell in
476 CE when a leader of a German tribe, Flavius
Odoacer (433–493 CE), took control of Rome.
He became king of Italy and forced the last
emperor, Romulus Augustulus, to step down.

I can
see the end
coming!

Britain had been part of the Roman Empire for over 350 years. From around 250 CE onwards, the Romans were trying to deal with growing attacks from enemies outside the Empire. By the year 410 CE, the Romans could no longer rule Britain. They had to leave the Britons to defend themselves as best they could against enemies from across the sea.

With no Roman army to help them the British people were soon overrun by the Anglo Saxons ... but that's another story!

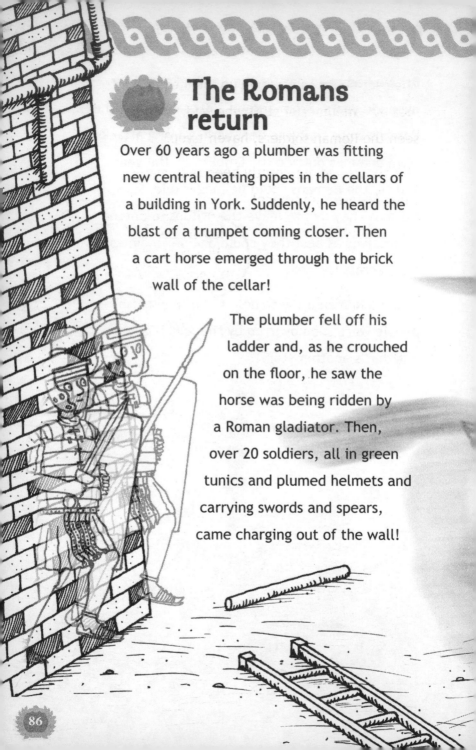

The Romans return

Over 60 years ago a plumber was fitting new central heating pipes in the cellars of a building in York. Suddenly, he heard the blast of a trumpet coming closer. Then a cart horse emerged through the brick wall of the cellar!

The plumber fell off his ladder and, as he crouched on the floor, he saw the horse was being ridden by a Roman gladiator. Then, over 20 soldiers, all in green tunics and plumed helmets and carrying swords and spears, came charging out of the wall!

The petrified man escaped up the steps to be met by a member of staff who said, "You've seen the Roman soldiers, haven't you?"

The ghosts had apparently been seen many times before... and since!

My horse is a real nightmare!

What is your total score from the Survival Quizzes at the end of the chapters? Add up your points from all 18 questions to see how long you would survive under the Romans.

Over 150	WOW — you'd make a great Roman! Your chances of making it to old age are promising. There again, were your answers strictly honest?
100 — 150	Fairly good. You'd be a Roman with a fair chance of reaching middle-age... just about.
80 — 100	Not bad. You'd make a fairly average Roman but don't plan for a peaceful old age.
50 — 80	Ooer — you're high risk! Roman life isn't for you. Low survival chances.
Below 50	AAH! Give up now. You wouldn't make a successful Roman. Only a dead one.

If your scores were a whole mixture, that means you'd probably be a fairly normal Roman. You'd have no idea if or when something horrible would strike. And it surely would! In fact, the Roman guards are already on their way ...

Quam operor vos rate Romanorum? (How do you rate the Romans, then?)

Funditus dementis, nocens quod periculosus! (Totally mad, bad and dangerous!)

753 BCE   The city of Rome is founded – named after Romulus who killed his twin brother Remus (according to legend). Rome was ruled by kings for the next 240 years.

509 BCE   The last king is overthrown and Rome is now a republic ruled by elected senators.

264 BCE   The first games for gladiators are held.

73 BCE   Spartacus the gladiator leads the slaves in an uprising.

44 BCE   Julius Caesar was the first Roman leader to be declared a dictator for life. Within a year he was assassinated by a group of senators.

27 BCE   The Roman Empire begins as Caesar Augustus becomes the first Roman Emperor.

I've got a date for dinner. Yum!

0	Jesus Christ is born.
33 CE	The crucifixion of Jesus in the Roman province of Jerusalem and the start of Christianity.
43 CE	Emperor Claudius sends 40,000 troops to Britain.
64 CE	Much of Rome burns. Legend has it that Emperor Nero watched the city burn while playing a lyre.
70 CE	Building of the Colosseum begins.
79 CE	The volcano Mount Vesuvius erupts, destroying the cities of Pompeii and Herculaneum and killing everyone who lived there.
80 CE	The Colosseum is opened in Rome by Emperor Titus. The games were paid for by emperors and wealthy Romans to make them popular with the people. The arena has a sand floor to soak up the blood of victims.
117 CE	The Roman Empire reaches its greatest extent under Emperor Trajan.
122 CE	Emperor Hadrian builds a very long wall across northern England to keep out invading tribes, such as the Picts and Scots.
313 CE	Emperor Constantine allows Christians to worship openly.
380 CE	Theodosius I declares that Christianity is to be the religion of the Roman Empire.
410 CE	The Romans have to leave Britain to deal with attacks from barbarians on the Empire and on Rome.
476 CE	The end of the Western Roman Empire and the fall of Ancient Rome.

Gruesome Glossary

ammonia a gas with a sharp smell. When dissolved in water it can be used as detergent

amputation cutting off an arm or leg from the body

aqueduct a bridge-like structure that carries a channel or pipe of water across a river below. They were built to take water to areas where there was none.

arena an enclosed area used for public entertainment

assassination the murder of an important person or leader in a surprise attack

banquet a special dinner for many people, sometimes in honour of an event or person

barbarians a group or tribe of people who lived outside the Roman Empire. The Romans thought they were savage and like animals.

battering ram a huge heavy log or tree trunk used by soldiers to batter down walls and gates

centurion a commander of 100 men in the Ancient Roman army

diarrhoea when poo is very loose and runny

dictator a ruler who has total authority, one who is often cruel or brutal

dynasty a series of rulers from the same family

Learn your words or you'll be 'saw'ry!

epilepsy electrical discharges in the brain that can cause a fit or loss of consciousness

leeches small bloodsucking worm-like creatures

malaria a disease passed from one person to another by a bite from an insect called a mosquito, causing a fever

myths stories describing the origin of a people's customs, often with superhuman beings

philosopher a person who thinks about life and wisdom

republic a government that has a head of state who is not a king or queen

River Styx in Greek mythology dead souls were carried across the River Styx to the underworld

senator a member of a senate – the supreme governing council of the Ancient Roman Empire

superstition a belief people have when they fear the unknown

thunderbolt a flash of lightning followed by a blast of thunder

tyrant a person who uses power harshly or violently

urine wee; liquid waste from the body

warts small hard growths on the skin

Weird Websites

Pssst. There's something you need to know. This book is a fun look at just some of the mad, bad and dangerous Roman goings-on. The Romans did many great things, too. Take a peep at:

http://www.bbc.co.uk/schools/primaryhistory/romans/
Learn more and play games.

http://superbrainybeans.co.uk/history/videos/rotten-romans.html
Fun, facts and some great songs!

http://www.brims.co.uk/romans/
Read up on the Romans and then try the quiz

www.bbc.co.uk/history/ancient/romans/launchgms_deathrome.shtml
Play the game and solve the mystery.

Infernal Index

> What was I used for? Slither to page 55 to find out.

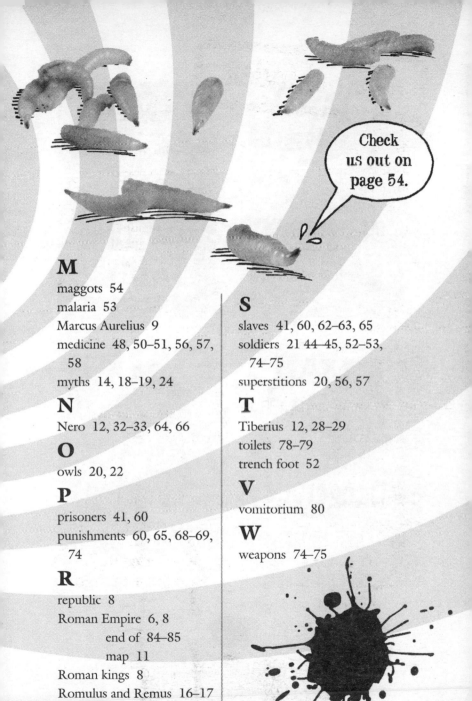

Check us out on page 54.

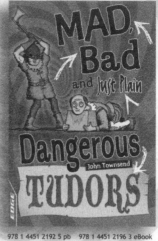

978 1 4451 2191 8 pb   978 1 4451 2195 6 eBook

978 1 4451 2192 5 pb   978 1 4451 2196 3 eBook

978 1 4451 2193 2 pb   978 1 4451 2239 7 eBook

978 1 4451 2194 9 pb   978 1 4451 2240 3 eBook

www.franklinwatts.co.uk